The Multidimensional DATA MODELING *Toolkit*

Making Your Business Intelligence Applications Smart with Oracle OLAP

JOHN PAREDES

The Multidimensional Data Modeling Toolkit: Making Your Business Intelligence Applications Smart with Oracle OLAP

Copyright © 2009 John Paredes

All rights reserved. No part of this book may be reproduced or transmitted in any form or by any means, electronic or mechanical, including photocopying, recording, or by any information storage and retrieval system, except for inclusion in a review, without permission in writing from the publisher.

ISBN: 978-0-9817753-0-2
Library of Congress Control Number: 2009922778

Published in the United States of America by
OLAP World Press
545 Eighth Avenue
New York, NY 10018
(212) 502-7980
www.OLAPWorldPress.com

This book is intended for informational purposes only. While every effort has been made to ensure the correctness of the information in this book, no guarantee is made of it; the information contained in this book is provided without any express, statutory, or implied warranties. This book does not include any offer of software support. The author has never been an employee of Oracle Corporation; the opinions expressed herein are exclusively those of the author. Various trademarks have been used throughout the text and are the property of their respective owners.

www.AnalyticalAlchemy.com

To my wonderful parents who are always there for me.

Contents

Part I: Preparing for the Journey

1 Overview — 3
- Who is the Book's Audience? — 4
- The Book's Approach — 5
- Thinking Inside the Cube — 6
- Engineering Tradeoffs — 7
- Section Overviews — 9

2 What is OLAP? — 11
- What: OLAP and FASMI — 12
- How: ROLAP, MOLAP, and HOLAP — 12
- OLAP and Business Intelligence — 14
- OLAP's Position in the Data Food Chain — 14
- Military Intelligence, Business Intelligence, and Other Kinds of Intelligence — 15

3 What is the Oracle OLAP DML? — 17
- Contrasting the Relational World with the World of Analytic Workspaces — 18
- What Advantages Does OLAP Offer? — 19
- What is the Oracle OLAP Option? — 20
- Software Required for This Book — 21
- The 30,000-Foot View — 21

4 Pit Stop: Analytic Workspace Manager Administration Basics — 27
- Creating an Analytic Workspace — 28
  - How to Graphically Create an Analytic Workspace — 28
  - How to Create an Analytic Workspace from the Command Line — 32
- Understanding the Different Access Modes — 33
- Changing Access Modes — 34
- Saving Changes Permanently — 34
- Listing the Objects in an Analytic Workspace — 35
- Deleting an Analytic Workspace — 35
- Ordering Multiple Analytic Workspaces — 35

Getting Information About an Analytic Workspace 36
Using the OLAP Worksheet as a Calculator 37
Using Shortcuts 38

Part II: Mastering Dimensions

5 Creating Dimensions — 41

Defining and Maintaining Dimensions. 42
Choosing Codes for Dimension Members 43
Getting Information About Dimensions and Dimension Members 45
The Order of Dimension Members. 46
The Concept of Status 47
Comparing the OLAP DML LIMIT Command to the SQL SELECT Command . . . 51

6 Describing Dimension Members with Labels — 53

Creating Labels for Dimension Members 53
Implicit Looping 56
Qualified Data References 57
Setting Status Based on Labels 58
Labels in More than One Language 60
Numerical Descriptions 62
Using Properties to Describe the Dimension Itself 62
Sorting Dimension Members 63

7 Categorizing Dimension Members with Attributes — 65

Object Attributes 66
Using Relations 67
Dimension Profilers 69
Other Uses of Relations 73
  Performance Attributes 73
  Treatment Attributes 74
  Attributes as Application Data 75
Multidimensional Relations 75
The Versatility of Relations 76

8 Organizing Dimension Members into Hierarchies — 77

Developing a Customer Hierarchy 79
Representing Hierarchy Information in a Tabular Format 81

	The DML Representation of a Hierarchy	84
	Representing Multiple Hierarchies	85
	Not All Self-Relations Define Hierarchies	88
	Hierarchically Based Filtering	88
	Working with Levels	92
	Level-Based Filtering	94
	Reporting Hierarchy Information	94

9 Representing Unnatural, Ragged, and Other Hierarchy Variations — 97

	Natural Versus Unnatural Hierarchies	97
	Qualitative Differences Between Natural and Unnatural Hierarchies	99
	Creating an Unnatural Hierarchy	102
	Balanced Hierarchies Versus Ragged Hierarchies	103
	Representing a Ragged Hierarchy in the DML	104

Part III: Designing Multidimensional Data

10 Storing Data in Analytic Workspaces — 109

	Determining Dimensionality	110
	Defining Variables	110
	Getting Information About Variables	111
	Multicube Approach	112
	Data Storage Order	113
	Using the Random Number Generator to Create Test Data	115
	Value-Based Filtering	115
	Choosing Dimension Order to Maximize Performance	117
	Measure Dimensions	118
	Display Dimensions	120
	Sparsity Happens	122

11 Calculating Data On-the-Fly — 125

	Calc This, Not That	125
	Defining a Formula	126
	Changing a Formula's EQ	127
	Formulas for Common Calculations	128
	Formula 1: Revenue Index	128
	Formula 2: Percent of Revenue (Customer)	128
	Formula 3: Percent of Revenue (Product)	128

Formula 4: Percent of Revenue (Category)	128
Formula 5: Ampersand Substitution	130
Formula 6: Substituting a Forecast Value for a Missing Actual	130
Formula 7: Relative Time	131
Formula 8: Revenue a Year Ago	132
Formula 9: Revenue Delta	133
Formula 10: Hiding a Dimension from a Measure	134
Formula 11: Stitching Variables Together	134
Formula 12: Smoothing a Time Series with Moving Averages	135
Formula 13: Implementing Finite Impulse Response Digital Filters	136

12 Filtering, Relationships, and Combinations — 139

Limit Types	139
The Three Different Types of Relationships	141
One-to-One Relationships	142
One-to-Many Relationships	142
Many-to-Many Relationships	142
Working with Combinations	143
Some Practice Working with Counting and Combinations	145
Counting and Selecting with Combinations	146
Example 1. Find the Distinct Items in a Given Order	146
Example 2. Find the Distinct Items Contained in Any (of More than One) Specified Orders	148
Example 3. Find Which Orders Contain at Least One of the Specified Items	148
Example 4. A Formula That Tells If an Item Is in an Order	149
Example 5. Calculate the Number of Distinct Items per Order	149
Example 6. Trend Report on the Number of Distinct Items Ordered	150
Example 7. Trend Report on the Average Number of Items per Order	151
Switching Between Multidimensional and Relational Data Presentations	151

13 Working with Sets — 157

Similarities Between Valuesets and Variables	157
How Sets are Used in Business Intelligence Applications	158
Saving the Results of a Filter into a Named Set	159
Using a One-Dimensional Valueset to Store a Series of Filtering Results	160
Limiting the Valueset Directly	161
Storing Information in Multidimensional Valuesets	161
Many-to-Many Relationships with Valuesets: A Healthcare Example	162
Another Way to Save a Status List: The Push-Down Stack	163

14 Aggregation — 165

- Core Principles of Aggregation 166
- Group Specification Methods 167
- Hierarchies 168
- Custom Groupings 176
- Attributes 178
- Accumulations 182

Part IV: Graphical User Interfaces for OLAP

15 Exploring Metadata — 189

- What is Metadata? 190
- Creating the Demo Application 191
  - Creating Dimensions and Their Descriptions 193
  - Creating Cubes and Measures 200
- Exploring Objects Created from AWM's GUI 203
- Metadata Structures 208

16 The Star Schema and Beyond — 211

- What Is a Star Schema? 211
- The Fact Table 213
- Dimension Lookup Tables 215
- Populating DML Objects from the Data Warehouse 216
  - Loading the Dimension Table Data 216
  - Loading the Fact Table Data 221
- The Classic Business Intelligence Application 225
- Analytic Workspace as Information Foundry 225
  - Breaking Out Data by Related Dimensions 226
  - Behavior-Based Attributes 226
  - Dimension Profiler 227
- OLAP by Bill Blass 227
- Making Data Visible in the GUI 228

17 Selectors — 229

Part V: OLAP DML Programming

18 Writing DML Programs — 241
- The Reasons for Writing Programs — 241
- Creating a DML Program — 242
  - Program 1: A Simple Aggregation Program — 242
  - Program 2: Meta-business Intelligence — 245
  - Program 3: The Accumulation Program — 248
  - Program 4: Populating the Relative Time Variable — 250
  - Program 5: Creating Random Samples — 252
  - Program 6: Creating Random Combinations — 253
- What Determines Program Output? — 254

19 Getting Data In and Out of Analytic Workspaces — 257
- Writing Programs to Read Data from an External Source — 258
  - Program 7: Maintaining a Dimension from a Text File Using FILEREAD — 258
  - Program 8: Populating Relations from Data in a Flat File — 260
  - Program 9: Reading in Combinations — 261
  - Program 10: Loading in Programs, Aggmaps, and TheKitchenSink — 262
  - Program 11: Exporting Data to a Text File — 263
  - Program 12: Loading Data from a Relational Table Using Embedded SQL — 264
  - Program 13: A Program That Writes a Program — 264
  - Program 14: Loading Valuesets — 266

20 Tune-Up: Working with Analytic Workspaces — 269
- Backing Up an Analytic Workspace — 269
- Using Export-Import Cycles to Defragment an AW — 271
- Saving AW Information with AWXML — 272
- Estimating Storage Usage — 273
- Working with Multiple Analytic Workspaces — 274
- Event-Driven Programs — 275

Part VI: Analytical Alchemy

21 Design Principles for Creating Multidimensional Information — 279

- The OLAP Advantage: Dimensionalizing an Analysis — 281
- The Presentation of OLAP Data — 282
- The Genesis of OLAP Data: Dimensions — 283
- Designing Measures — 286
- Filters-to-Measure — 286

22 Migrations: Tracking Changes in Customer Choices — 289

- The State-Transition Analysis Framework — 290
- A Sales Application — 292
- Getting the OLAP Advantage — 295
- Using State-Transition Analysis — 295
- Displaying the State-Transition Information in Tabular Format — 297
- Creating the State-Transition Report with DML — 298
- Extending the Transition Analysis — 300
- Customer Loyalty — 300
- DML Code for the Extension — 302
- Measuring Changes in Customer Composition — 303
- Different Plays Leading to the Same End Score — 304
- Dimensionalizing the State-Transition Analysis — 306
- Other Applications of State-Transition Analysis — 307
  - University Graduation Rate Analysis — 308
  - Drug Treatment Program Assessment — 308
  - Store Incentive Program Analysis — 309
  - RFM Analysis — 309

23 The Relationship Between OLAP, Statistics, and Data Mining — 311

- MOLAP is from Mars, Statistics is from Venus — 312
- Data Mining is from Pluto — 314
- Synergy Between OLAP and the Other Analysis Platforms — 316

Index — 319

Figures

Figure 2.1.	The Essential Difference Between ROLAP and MOLAP Is How the Data is Stored	13
Figure 2.2.	Locating Our Concerns in the Data Food Chain	15
Figure 8.1.	A Simple Organizational Hierarchy	77
Figure 8.2.	Alternate Representation of the Organizational Hierarchy	78
Figure 8.3.	How the Hierarchy Looks From a Graphical Interface	80
Figure 8.4.	A Hierarchy Based on Where the Customer Enrolled in the Loyalty Program	81
Figure 8.5.	A Geographical Hierarchy	86
Figure 8.6.	The Children of 33634	89
Figure 8.7.	The Descendants of Carrollwood	90
Figure 8.8.	The Parents of Tampa	91
Figure 8.9.	The Ancestors of Kathleen Riley	92
Figure 8.10.	All Values at the Zip Code Level	94
Figure 9.1.	Hierarchy of Figure 9.2 Displayed from AWM	98
Figure 9.2.	Using Attributes to Define a Hierarchy	99
Figure 9.3.	Interchanging Marital Status and Gender Levels	100
Figure 9.4.	Balanced but Not Regular Hierarchy	103
Figure 9.5.	Ragged Hierarchy	104
Figure 11.1.	Equation 1: Moving Average with Three Data Values	135
Figure 11.2.	Equation 2: FIR Filter with N Weights	136
Figure 12.1.	LIMIT ADD as a Venn Diagram	140
Figure 14.1.	Promotion Dimension: Hierarchy	183
Figure 15.1.	Choosing Model View as the Display Style	191
Figure 15.2.	Expanding an Analytic Workspaces Node in Model View	192
Figure 15.3.	Expanding the Analytic Workspaces Node in Object View Versus Model View	192
Figure 16.1.	Star Schema Database Design for the Demo Application	212
Figure 16.2.	Graphical Representation of the Fact Table	213
Figure 16.3.	The RFM Displayed in Relational Format is Equivalent to the Rows of Data in a Fact Table	214
Figure 16.4.	Dimension Lookup Tables	215
Figure 16.5.	Mapping Data Warehouse Objects to AW Objects	217

Figure 16.6.	Mappings are Made by Connecting the Associated Objects with an Arrow	218
Figure 16.7.	Bringing Up the Maintenance Wizard to Populate the Product Dimension	219
Figure 16.8.	Loading Dimension Members with the Maintenance Wizard	219
Figure 16.9.	Inspecting the Product Dimension	220
Figure 16.10.	Mapping Fact Table Columns to AW Objects	221
Figure 16.11.	Using the Measure Data Viewer to Create Reports and Charts	222
Figure 16.12.	Basic Report of the Four Dimensional Units Measure	222
Figure 16.13.	Swapping the Store and Products Dimensions	223
Figure 16.14.	Report of Units with Store on Rows and Product on Columns	223
Figure 16.15.	3D Bar Graph	224
Figure 16.16.	Trend Display	224
Figure 17.1.	Query Wizard: Items Tab Displayed on Open	230
Figure 17.2.	Query Wizard: Layout Tab (Layout Manager)	231
Figure 17.3.	Query Wizard: Dimensions Tab (Dimension Selector)	231
Figure 17.4.	Choosing Which Dimension to Work With	232
Figure 17.5.	Choosing Which Hierarchy to Work With	233
Figure 17.6.	Filtering Tools	234
Figure 17.7.	Anchoring the Non-filter Dimensions	235
Figure 17.8.	Hierarchy Selection Tools	236
Figure 17.9.	Setting Parameters for Hierarchical Selections	236
Figure 17.10.	Selecting Based on Attributes and Descriptions	237
Figure 17.11.	Setting Parameters for Attribute Selection	237
Figure 18.1.	Edit Window	243
Figure 18.2.	Simple Input-Output Process	254
Figure 18.3.	Realistic Input-Output Process	256
Figure 20.1.	Saving Metadata to an XML File	272
Figure 22.1.	State-Transition Diagram Representing a Change from A to B	291
Figure 22.2.	State-Transition Diagram Showing Transitions for Many Customers at Once	292
Figure 22.3.	The Data Depicted as a State-Transition Diagram	296

Tables

Table 4.1.	Access Modes for AWs	33
Table 6.1.	OLAP DML Comparison Operators	58
Table 7.1.	Recency Categories	73
Table 8.1.	Documenting Hierarchy Information in a Tabular Format	82
Table 8.2.	Hierarchy Information Including the Underlying Codes	83
Table 9.1.	Hierarchy Data for Creating the Hierarchy of Figure 9.2	102
Table 9.2.	Data for the Ragged Hierarchy of Figure 9.5	105
Table 9.3.	Comparison of the Two Formats: Balanced Hierarchy Only vs. Any Hierarchy	105
Table 14.1.	Promotion Dimension: Sample Data with Non-mutually Exclusive Sets	183
Table 15.1.	Object View Worksheet vs. Model View GUI	204
Table 21.1.	Identifying Base Dimensions	284
Table 21.2.	Identifying Attributes for Base Dimensions	285
Table 22.1.	The States Associated with the Sales Process	291
Table 22.2.	Basic Fact Data for a Sales Application	293
Table 22.3.	Conventional Summary Report ("Basic Report")	293
Table 22.4.	State-Transition Diagram Data in Tabular Format	297
Table 22.5.	Adding the Row Totals to the State-Transition Diagram Data	300
Table 22.6.	The "To" Percentages	301
Table 22.7.	Customer Loyalty Broken Out by Manufacturer	301
Table 22.8.	Adding the Column Totals to the State-Transition Diagram Data	303
Table 22.9.	The "From" Percentages	303
Table 22.10.	Percent of Customer Base Who Bought from Some Other Manufacturer Last Time	304
Table 22.11.	State-Transition Report for a Contrasting Report	305
Table 22.12.	The "To" Percentages for the Contrasting Report	305
Table 22.13.	Comparison of the Extended State-Transition Data for the Two Datasets	306
Table 22.14.	The Path of Students	308
Table 22.15.	The Path of Patients	309
Table 22.16.	The Path of Stores	309
Table 23.1.	Multidimensional Analysis (OLAP) vs. Statistics	313
Table 23.2.	Multidimensional Analysis (OLAP) vs. Data Mining	316

Acknowledgements

I'd like to thank Katarzyna Mikoluk for her brilliant support of multiple aspects of the preparation of this book. She worked through many of the examples, asked lots of great questions, and gave insightful feedback as well as many challenges, all of which significantly contributed to the quality of the book. Without her support and encouragement it is doubtful that this book would have been born. She is living proof that even a molecular biologist can understand OLAP. I'd also like to thank Jill Cooper for her incredible, meticulous review of the final manuscript and preparation of the index. She is a true jack-of-all-trades and master of all of them! I only wish I had met her sooner. And thank you to Clint Sutton for his superb job of transforming the whimsical OLAP musings that popped into my head into cartoons.

Thank you to the many people who supported me in various important ways through the process of writing this book. In particular, I would like to thank Dr. John Baker, Jorge Liñero, and Debora McLaughlin. I would also like to thank all of my past clients—I learned from each of them—and my fellow multidimensional road warriors, especially, Dan Vlamis, Mark Cawi, Steve Taylor, and Kim Moulton.

Finally, I wish to thank my parents for their wonderful support and my children John and Michael and the family pet, Chester, for their inspiration.

Part I:
Preparing for the Journey

1 | Overview

The book you are about to read is an invitation—and a ticket—for you to go on a journey with me deep into the world of *multidimensional data analytics*. On this journey, you will gain an in-depth knowledge of a specialized programming language designed specifically for conducting analyses in a dimensional framework. You will also learn powerful analysis techniques and principles that stand on their own, independent of any particular implementation language.

The realm through which we'll chart our course was defined by a computer-aided style of analysis that emerged in the late 60s and early 70s from the then relatively inconspicuous field of decision support. Observations of business analysts framing their world in terms of breakout categories—time frames, products, markets—led researchers to develop computational frameworks whose elements mapped directly to the conceptual framework and other distinctions they saw being employed to perceive, reason with, and analyze business performance.

Through waves of societal evolution and technological explosions, *the field of decision support has grown-up into business intelligence (BI) and has become mainstream and is acknowledged as being mission-critical.* Indeed, many of today's best-known industry leaders achieved their prominence as much through the innovative application of analytics as through the uniqueness of their core products. Business intelligence is more inclusive than its decision-support forerunner. It encompasses a variety of analytical approaches and novel ways of displaying and interacting with data. However, if there is an analytical paradigm that lies at its core, it is that of working with multidimensional data (or data cubes), which is referred to as *online analytical processing or OLAP*.

In this book you will see OLAP in detail. You will venture into the rarefied world of data stored in a native multidimensional format. You will find out what that means, both from a technical standpoint (what it is and how to do it) and an analytical standpoint (what it can do with data), and you will learn design principles that will empower you to use its capabilities fully.

Overshadowed by the explosive growth of the relational database, information and expertise concerning multidimensional data stored in a native multidimensional format is hard to find! Its interdisciplinary nature—with both a technical and an analytical face—adds to the challenges of learning it. Having worked with the technology for more than 15 years; however, I am convinced that multidimensional OLAP is well worth learning, now in fact more than ever. With the continuing growth in the importance and pervasiveness of analytical software, its timeliness is difficult to argue.

In this book, I strive to introduce the concepts and programming techniques that support development of advanced analytic applications in a natural order, an order that streamlines the learning process, making it easy to see the logic, power, and potential of OLAP in its native multidimensional format.

Even if Oracle OLAP is little more than a mystery to you now, by the end of this journey you'll be armed with all of the tools you'll need to put it to work for you! And you will not just learn language syntax, you will learn analytical techniques and application development *secrets*. The examples shown will truly showcase the power of an impressive language with a distinguished history.

Who is the Book's Audience?

This book was written for individuals working in the field of business intelligence who want to learn about OLAP: what it is, why it is valuable, and how to use it. It should be of special interest to individuals who fall into any of the following categories:

- People who have been looking for a book that will **explain the Oracle OLAP DML (Data Manipulation Language)**.

- **Power analysts who want to know what OLAP can do for them.** This means statisticians, data miners, and database marketers—professionals who use SAS, SPSS, Minitab and data mining software.

- **Managers who want to understand the value and potential of multidimensional analysis** and who want to maximize the value of their investment in this technology.

- **Developers of OLAP tools and applications,** including open-source developers who want to survey the capabilities of other product sets.

- Developers who need to **port an application** from legacy Express-based systems to 10g, or from Microsoft toolsets to Oracle OLAP, or vice versa.

- Developers who want to **optimize the performance of OBIEE** (Oracle Business Intelligence Enterprise Edition).

- **Students or faculty in university programs** in computer science or quantitative MBA programs seeking a principled explanation of what can be done with multidimensional analysis.

While this isn't a product book, the discussion does revolve around a real product, the OLAP DML as it exists in Oracle's 10g Release 2 database. You will find the material that relates to this programming language applicable to related products like Oracle 9i OLAP, Oracle 11g OLAP, and Oracle Discoverer PLUS OLAP, as well as legacy systems that include Oracle Express, Oracle Financial Analyzer (OFA), and Oracle Sales Analyzer (OSA).

The Book's Approach

There's a tremendous difference between learning to hit keys on a piano and learning to make music with it; similarly, there's a tremendous difference between knowing the syntax of a computer language and knowing how to create powerful applications with it. In this book, I'll be guiding you step by step through a series of stages designed to not only teach the language, but also to show how its various elements are used in context, so that you'll learn how to develop meaningful analytical frameworks with this technology.

We'll begin with the most fundamental operation: creating a dimension. Then we'll build upon and expand that foundation, creating an arsenal of techniques for working with multidimensional data. In covering analysis techniques, rather than give general discussions, I'm going to show concrete methodologies and specific programming techniques. Through seeing and working through example after example, you will build up a repertoire of techniques until you know everything you need to know to be able to create powerful, leading-edge analytical applications that can address the most exotic of requirements. The examples you'll see will be realistic in structure but will be built from small datasets, so they can be easily displayed on the page.

I'll make occasional comparisons of the OLAP DML with SQL to address the questions anyone with a relational database background will naturally have. However, you don't have to have a background in relational databases and SQL to follow the essential content of this book, and you won't lose much value by not having one.

I won't show every option for a given programming statement; there's no need, as those options are covered quite thoroughly in the product documentation. *Instead, I'm going to give you what the documentation doesn't: a path for learning the language and the elements of the discipline of OLAP analysis.* I will answer the important questions; questions such as, How is this feature used in practice? Why would I do this? How can I use this?

The book is divided into six sections. Part II: *Mastering Dimensions* is the first to dive headfirst into the language and every statement that you need to run the examples is there. In subsequent sections as things become more complex, it won't always be practical to give every single detail, so some statements may be left out. By that time, however, you will have the knowledge to see what they are and fill in the blanks yourself. Some supporting files are available at www.learn-oracle-olap.com.

I strongly encourage you to gain access to the software and try the examples out for yourself while reading the text. I'll tell you what software is required in the next chapter.

Thinking Inside the Cube

Don't be afraid to be creative! Try making variations or adaptations as you read. Why is this important? Because I want you to start honing your ability to think multidimensionally. An accomplished object-oriented programmer knows there's a certain mindset, or way of thinking, that goes with it. The proper mindset makes the process of writing code that realizes the advantages of the programming paradigm, come naturally. That's the way it is with the Oracle OLAP DML. Think of it as not just a language, but also a mindset, one that you'll learn. Developing proper thinking starts with learning the principles, then seeing examples of their application, and finally—through actual practice and firsthand experience—using them. This book provides the first two and opportunities for the third for the motivated reader.

This book isn't a "guide for dummies" or "manual for idiots"; it's written for intelligent, inquisitive people who aren't looking to avoid a learning curve; people who embrace learning opportunities. We won't spend much time learning how to enter parameters into templates and wizards—*our goal is to become the wizard!*

Every real application has stress points. Either it will have to operate fast with very large amounts of data, or it will need to accommodate some nonstandard computation or some exotic hierarchy that doesn't fit into the standard mold. What do you do when that happens? By focusing on learning to think rather than on what to do, you will know what to do!

Engineering Tradeoffs

As is true of any development effort, there are engineering tradeoffs in developing business intelligence applications. You might think of it in terms of four competing factors: *speed, size, functionality, and maintainability.*

For instance, as the amount of data included in a system increases, a larger space must be searched—and that larger size tends to make response time slower. To mitigate this, you might employ a more sophisticated data-access strategy. It might be possible to identify the most common data requests and create a small, nimble subuniverse and direct those requests there behind the scenes. This would result in a more complex design, but it would improve the end-user experience.

On the other hand, your goal may be to streamline system management to make it as easy to develop or maintain as possible. This goal might lead you to choose the simplest of designs using conventional, standardized approaches or to conform to a strict set of standards. Approaches that use a minimum of customization will more likely be more amenable to existing standard tools and administrative interfaces. Thus, as complexity goes down, size and speed may be limited but maintainability will be enhanced.

Finally, imagine there's a need for some metric that is a little off the beaten path. Maybe you want a customer segmentation model based on behavior qualified by some multistep process. Or maybe you need a derived quantity involving a sophisticated calculation process. This higher level of functionality means a more difficult system to maintain.

There's actually one more engineering tradeoff in the overall equation, and it has nothing to do with hardware, software, or methodologies—*it has to do with people*. The level of expertise in using the tools and in understanding how to apply the technologies is critical. With expertise, difficult tasks can be taken on and problems solved. With the right skills, you might figure out how to arrive at speed and simplicity at the same time.

How are these skills acquired? Unlike other software technologies, the core competencies for developing applications for multidimensional analytics are difficult to find in university curricula. Though this is changing, the requisite conceptual elements are often not available in the classroom, and the practice of developing OLAP data models for analysis has been largely developed in the trenches by practitioners. In the most favorable cases these skills are acquired through a mentoring process, one-on-one with a seasoned practitioner who has mastered the craft. I was fortunate to have learned this way—and to have had the opportunity to teach as well. And that's one of my greatest motivations for writing this book. I'm trying not so much to provide information as to share expert experiences, taking you on the path that I believe needs to be traveled to develop advanced expertise in this fascinating area. I hope you'll find your journey while reading this book to be like working alongside an actual human mentor.

As part of your management process involved in developing business intelligence capabilities for your firm, remember:

- You need someone with an analytical mindset on your development team.
- You need analytical people to help gather requirements and train end users.
- There's a huge advantage in having a mentor.
- In addition to technological foundations, you will want to grow human capital of analytical expertise.

Section Overviews

This journey has been divided into six major destinations. Here is your itinerary.

PREPARING FOR THE JOURNEY

In this section, you will be introduced to the idea of multidimensional analysis. You will get a glimpse into what OLAP has to offer for business analysis and what its defining characteristics are. You will get a concrete illustration of its capabilities using a sample four-dimensional report developed using Oracle OLAP. You will get your first peek into the analytical environment inside which the succeeding explorations will take place and get your introduction to the Oracle OLAP programming language.

MASTERING DIMENSIONS

Next, you'll zero in on the element that underlies everything: the dimension itself. You'll find out how to use dimensions as a powerful tool for structuring data for doing analysis. You'll see the process of creating, describing, relating, and categorizing dimensions. You'll see how to organize dimensions into hierarchies and explore practical issues that sometimes lead to complications.

DESIGNING MULTIDIMENSIONAL DATA

In this section, you'll look at the core elements of the OLAP framework: how multidimensional data is stored, how data can be calculated at display time, how to perform filtering operations, and how to work with sets and combinations. You'll also see what can be done with data: multidimensional data breakouts, dimension profilers, calculating shares and percentages, time series smoothing and digital filters, segmentations, manipulations with non-numerical data, and aggregations.

GRAPHICAL USER INTERFACES FOR OLAP

Until now, the focus has been on data modeling and creating analytical components within the multidimensional framework. But what about getting the information out through a graphical user interface (GUI)? In this section, you'll get a very practical introduction to using the graphical interface of Analytic Workspace Manager (AWM) to create objects in a format that makes that possible. You'll see how the filtering operations you learned translate into a graphical representation.

OLAP DML Programming

Here's where you'll learn to write DML programs. You'll already have a great background in the language by this point, so writing programs will be but a small step forward. We won't just go over the syntax of how to create, save, and run a program; we'll look at what are the typical kinds of things done with programs in the business intelligence arena. You'll learn practical programming techniques through a series of examples based on those very applications.

Analytical Alchemy

Here's where you'll learn the secrets of analytical alchemy with multidimensional data. I'll introduce two key ideas: the OLAP advantage and dimensionalizing an analysis. Through them, I'll characterize the benefit that OLAP offers and articulate a key design principle that you can use to create unique and powerful measures. Application of the principle will be thoroughly illustrated via a powerful OLAP-based customer-tracking model.

Given a full-fledged OLAP analysis platform, you may be curious to know how it compares to the other analysis platforms—statistics and data mining. In the final chapter of this section, I will discuss the relationship between these differing approaches.

2 | What is OLAP?

In this chapter, I will clarify a few critical terms that are needed to set the stage for everything else that follows. This will be accomplished in the manner of the proverbial peeling of an onion, with the issues examined layer-by-layer, delving a little deeper with each.

First, I will introduce and examine the acronym that is the centerpiece of the book: OLAP. Then we'll take a quick look at the two fundamentally different approaches for creating OLAP-based solutions noting the one we'll be taking. Finally, I will make a few remarks about how OLAP fits into the overall picture of business intelligence applications.

In the next chapter, the big picture will be completed. You will learn the distinguishing characteristics of the Oracle OLAP DML itself. You will find out where it fits into Oracle's OLAP option. In the second part of the chapter, I'll provide a down-to-earth explanation of the essential OLAP basics: what a dimension is and what a multidimensional data measure is. Through a sample illustration you will get a good look at results of the data modeling. You'll see how your work gets displayed to a user in an OLAP-aware interface. You'll see some typical display manipulations that are an important part of OLAP's power.

With a big picture of OLAP in place, you will have a North Star to follow for the rest of the journey.

What: OLAP and FASMI

We've used the term OLAP without formally defining it, so in case you are not familiar with it, OLAP is an acronym that stands for online analytical processing. The term OLAP was coined by renowned computer scientist Dr. E.F. Codd in 1993 well after the use of multidimensional database systems had been firmly established. Clearly, the term was chosen to contrast it from OLTP (online transaction processing).

It is unfortunate that the OLAP acronym fails to include explicit reference to the essence of what it was meant to describe—multidimensionality—and it mentions elements that are arguably not essential: you don't have to be online to work with multidimensional data. Also, does it help to call analytical analysis *processing*?

The shortcomings of the OLAP acronym have not gone unnoticed by others. Longtime industry observer Nigel Pendse found that the term could not be used to determine which products fell into the OLAP category. On his olapreport.com website, he says the term gives no indication of why you would want to use an OLAP tool or what an OLAP tool actually does. Mr. Pendse undertakes to rectify these shortcomings by proposing an alternate formulation encapsulated in the acronym FASMI (fast analysis of shared multidimensional information). His formulation emphasizes not technology, but the goals of OLAP.

I don't like to start out on a blue note, but I think it is important to point out the weakness of the OLAP acronym, because without it we're working with an unacknowledged handicap. By recognizing it, we can easily clarify and move forward unhandicapped.

How: ROLAP, MOLAP, and HOLAP

Originally, OLAP implied a multidimensional database. As the relational database evolved and grew in popularity, work was performed (most notably by Ralph Kimball) to define design approaches so that they could be adapted for creating dimensional applications as well. This led to two different approaches for realizing OLAP solutions: ROLAP and MOLAP.

ROLAP is the approach for developing dimensional systems based on data stored in *relational* database tables, thus the "R" for relational. MOLAP is the original approach based on data stored in a *multidimensional* database, ergo the "M." A multidimensional database stores the specialized data structures created specifically for working with multidimensional data; it doesn't use tables or SQL. MOLAP data is not only stored differently, it is accessed with a different language!

There is also a hybrid approach—HOLAP—in which a single database accommodates both types of data storage. This is the approach that the Oracle database takes. In this book we will be working with the MOLAP portion of the Oracle database, embodied in an *analytic workspace* that is embedded as a part of the relational database. Using the Oracle OLAP option means you will be making use of AWs.

Other products offer MOLAP environments, such as Oracle Essbase and Microsoft Analysis Services, but because the multidimensional database approach did not standardize in the way that the relational database did, *it is not possible to take a product-agnostic approach in this book without losing the concreteness*. While most of the principles in this book will be helpful in working with other products, the focus in this book will be directed squarely on the Oracle OLAP DML.

Figure 2.1 depicts some typical examples of data storage platforms for the two basic competing approaches.

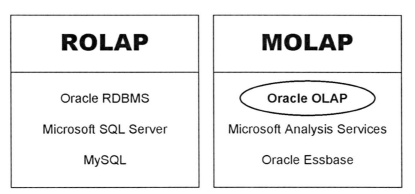

Figure 2.1. The Essential Difference Between ROLAP and MOLAP Is How the Data is Stored

OLAP and Business Intelligence

In *Successful Business Intelligence: Secrets to Making BI a Killer App,* Cindi Howson describes the value of business intelligence:

> Business intelligence allows people at all levels of an organization to access, interact with, and analyze data to manage the business, improve performance, discover opportunities, and operate efficiently.

Wikipedia gives this definition of business intelligence:

> Business intelligence (BI) refers to technologies, applications, and practices for the collection, integration, analysis, and presentation of business information and sometimes to the information itself.

So what is the relationship between OLAP and business intelligence? OLAP is one of those technologies; it is one of those practices.

OLAP's Position in the Data Food Chain

The way business data moves and evolves can be likened to a food chain. It starts life in some business process where small, simple bits of detailed data are generated. In a modern enterprise these data enter into a transaction processing system where they are recorded and used to produce some specific result, such as dispensing cash from an ATM or checking out a customer at a cash register. At some point, the multitude of transactions that have entered into the system are organized and reported on, at minimum to create accounting reports so that financial management of the firm is possible.

The purpose of business intelligence systems is to further enhance the understanding and insight that can be gleaned from such data. Because they are dealing with the presentation of summarized, historical data, there are systems in place to clean and restructure the data that was generated to put it in a usable format for them. This is a role of data warehousing.

At the end of the food chain are software technologies that further refine the information, making more sophisticated quantitative metrics available to a user at the front end.

And so we see the beginnings with small, simple data, like single-cell organisms. They are aggregated into larger, more sophisticated structures for accounting and other purposes.

Finally sophisticated structured summaries or other derived measures may be created for reporting and analysis purposes.

This process is illustrated in Figure 2.2. This diagram breaks the process out into conceptual steps, starting with the genesis of the data and ending with the business intelligence user's screen.

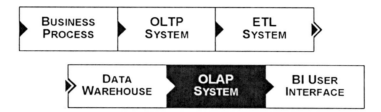

Figure 2.2. Locating Our Concerns in the Data Food Chain

The OLAP system stores the structured, multidimensional data that we'll be working with. In Oracle OLAP, it is called an analytic workspace (AW).

Military Intelligence, Business Intelligence, and Other Kinds of Intelligence

Long before the term *business intelligence* appeared, there was *military intelligence*. Let's take a few minutes to look at it because I think there is a lesson to be learned there, just as many a businessperson has benefitted from a read of Sun Tzu's *Art of War*.

NationMaster.com's online encyclopedia defines military intelligence as:

> A military discipline that focuses on the gathering, analysis, protection, and dissemination of information about the enemy, terrain, and weather in an area of operations or area of interest.

Military intelligence is not fighting the battle, it's gathering information that would maximize the chances of its success. It's about supporting the combat commanders' decision-making process by providing intelligence analysis of data to ensure that resources are applied in the most expedient manner.

The parallels between the goals of military intelligence and business intelligence are compelling; the difference is the nature of the mission, national security rather than commerce. Don't think of *business intelligence* as simply a replacement for the term *decision support*; think of it as the application of the principles of military intelligence to business.

And actually, even though we use the term *business intelligence,* any process that generates data could potentially make use of the techniques of OLAP analysis that you will learn in this book. This includes data that you might not think of as business data such as weather data, crime data, student performance data, medical data, or science data—the possibilities are endless.

3 | What is the Oracle OLAP DML?

Let's start at the beginning: what exactly is the OLAP DML language? The name itself can be confusing. First, while it is a programming language, one specifically designed for doing analytics on multidimensional data, it's actually more than that. *It doesn't just manipulate the data, it contains the data.*

In the relational world you could say, "here is a database and I will use SQL to query the data in it." But you wouldn't say that the data itself is stored in SQL, because it isn't: the data is stored in relational data tables. In the Oracle OLAP DML, *the data is stored within the language elements themselves!* There is no separation between the programming language and the data: they're parts of the same system.

There's a second point of potential confusion if you're familiar with SQL. SQL is divided into four components: DML, DDL, DCL, and queries created using SELECT statements. DML commands (INSERT, UPDATE, and DELETE) are used to change the data stored in the tables. DDL commands (CREATE, ALTER, and DROP) are used to create or modify the table structures themselves. DCL commands (GRANT and REVOKE) are used to set user access privileges. Finally, the SELECT statement is used to retrieve data.

So you might think, okay, OLAP DML is a language that does something analogous to the INSERT, UPDATE, and DELETE commands of SQL… right? Actually, the Oracle OLAP DML does *everything*. It does the functions analogous to *all four* components of the SQL language. It acts like a database *and* a complete data manipulation language all wrapped up in one package.

I'd like to make a final comparison here between the Oracle OLAP DML and Oracle's proprietary extension to SQL, PL/SQL. SQL is classified as a "fourth-generation" or "declarative" language. This means it's a language in which the user specifies *what* they want and the language figures out *how* to get it. PL/SQL is a "third-generation" extension developed to address SQL's lack of procedural control. PL/SQL has all the standard program control statements, such as *for loops, goto statements, procedural blocks, etc.* Like PL/SQL, the Oracle OLAP DML is also a procedural language with all the standard program control elements; like SQL, it contains a command, the LIMIT command, which in some respects plays the role of the declarative SQL SELECT command.

Contrasting the Relational World with the World of Analytic Workspaces

Analytic workspaces (AWs) are the physical storage element for the multidimensional world of the Oracle OLAP DML. AWs were designed explicitly to handle multidimensionality and are based on an indexed array model that provides direct cell access. I want to take another step in the direction of the multidimensional world embodied in the AW by taking a square look at the object types dealt with in these two different worlds.

In the relational database, you would be working with object types such as:

- Tables
- Indexes
- Sequences
- Views
- Stored Procedures
- Triggers

The AW has different object types, such as:

- Variables
- Dimensions
- Relations
- Formulas
- Programs
- Valuesets

There is no straightforward mapping between these two sets of objects, though some comparisons can be made. I've taught five-day courses in this language and occasionally, after a couple of days, a student asks me how to join tables or set up indexes in the language. So let me make this clear from the beginning: there are no tables and no joins, no WHERE clauses or GROUP BYs in the Oracle OLAP DML. There will be something else, however, and that's what this book is about!

And although you're looking at two different worlds here, there's a way to connect them. There's a way to read data from an AW using SQL, and there's a way to read data from a relational table using the Oracle OLAP DML. Typically, the AW reaches out to the relational world during the load process. It's quite possible to store all data being manipulated within the AW and never go back to the relational source tables during the operation of the system. This is a great strength of Oracle's product offering. It provides a mechanism for taking advantage of the strengths of each approach from within a single database.

What Advantages Does OLAP Offer?

There are several major advantages to using OLAP.

- PERFORMANCE—OLAP can give very substantial boosts in reporting and filtering performance over what you could achieve with a pure ROLAP solution. Execution speed is a critical success factor for analysis systems. Remember that these systems are used interactively with live users. Often they are used to explore data, with the user switching frequently from one scenario to another. As the user switches data presentations, the new data should be rendered quickly; delays of even tens of seconds disrupt the kind of thought process that needs to take place. In the same way, if filtering operations take a long time, the user will avoid them, exploring fewer possibilities. Needless to say, slower performance translates into more time required to complete an analysis.

- THE OLAP DML's COMPUTATIONAL RICHNESS—The DML is a full-featured programming language designed specifically for working with multidimensional data. It's a mature language, having evolved over the span of several decades. The DML has built-in functions for streamlining typical operations like aggregations, as well as a full complement of programming constructs that give developers the ability to create virtually any custom measure a specific application may need.

- THE OLAP DML PROVIDES A STREAMLINED ENVIRONMENT WITH A NATURAL FLOW FOR DOING DIMENSIONAL ANALYTICS—The DML was invented solely for the purpose of providing multidimensional analytics, so it supports all the fundamental needs of the activity: data structures for representing multidimensional data are native elements of the language; dimensional relationships are created with indexing automatically generated behind the scenes; and constructs for working with sets and orderings are included.

Compare this to SQL, which is, in the end, a world of rows and columns. The expression itself—rows and columns—refers to positions on a two-dimensional display, not functional categories (such as PRODUCT, GEOGRAPHY, and TIME) that you find in the native multidimensional platform. Also, there's a symmetry between dimensions in OLAP that doesn't exist with relational rows and columns. If you add a row to a SQL table that's just data, but to add a column you have change the table's definition. Add a product to the product dimension, that's adding a dimension member; add a region to the geography dimension, that's adding a dimension member!

We tend to gravitate toward that which is familiar. Hopefully this book will make the DML a familiar thing to you, which you will use and with which you will set yourself apart. But even if you go back to SQL and never return to OLAP DML, I believe you will find that your tour-of-duty through the AW was worthwhile, helping you to develop the mindset that is adept at working with multidimensional analytic systems.

What is the Oracle OLAP Option?

The OLAP DML is part of Oracle's OLAP option. All the components of the Oracle OLAP option are nicely described in the *Oracle® OLAP Application Developer's Guide,* 10g Release 2 (10.2.0.3), part number B14349-03 that outlines the following six major components installed in the database:

- OLAP ANALYTIC ENGINE—The OLAP analytic engine supports filtering operations and rapid calculation of multidimensional data.

- ANALYTIC WORKSPACES—AWs store the data in a native multidimensional format.

- OLAP DML—OLAP DML is the native language of AWs (this is what this book explores in depth).

- SQL INTERFACE TO OLAP—The SQL interface to OLAP provides access to AWs from SQL using PL/SQL.

- ANALYTIC WORKSPACE JAVA API—The Analytic Workspace Java API provides a way to create an AW (including the logical dimensional model) from a Java program.

- OLAP API—The OLAP API is a Java-based programming interface for developing OLAP applications. It supports Oracle BI Beans.

There are also two client-based components:

- ANALYTIC WORKSPACE MANAGER—The Analytic Workspace Manager (AWM) provides a GUI for creating and managing AWs. It can be used to create workspaces in database standard form. Being in "standard form" means the objects in the AW comply with Oracle's metadata standard so their data is accessible from standard front-end tools, such as OracleBI Discoverer Plus for OLAP, OracleBI Spreadsheet Add-In, and Oracle BI Beans. It is also possible to create AWs without the metadata information and they are much simpler in structure. We will work with both types in this book.

- OLAP WORKSHEET—The OLAP Worksheet is an interactive environment for working with AWs that is accessed from AWM. It is the primary interface you will be using in this book for entering DML commands and retrieving output. The OLAP Worksheet contains a help menu item that includes an "OLAP DML Language Help F1" choice.

Software Required for This Book

To follow along with the examples in this book, you'll need access to the Enterprise Edition of the Oracle 10g Release 2 database and the AWM client application. The purchase of this book includes no offer of software support; you are referred to the Oracle website for downloads and documentation for Oracle products. You might start at www.oracle.com/technology/software/index.html.

The 30,000-Foot View

Before getting into the nuts and bolts of the DML, it will be helpful for you to have an idea of the end product of your efforts. In this section you will see an important part of the end goal of OLAP development—we will explore a report of four-dimensional data (the Demo Application). Using that report as an example, I'll show some of the characteristic ways that OLAP reports can be manipulated by an end user to reconfigure the data presentations. The flexibility of presentation you will see is an important part of the value of the OLAP approach.

To begin, you will need to have a clear notion of *categorical* versus *quantitative* information:

- CATEGORICAL INFORMATION—Categorical information captures discrete entities, qualities, or characteristics. Examples of categorical information include products, customers, accounts, cities (or other geographical terms), markets, gender, and time frames such as weeks or months.

- QUANTITATIVE INFORMATION—Quantitative information is *numerical*. It's generally the measurement of the process of interest—or what could be called the application data. This might be the number of products sold, the amount of revenue earned, the cost of producing a product, or the number of customers.

In the multidimensional framework, categorical entities correspond to *dimensions* and quantitative information corresponds to *measures*. One of the most basic operations that is performed in multidimensional data processing is to collect numerical data along with the categorical information that applies to it, then to calculate summary values corresponding to even broader categories.

Now let's look at the hypothetical Demo Application. Suppose you were to collect sales activity data, noting what product was purchased, in which store the purchase was made, what payment method was used, and when the sale was made. In OLAP terminology, you would say you have four dimensions: *product, store, payment method, and time*.

The figure below is a display of summarized data with these four *breakout dimensions*, showing a Units measure.

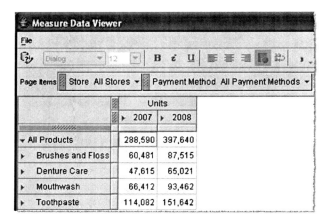

In this report, you see that a grand total of 288,590 items were sold during 2007. You see that numerical data constitutes the body of the report and the breakout categories—or dimensions—make up the various headings. You see Products as the row headings and time as the column headings. This report actually consists of numerous "pages," which are a function of the store and payment method.

Assume the data was collected on a weekly basis. It was summarized so that yearly figures are available. The same principle applies for the other dimensions. As you will see shortly, the information can be presented at various degrees of granularity for all the dimensions.

In an OLAP application, you can typically *choose from a variety of measures*; in addition to units, a sales application like this might have measures such as revenue, cost, or number of customers.

The OLAP-aware interface will provide a mechanism so you can *choose a slice of data*. In the figure below, the user has clicked on the triangle to the right of the "All Stores" tile to reveal some choices for the value of the store dimension.

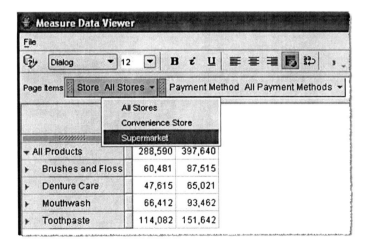

The user selects "Supermarket" to get the supermarket-only figures. That slice of data is shown below.

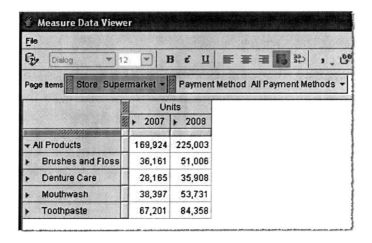

In addition to selecting which slice of data to show, OLAP interfaces allow you to *swap dimensions to exchange their display role*. In the figure below, Time has been swapped with Store so now time values are used to define the pages rather than label the columns.

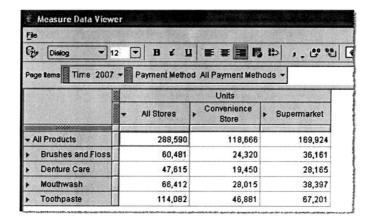

You can perform a *rotation*, which is just swapping the row and column dimensions. These operations are performed using the mouse by dragging and dropping control panes to different places on the display. This gives the next display.

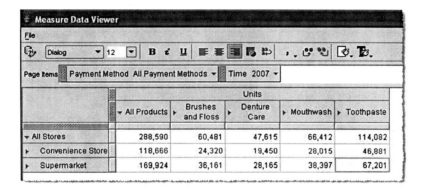

OLAP reports also let you *drill down into a hierarchy* to see more detailed information. The Product hierarchy has already been expanded once, but it has one more level. The next display is a report with all levels of the Product hierarchy showing.

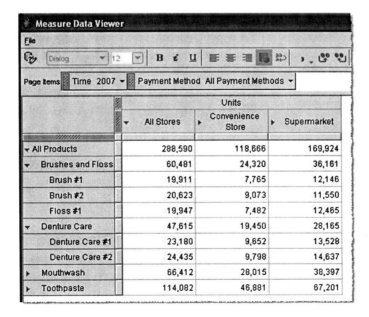

The last manipulation you'll see demonstrates the ability to put *multiple dimensions along an edge*. In the report below, Time and Store were both dragged to the top edge of the report.

	Units					
	All Stores		Convenience Store		Supermarket	
	2007	2008	2007	2008	2007	2008
All Products	288,590	397,640	118,666	172,637	169,924	225,003
Brushes and Floss	60,481	87,515	24,320	36,509	36,161	51,006
Brush #1	19,911	28,473	7,765	11,850	12,146	16,623
Brush #2	20,623	30,642	9,073	12,991	11,550	17,651
Floss #1	19,947	28,400	7,482	11,668	12,465	16,732
Denture Care	47,615	65,021	19,450	29,113	28,165	35,908
Denture Care #1	23,180	32,378	9,652	14,918	13,528	17,460
Denture Care #2	24,435	32,643	9,798	14,195	14,637	18,448
Mouthwash	66,412	93,462	28,015	39,731	38,397	53,731
Toothpaste	114,082	151,642	46,881	67,284	67,201	84,358

Reports like this are very powerful tools for an analyst who wants to gain insight into a business process. OLAP reports show how results vary as a function of key drivers. The analyst has the ability to orient the reports to display trends or to compare and contrast the performance of two entities. The analyst can choose the level of detail they want to see.

This illustration is just the tip of the business-intelligence iceberg, but it represents an important element of what the OLAP model offers and gives a concrete illustration of functionality available to an end user.

So, how is data stored and organized to make it easy to create presentations like this? What are the design choices and issues involved in working with dimensions and measures? What other functionality does OLAP have to offer?

These questions will all be addressed in this volume. By the middle of the book, you'll be able to create the application that generated these displays. In the end, you will understand a rich analytical platform that has far more to offer than this simple demonstration can show.

4 | Pit Stop: Analytic Workspace Manager Administration Basics

Before you begin your journey into the world of data modeling techniques and multidimensional analytics, you'll need to know a few things about working with the container of those activities: the AW. In this chapter, you will learn the basic operations with AWs such as the following:

- Create and delete.
- Attach and detach.
- Reorder.
- Set access mode.
- Save changes.
- Get information about them.

Oracle's HOLAP platform can be thought of as a *world within a world approach*. AWs constitute the multidimensional world. Although AWs are, in fact, stored in rows of a relational database as a large object binary (LOB), in some respects AWs operate like a database unto themselves. In this chapter, you'll learn some administration basics for them.

Before creating your first AW, I would like to call your attention to the idea of a *standard-form* AW that was introduced in the last chapter. A standard-form AW contains the supporting objects required to ensure its data can be accessed through standard graphical front-end tools.

The number of supporting objects and properties required to do so is quite large and entails significant complexity. For this reason, we will start by creating a non-standard-form AW. This will greatly simplify the environment and make it easier to focus on data modeling and analytics—the issues we want to focus on. By pushing this complexity out of the way, statisticians, data miners, and analytically oriented readers who want to learn about the analytical value of OLAP but who are not concerned with technical issues surrounding the creation of GUIs will find the material in this book far more accessible.

So for now, you will be accessing data through the command-line interface. Then, in Part IV: *Graphical User Interfaces for OLAP* we will create standard-form AWs so you will see that part of the equation as well. By that time, you will have built up a substantial knowledge base on the OLAP DML, which you can apply to understanding the objects and properties that are created by the system when a standard-form AW is created.

Creating an Analytic Workspace

There are two ways to create an AW—through mouse interactions with the graphical user interface of AWM and through commands entered into the OLAP Worksheet, OLAP's command-line interface—you'll be examining both.

How to Graphically Create an Analytic Workspace

To create an AW graphically, start AWM to get a window like the one below.

Next, from the main menu select View | Object View. *It's very important that you make this choice!* Also I'll warn you now, if you create an AW under Object View as we are about to do and then get out of the system and then get back in under Model View, you won't see your AW and you may think that it disappeared. Don't worry. Just switch to Object View and you'll see that it's still there.

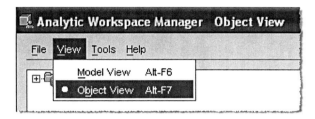

Now, open the Databases icon, click on the + by the database name, enter your username and password, and click OK to log on.

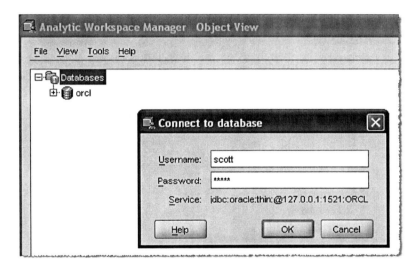

Now keep opening up the Databases hierarchy until you get to the Analytic Workspaces node. Right-click Analytic Workspaces and select Create Analytic Workspace. Your screen should look something like the one below:

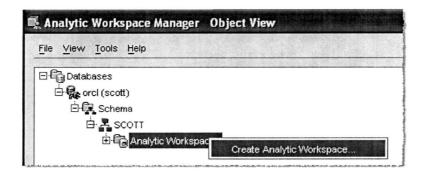

Name your AW, SALES. When an AW is being created, there will be an opportunity to select which tablespace it goes into, and it's recommended that you (or your DBA) set up one for that purpose.

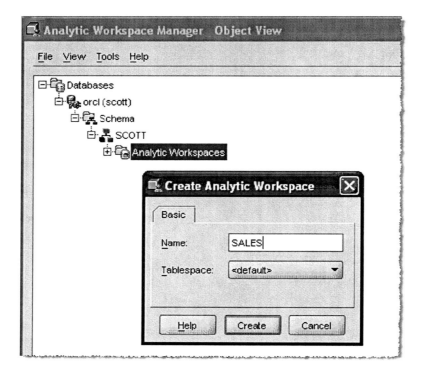

A child node in the hierarchy representing the new AW appears. Click on that node to highlight it. Now from AWM's main menu select Tools | OLAP Worksheet and the OLAP Worksheet window will appear.

You're ready to execute your first DML command; type this in as shown below:
Aw list

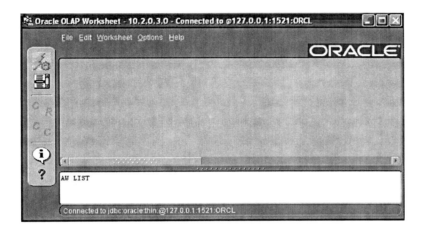

Press Enter to get the output:
->AW LIST
SALES* R/W UNCHANGED SCOTT.SALES
EXPRESS R/O UNCHANGED SYS.EXPRESS

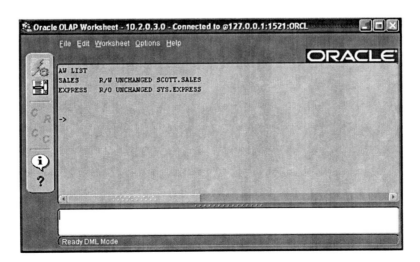

The first line of output lists the AW you just created. Subsequent lines show any required system AW that was attached automatically. The output gives the name of the AW, followed by its access mode. In the screen above, "R/W UNCHANGED" tells you that you're attached read/write and that nothing in the AW has changed since the last time it was updated. This is followed by "SCOTT.SALES" which is the schema name followed by a period and the AW name, which is the fully qualified name of the AW.

Notice the "->" in front of the AW LIST command. I'll use this as the convention for showing all commands the user enters whenever I show the system output. This will make it clear what the user enters and what the machine responds with, since any output generated will not be prefaced with the arrow. *(Warning: Don't type in the arrows; they will generate an error message!)* If the command is not prefaced with an arrow, then I'm not showing the output, which might be too voluminous. Also, keep in mind that many commands do not generate output. Also, the continuation character is a hyphen ("-") so if the last character in a line is a hyphen, then the next line is a continuation of that line.

How to Create an Analytic Workspace from the Command Line

To create an AW from the command line, the AW command is used. Create a second AW called "MARKETING" like this:

```
AW CREATE MARKETING
```

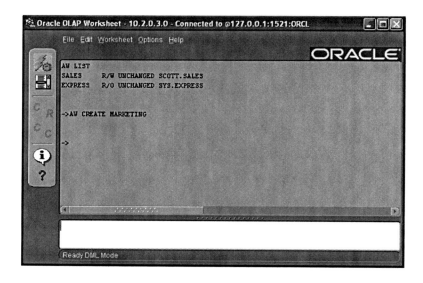

Now you have a new AW called MARKETING. You could issue the AW LIST command to see that it's there.

At any given time, an AW can be either attached or detached. When an AW is attached, it is available for use—you can query it, look at the objects in it, or modify it. When an AW is not attached, it is not available for use. When an AW is created, it is automatically attached read/write.

To make better use of space, subsequent material will not show a screenshot, but I think you get the picture by now.

Understanding the Different Access Modes

There are different access modes associated with the attachment process. When you create an AW, you're automatically attached as read/write, which means you have the privilege to make permanent changes to it. There are four types of access modes and they are shown in Table 4.1 below.

Table 4.1. Access Modes for AWs

Access Mode	Description
Read-Only (RO)	Can read, but cannot make permanent changes to the AW.
Read/Write (RW)	Can read and can make permanent changes to the AW. Only one user can have this mode at a time.
Read/Write Exclusive (RWX)	Can read and can make permanent changes to the AW, but no one else can connect to the system at the same time. This can be useful for keeping other users out when you are building an AW. Allowing users to access an AW where significant additions are being made can cause inflated disk storage usage.
Multi (MULTI)	Can be accessed simultaneously by several sessions and can be simultaneously changed by several users by using special statements for managing objects in this mode.

Changing Access Modes

To change the access mode, you detach and then reattach with the new access specification. For instance, try this out:

```
AW DETACH SALES
```

There won't be any output, but if you then type AW LIST, you'll see it's no longer attached. Next, do this:

```
AW ATTACH SALES RO
```

SALES is now attached read-only. Now do AW LIST again and you will see:
```
->aw list
SALES* R/O UNCHANGED SCOTT.SALES
SYS.AWCREATE* R/O UNCHANGED SYS.AWCREATE
EXPRESS R/O UNCHANGED SYS.EXPRESS
```

In read-only mode, you can still make changes to the AW; you just can't save them. Sometimes this is used as a way to experiment, with the confidence that the underlying system will not be changed.

You switch back to read/write mode with the commands:
```
AW DETACH SALES
AW ATTACH SALES RW
```

Saving Changes Permanently

If you're attached read/write, you can save your changes with the commands UPDATE and COMMIT.

Try this out:
```
UPDATE
COMMIT
```

The changes committed won't be seen by another user working with the same AW until that user detaches then re-attaches the AW. If you're attached read/write, the other user will of course be attached as read-only, since only one person at a time can be attached read/write.

Listing the Objects in an Analytic Workspace

So far you've only created AWs; you haven't actually put anything in them, so the "save commands" haven't had much to save. You can see what is in an AW by using the LISTNAMES command.

```
->LISTNAMES
There are no objects in the analytic workspace.
```

If you got a long list of objects rather than the above message, it is probably because you were attached in Model View when you created the AW. If that's the case, delete the SALES AW, switch to Object View, then create it again. You'll be working with in Model View in Part IV: *Graphical User Interfaces for OLAP,* but for now we're working in Object View.

Deleting an Analytic Workspace

There are two ways to delete an AW: from the command line or using AWM's graphical interface. We'll look at both ways.

From within the OLAP Worksheet, you would first have to detach the AW if it's attached:
```
AW DETACH MARKETING
```

Now you can delete it:
```
AW DELETE MARKETING
```

From the graphical interface, right-click the AW icon and select Delete Analytic Workspace MARKETING. That'll do it.

Ordering Multiple Analytic Workspaces

As you've seen, it's possible to attach more than one AW at once. When multiple AWs are attached, the order does make a difference since new defined objects are placed in the AW that is first in the attachment list. When the AW LIST command is issued, you'll see what the ordering is.

To put an AW first, you can type:
```
AW ATTACH SALES FIRST
```

...or actually, just doing:
```
AW ATTACH SALES
```

...will put it first. There are other variations possible, for instance:
```
AW ATTACH EXPRESS BEFORE SALES
```

If you use one of these statements to reorder an AW that's already attached, its attachment mode will not change; if it was attached read/write before the statement, it will continue to be read/write. If it was attached read-only, it will remain read-only.

Getting Information About an Analytic Workspace

So far, you've been working with the AW *command*. This command, like many other DML commands, has a corresponding *function* form:

- The command form makes something happen. It starts with the command name.

- The function form returns information about something. The function form uses parentheses and will follow a reporting command or an assignment statement.

For example, here is the AW command; it attaches the AW:
```
->AW ATTACH SALES
IMPORTANT: Analytic workspace SALES is read-only. Therefore,
you will not be able to use the UPDATE command to save
changes to it.
```

And here is the AW function; it tells you if it is attached:
```
->REPORT AW(ATTACHED 'SALES')
AW(ATTACHED 'SALES')
----------
    yes
```

It will be useful at this point to introduce a command similar to the REPORT command, namely the SHOW command. The SHOW command doesn't produce any heading information and can only be used to display one item, whereas the REPORT command can take a list of items to display in a single statement.

```
->SHOW AW(ATTACHED 'SALES')
Yes
```

Or using lowercase:
```
->Show aw(attached 'sales')
yes
```

You'll observe that *the AW name is not case sensitive, though capitals are recommended.* You can also find out if an AW exists using the AW function like this:

```
->Show aw(exists 'marketing')
no

->Show aw(exists 'SALES')
yes
```

You can get the full name of the AW:
```
->show aw(fullname 'sales')
SCOTT.SALES
```

You can find out the date it was last updated:
```
->SHOW AW(DATE 'SALES')
19OCT08
```

Using the OLAP Worksheet as a Calculator

Here are a few examples of the SHOW command with some simple arithmetic operations:
```
->SHOW (10-6)/2
2.00
```

You can change the number of decimals showing with the DECIMALS option:
```
DECIMALS = 4
```

Here's an example using the built-in function for square roots:
```
->SHOW (-5 + SQRT(25-8))/2
-2.9384

DECIMALS = 2
```

And here's an example of generating a random number between 0 and 1 from a uniform distribution:

```
->SHOW RANDOM(0,1)
-0.57
```

Here's a simple use of the SHOW command to display a literal (single quotes are used to encapsulate literals):

```
->SHOW 'Hello World'
Hello World
```

Generally speaking, DML commands and functions are not case-sensitive literals. The arguments to the built-in functions, when they are AW names or dimension names, are not case sensitive.

Using Shortcuts

Most commands have an abbreviated name as well; for instance, we could have written:
```
UPD
CMM
```

…instead of:
```
UPDATE
COMMIT
```

Or:
```
RPR LOG(10)
```

instead of:
```
REPORT LOG(10)
```

The basic rule for creating a command abbreviation is:

- Discard vowels, except if it's the first letter of the word.
- Discard consonants beginning at the end.
- When you are left with three characters, you are finished!

You can put more than one command on a line by separating them by a semicolon:
```
UPD; CMM
```

By the way, if you put several commands on a line like this and one of them fails, the subsequent ones will run anyway; they won't be ignored. This can be important to know in situations where one step is a setup for a subsequent step, so please exercise care!

Part II:
Mastering Dimensions

5 | Creating Dimensions

In Chapter 3: *What is the Oracle OLAP DML?* you learned that dimensions are used to model discrete entities, qualities, or characteristics. Dimensions are organizers of information! Fasten your seat belts, because I'm going to spend significant time working with dimensions as they are the basis for everything that follows. I hope you'll enjoy this part of the journey; there's a big payoff at the end for understanding not only the mechanics of how to create dimensions and their associated elements, but for understanding the modeling issues that arise in translating a real-world problem into a dimensional framework.

Before launching into the DML elements, I will provide a comparison point about relational data storage. In the relational world, there's one basic object for storing information, the table. In the native multidimensional world of the AW, there are several distinct types of objects that store information. The different object types can be thought of as being specialized for performing a particular type of function in the multidimensional analysis process. Not surprisingly, there is a *dimension* object type in the DML.

The DML provides many commands and structures for working with, organizing, and managing dimensions, things specific to what you would typically do with dimensions.

Dimensions are usually the first objects defined when building an AW and this will be our starting point.

To follow along with the examples, you should be connected to 10g, have the SALES AW attached read/write, and have the OLAP Worksheet open. We will build up the SALES AW created in the last chapter step-by-step in this and in subsequent chapters.

Defining and Maintaining Dimensions

Dimensions have a data type associated with them. The most common data type is text, but the type can also be integer, ID, and number. Here's how to create a dimension:

```
DEFINE PRODUCT DIMENSION TEXT
```

If you type the LISTNAMES command, you'll see that you now have one object in the AW, your PRODUCT dimension:

```
->LISTNAMES
   1 DIMENSION
   ----------------
   PRODUCT
```

All the DEFINE statement does is create the PRODUCT dimension; you have to create dimension members for it to be useful. Suppose you have three products. You'll need three members to represent those three products. The member values will be codes, such as TP001, TP002, and TP003. You can add these values to the product dimension with the MAINTAIN command and the keyword ADD as follows:

```
MAINTAIN PRODUCT ADD 'TP001' 'TP002' 'TP003'
```

The MAINTAIN command produces no output. To inspect the values you just entered use the REPORT command:

```
->REPORT PRODUCT
PRODUCT
--------------
TP001
TP002
TP003
```

If you want to add a few more members, you could do this:
```
MAINTAIN PRODUCT ADD 'TP004' 'TP005'
```

So far you've added dimension members (also called *dimension values*) from the command line. In a production environment, you'd probably load dimension members from a flat file or a relational table. I'll show you that process in Chapter 16: *The Star Schema and Beyond* and also Chapter 19: *Getting Data In and Out of Analytic Workspaces*. For now, we will continue to enter dimension members manually from the command line.

If a dimension member is already there, you'd get an error if you tried to add it again:
```
->MAINTAIN PRODUCT ADD 'TP004'
ERROR: (ORA-34034) TP004 is already a value of
SALES!PRODUCT.
```

The members of a dimension are necessarily unique; that's an inherent part of the language design. You cannot add the same member more than once. Thus the number of unique members of a dimension is the same as the number of members it has.

Dimension values are deleted with the MAINTAIN command:
```
MAINTAIN PRODUCT DELETE 'TP003'
```

There's also a MERGE option that works similarly to ADD, but doesn't complain if you try to add a value that's already there.

Since TP004 is already there, this MAINTAIN command has no effect:
```
MAINTAIN PRODUCT MERGE 'TP004'
```

This one adds a value:
```
MAINTAIN PRODUCT MERGE 'TP003'
```

Another difference between ADD and MERGE is that you can ADD several values in a single statement, but you can only MERGE one value at a time. For example, you would get this error:

```
->MAINTAIN PRODUCT MERGE 'TP006' 'TP007'
ERROR: (ORA-33852) You provided extra input starting at
'TP007'.
```

Choosing Codes for Dimension Members

It is worthwhile to make a few remarks about choice of codes here. Normally, the codes are not the descriptive text that the end user would want to see. Descriptive labels can and should be contained in a separate object that is dedicated to describing the object that the code represents. You will see how to create them in the next chapter.

One reason it is a good idea to have a clear separation between a dimension member's code and its label is that it gives the ability to change the label without having to touch the underlying code. Also, shorter codes lead to better performance, and from a developer's viewpoint, they are generally easier to work with than lines of descriptive text.

All other things being equal, we would prefer the codes to be short, to contain no special symbols or blanks and, for good measure, contain all capital letters and/or numbers. Nevertheless, the DML does not actually impose these restrictions. Indeed, the dimension values can contain blanks; they can be long; they can contain ampersands and the like. Thus, if one wanted to make the dimension values descriptive lines of text, it is certainly possible to do so and there are certain points ahead where we will do just that.

Thus it would be legal to do this:
```
MAINTAIN PRODUCT ADD 'A&B Quality Toothpaste'
```

There's nothing wrong with the codes themselves possessing some descriptive content. Putting some descriptive content into the codes can actually make the developer's work easier when working with the data from the command line, because the developer can look at the code and know something about it without consulting the descriptions.

When you're trying to perform a task in the OLAP Worksheet, without use of the GUI, descriptive content in the codes can save significant time. Examples of these situations include tracking down data problems, unit testing, prototyping a solution approach, and performing a special "one-off" analysis at a client's request.

However, if descriptive content is built into the codes, it should be done as a convenience for the developer or power analyst; the *system itself* should not rely on any information embedded in the codes. The system should only rely on information that is coded in more formal ways.

To give us something concrete to work with, let's create a sample dimension based on toothpaste products. In the examples that follow, I'll use TP to stand for toothpaste—so you can look at the code and, without knowing specifically what it stands for, see that it is some kind of toothpaste.

Regardless of whether the codes used have any descriptive content or not, dimension members each correspond to something in the application universe. In the case of the PRODUCT dimension, they represent products.

Getting Information About Dimensions and Dimension Members

If you want to know how many dimension members are in the product dimension, you can find out by using the built-in function, OBJ:

```
->SHOW OBJ(DIMMAX 'PRODUCT')
6
```

This tells you that there are six different dimension members in the product dimension. The OBJ function is one of hundreds of built-in functions and is very important. This is your access into the data dictionary and provides a wealth of information about the AW and the objects in it. Various uses of the OBJ function will be sprinkled throughout the book to show how it is used in context; but refer to online documentation for a complete explanation of its many uses.

Suppose there's a situation where you want to add a value, but you don't know whether or not that value is already a dimension member. You could try to add it—and if you get an error message, you'll know it was already there (otherwise the value would get added). You could use the MAINTAIN MERGE if it's only one value. A more graceful way of accomplishing the same thing would be to use the ISVALUE function like this:

```
->SHOW ISVALUE(PRODUCT 'TP004')
yes
```

If we get a no, we could add the value; if we get a yes, we would know it was already there. (As you might guess, the real reason for demonstrating the ISVALUE function is that it can be useful in DML programs handling dimension members in some automated process that may need to know if the dimension member is there or not.)

Next, notice what we get if we type:
```
->SHOW ISVALUE(PRODUCT 'tp004')
no
```

As you can see, *the dimension values are case sensitive.*

The Order of Dimension Members

The order in which the dimension members are added establishes the order in which they are stored. Unless you explicitly reorder them (with the SORT command, discussed in the next section), they will always appear in the same order when you do a REPORT on them.

If that default order is important to you, put the values in the desired order, and add them in that order. This is usually a good idea, because if the dimension values are in a random order, working with the system can become cumbersome and you'll be doing lots of SORT commands to get values to report in a meaningful order.

And let me make this clear: I'm talking about reports generated in the OLAP Worksheet using the REPORT command, not what happens in a graphical user front end. When you have an emergency with a deadline, you'll appreciate making the system easy to work with from the developer's standpoint. User friendly, good, but let's make it developer friendly, too! Storing dimension members in a useful order is a step towards that.

After the dimension values have been loaded, you can still change the default order. Here is the default order now:

```
->rpr product
PRODUCT
--------------
TP001
TP002
TP004
TP005
TP003
A&B Quality
Toothpaste
```

To change the default order, use MAINTAIN with the MOVE option:
```
MAINTAIN PRODUCT MOVE 'TP003' BEFORE 'TP004'
```

Now you get:
```
->RPR PRODUCT

PRODUCT
--------------
TP001
TP002
```

```
TP003
TP004
TP005
A&B Quality
Toothpaste
```

A MAINTAIN MOVE command will permanently change the dimension members' default order; this is not the same thing as doing a sort, which is temporary!

Using the MAINTAIN MOVE command doesn't actually change the way the data is stored; instead, it creates an internal pointer that redirects the order in which the values are accessed. Be careful, however, because if a lot of these pointers are created there can be noticeable performance degradation. Finally, if you are in a situation where you must do a lot of "maintain moves," there's a way to clean things up after the fact using what's called an EIF export-import cycle. This will be discussed in Chapter 20: *Tune-Up: Working with Analytic Workspaces*.

This process of populating a dimension with values is called *dimensional maintenance*. What typically happens when a system is built is that the dimension values are loaded in and there's a minimal amount of dimensional maintenance after that. If you find that the operation of your systems includes a lot of adding and removing dimension values, there may be something amiss with the overall design.

Dimensional maintenance can be slow, and if a lot of it is done after the system is built, it can lead to inefficient usage of storage or poor performance.

The Concept of Status

One of the unique aspects of the DML is described by the concept of *status*. Inside an OLAP session, every dimension has a status list associated with it. The status list tells what is "in status." You haven't done anything to set status so far, so you've always been getting the default status setting, which is all values. In terms of our example, this means all products—or, more precisely, all product dimension values.

Status is a way of telling the system, "these are the values I want to work with." There is really no counterpart to status in SQL.

Filtering and the LIMIT Command

Now you're ready to learn one of the most important commands in the DML language, the one that sets status. This is the LIMIT command. Setting status is a very common operation and is essentially the same thing as what you might call "running a filter." It is done to identify a set of dimension members meeting a criterion.

The LIMIT command has many options and variations. Here are a few examples:
```
LIMIT PRODUCT TO ALL
```

This command sets status to all values. The term "ALL" is a special reserved word. The LIMIT command generates no output. If you were to report on product:

```
->REPORT PRODUCT

PRODUCT
--------------
TP001
TP002
TP003
TP004
TP005
A&B Quality
Toothpaste
```

...you'd get a list of all values. Here's another example of the LIMIT command:
```
LIMIT PRODUCT TO FIRST 2
```

As you might guess, this gives you the first two values (working with the default order). You can report on product again to see the new result:

```
->REPORT PRODUCT

PRODUCT
--------------
TP001
TP002
```

Similarly, we have:
```
LIMIT PRODUCT TO LAST 3
```

We can also do:
```
LIMIT PRODUCT TO 3
```

This gives you the third value. Make sure you note the difference between LIMIT PRODUCT TO 3 and LIMIT PRODUCT TO FIRST 3.

If you tried to limit to the 10,000th and there was no such value, you'd generate an error message and status would not be altered:

```
->LIMIT PRODUCT TO 10000
ERROR: (ORA-33158) The SALES!PRODUCT dimension does not have a value numbered 10000.
```

Is it possible to have no dimension members in status? Yes, you can have null status as long as the option OKNULLSTATUS is set to yes.

```
OKNULLSTATUS = YES
LIMIT PRODUCT TO NA
```

On the other hand, we would get this:
```
->OKNULLSTATUS = NO
->LIMIT PRODUCT TO NA
ERROR: (ORA-35654) The status of the SALES!PRODUCT dimension cannot be set to null.
```

If the status of a dimension is set to NA, and you do a report on that dimension, no output will be generated. If the status of a dimension is NA and you switch OKNULLSTATUS to No, it remains with null status and no error is generated.

More examples:
```
LIMIT PRODUCT TO 2 TO 4
```
(This sets status to the second through the fourth dimension value.)

```
LIMIT PRODUCT TO 'TP004'
```
(Sets status to the value TP004.)

```
LIMIT PRODUCT TO 'TP003' TO 'TP005'
```
(Sets status to every value between TP003 and TP005 inclusive.)

FINDING OUT ABOUT STATUS

If you want to know how many values you have in status at any given time, you can use the STATLEN function to find out.

```
->SHOW STATLEN(PRODUCT)
3
```

If you want to know what they are, you can REPORT on them as we have been doing:
```
->REPORT PRODUCT

PRODUCT
--------------
TP003
TP004
TP005
```

...or use the STATUS command:
```
->STATUS PRODUCT
The current status of PRODUCT is:
TP003, TP004, TP005
```

If you want to know if a particular dimension value is in status or not, you can use the INSTAT built-in function:

```
->SHOW INSTAT(PRODUCT 'TP001')
no
```

You'll continue to expand your knowledge of the LIMIT command as we move forward; these examples show some of its most basic uses. For now, make sure you see the difference between dimensions and dimension members and between the MAINTAIN command and the LIMIT command. By the way, if you issue a MAINTAIN command, it sets status of the dimension to ALL.

Hopefully you've been following along with the examples discussed above by getting into AWM and trying the statements. If you haven't, take some time now and try it.

Comparing the OLAP DML LIMIT Command to the SQL SELECT Command

Let's take a moment now to compare the SQL SELECT command with the DML LIMIT command. Imagine you have a table called PRODUCT_LOOKUP that has a column named PRODUCT.

Then the SQL query:
```
SELECT PRODUCT FROM PRODUCT_LOOKUP
```

...would be similar to the DML commands:
```
LIMIT PRODUCT TO ALL
REPORT PRODUCT
```

A difference between the LIMIT command and the SELECT command is that the SELECT statement returns a list of all PRODUCT values, where the LIMIT doesn't return anything: it just identifies all the product values as the group of values in which you're interested.

The LIMIT command functions in many ways like a freestanding WHERE clause. It is used to designate which values are selected, and as a follow-up step, you tell the system what you want to do with them. So far, the only thing you've done is to REPORT values, but you'll see other choices later on. In fact, many commands besides the REPORT command operate only on values in status. You'll see examples ahead!

6 | Describing Dimension Members with Labels

So far, you have explored creating dimensions, adding dimension members, setting status, and ordering dimension members. In the next two chapters, you will be seeing other things that can be done with dimensions. Actually, you will be exploring the question, what can be done with information categories? You will see data modeling issues concerned with describing, categorizing, and organizing dimension members as well as learning how to actually mechanize things with Oracle OLAP DML.

The information used to describe and organize dimensions is often dealt with in the context of creating metadata. But we're not going to deal formally with the topic of metadata until Chapter 15: *Exploring Metadata*. The objective of this and the next two chapters is to engage you with the modeling issues surrounding the use of dimensions as information organizers all the while building up your vocabulary of DML statements.

None of the objects we'll be defining here are intended to be in compliance with any metadata standard, but to the extent we create objects that are normally part of metadata, I will choose names that will make them familiar to you when we do get to that topic later on in the book.

Creating Labels for Dimension Members

It's time to learn how to create descriptive labels for the dimension members. You can think of the codes used for dimension members as computer-friendly, and labels as user-friendly. To create labels, you'll be introduced to a second object type, the variable.

In the Oracle OLAP DML, variables are the primary object type used to store the numerical data that come from the business process. But variables can also store textual data: they can store the text labels for the dimension values.

Let's see how to create a variable. When you create a variable, you specify its dimensionality in the defining statement. To use a dimension, as you might expect, it must first be defined. So if you want to create a variable dimensioned by PRODUCT, the PRODUCT dimension has to have already been defined.

I'll illustrate this process by creating a text-valued variable called PRODUCT_LONG_DESCRIPTION.

```
DEFINE PRODUCT_LONG_DESCRIPTION VARIABLE TEXT <PRODUCT>
```

PRODUCT_LONG_DESCRIPTION is dimensioned by PRODUCT. There will be a value of the PRODUCT_LONG_DESCRIPTION variable for each value of PRODUCT.

It may be helpful to point out that PRODUCT_LONG_DESCRIPTION is similar to a one-dimensional text-valued array that you might create in any programming language such as Java or C++, except that rather than having integer-valued subscripts, the subscripts take on the values of the PRODUCT dimension.

Just as you've used the REPORT command to look at dimension values, you can use it to look at the values of variables. Let's use the REPORT command below with a width specification of 40 characters (the default is 10). If you issue the commands:

```
->LIMIT PRODUCT TO FIRST 3
->REPORT W 40 PRODUCT_LONG_DESCRIPTION
PRODUCT                 PRODUCT_LONG_DESCRIPTION
--------------          ----------------------------------------
TP001                   NA
TP002                   NA
TP003                   NA
```

…you'll see that the values of PRODUCT_LONG_DESCRIPTION are all NA, which is the way that null values are reported. Now assign some values, which will be the labels you want to create.

Suppose you start with the data in the table below.

Code	Label
TP001	Healthy Pro Toothpaste, Clean Mint
TP002	Children's Toothpaste, Glitter Mint
TP003	Revitalizing Toothpaste, Vanilla
TP004	Sensitivity Toothpaste, Fresh Mint
TP005	Whitening Toothpaste, Herbal Mint
TP006	Tartar Protection Toothpaste, Vanilla
TP007	Natural Toothpaste, Teatree

Take a look at the following assignment statement (note the use of the hyphen as a continuation character):

```
PRODUCT_LONG_DESCRIPTION = -
'Healthy Pro Toothpaste, Clean Mint'
```

Now do this:
```
->REPORT W 40 PRODUCT_LONG_DESCRIPTION
PRODUCT             PRODUCT_LONG_DESCRIPTION
--------------      ----------------------------------------
TP001               Healthy Pro Toothpaste, Clean Mint
TP002               Healthy Pro Toothpaste, Clean Mint
TP003               Healthy Pro Toothpaste, Clean Mint
```

If you don't already have them added, add in the last two dimension values:
```
MAINTAIN PRODUCT ADD 'TP006' 'TP007'
```

Since MAINTAIN will set status to ALL, you would now have:
```
->REPORT W 40 PRODUCT_LONG_DESCRIPTION
PRODUCT                 PRODUCT_LONG_DESCRIPTION
-------------------------------------------------
TP001             Healthy Pro Toothpaste, Clean Mint
TP002             Healthy Pro Toothpaste, Clean Mint
TP003             Healthy Pro Toothpaste, Clean Mint
TP004             NA
TP005             NA
TP006             NA
TP007             NA
```

Implicit Looping

The assignment statement automatically iterated over the values that were in status when the command was issued. This illustrates a very important characteristic of the DML. Whereas in many programming languages, iteration over a set of values must be accomplished with a FOR loop, in the DML, many statements do implicit iteration. This means the very statement implies iteration is desired, and its function is performed cycling over all dimension members in status without an explicit FOR loop.

Actually, you can accomplish iteration with an explicit FOR loop, and in Chapter 18: *Writing DML Programs*; you'll see the syntax for doing iterations that way. But it's always preferable to use an implicit FOR loop. The implicit FOR loop is typically much faster—maybe 10 or even 100 times faster! In addition, there are fewer lines of code.

Since you obviously do not want to give the same label to more than one product, you need to fix the above statement. Given what you've already learned, you could start setting the label values like this:

```
LIMIT PRODUCT TO 'TP001'
PRODUCT_LONG_DESCRIPTION = 'Healthy Pro Toothpaste, -
Clean Mint'
LIMIT PRODUCT TO 'TP002'
PRODUCT_LONG_DESCRIPTION = 'Children\'s Toothpaste, -
Glitter Mint'
LIMIT PRODUCT TO 'TP003'
PRODUCT_LONG_DESCRIPTION= 'Revitalizing Toothpaste, Vanilla'
```

You now have the first three labels set the way you want them:

```
->LIMIT PRODUCT TO 'TP001' TO 'TP003'
->REPORT W 40 PRODUCT_LONG_DESCRIPTION
PRODUCT            PRODUCT_LONG_DESCRIPTION
--------------     ----------------------------------------
TP001              Healthy Pro Toothpaste, Clean Mint
TP002              Children's Toothpaste, Glitter Mint
TP003              Revitalizing Toothpaste, Vanilla
```

Qualified Data References

There is another slightly more elegant way of accomplishing the same thing using a qualified data reference (QDR). To see how QDRs work, take a look at these examples:

```
PRODUCT_LONG_DESCRIPTION(PRODUCT 'TP004') = -
'Sensitivity Toothpaste, Fresh Mint'
PRODUCT_LONG_DESCRIPTION(PRODUCT 'TP005') = -
'Whitening Toothpaste, Herbal Mint'
PRODUCT_LONG_DESCRIPTION(PRODUCT 'TP006') = -
'Tartar Protection Toothpaste, Vanilla'
PRODUCT_LONG_DESCRIPTION(PRODUCT 'TP007') = -
'Natural Toothpaste, Teatree'
```

As you can see, the object name is followed by a parenthesis containing the dimension followed by the desired dimension member in single quotes. QDRs are a way of setting status locally to the statement in which they are contained. The above assignments will be made regardless of the status setting of the product dimension. Since QDRs give a way of making assignments without altering the dimension status, it's useful in a situation where you want to assign a value to an object but don't want to alter a status setting.

Setting Status Based on Labels

Now that you've got labels for the dimension values, there may be times when you need to set status for a dimension on the basis of one of its labels. For example, you may want to find the dimension member that has a given label. The following statement illustrates this process.

```
LIMIT PRODUCT TO PRODUCT_LONG_DESCRIPTION EQ -
'Healthy Pro Toothpaste, Clean Mint'
```

In the above statement, EQ means equal to. The comparison operators are shown in Table 6.1.

Table 6.1. OLAP DML Comparison Operators

Operator	Meaning
LT	Less than
LE	Less than or equal to
GT	Greater than
GE	Greater than or equal to
EQ	Equal to
NE	Not equal to

There is also a LIKE operator, which can be used to find labels containing a given substring. For instance:

```
LIMIT PRODUCT TO PRODUCT_LONG_DESCRIPTION LIKE '%Mint%'
```

…will find the products whose label contains the string "Mint."

This is a good time to introduce one of the more popular DML character manipulating functions: FINDCHARS. The FINDCHARS function returns the position of the beginning of a target literal within a given text expression. Suppose, for example, you want to find the position of the literal "Mint" within one of the labels. You could locate "Mint" this way:

```
->SHOW FINDCHARS('Healthy Pro Toothpaste, Clean Mint' -
'Mint')
31
```

…or "Healthy":
```
->SHOW FINDCHARS('Healthy Pro Toothpaste, Clean Mint' -
'Healthy')
1
```

…or a literal that isn't contained in the text expression:
```
->SHOW FINDCHARS('Healthy Pro Toothpaste, Clean Mint' -
'Snack')
0
```

Either one of the two arguments of this function could be an expression that evaluates to a literal; they don't have to be the literal itself. So, for example, instead of making the first argument a literal, you could do this:

```
->LIMIT PRODUCT TO 'TP001'
->SHOW FINDCHARS(PRODUCT_LONG_DESCRIPTION 'Mint')
31
```

You got this result since:
```
->SHOW PRODUCT_LONG_DESCRIPTION
Healthy Pro Toothpaste, Clean Mint
```

Or, using QDRs instead of setting the limit:
```
->SHOW FINDCHARS(PRODUCT_LONG_DESCRIPTION(PRODUCT -
'TP001') 'Mint')
31
```

Here's how to find all dimension values whose label contains a given character string (for instance, "Mint"):

```
LIMIT PRODUCT TO FINDCHARS(PRODUCT_LONG_DESCRIPTION -
'Mint') GT 0
```

Setting status by using dimension values directly is much faster than searching through the set of values, looking for the ones that have a given label, so if you can avoid searching through labels and use the codes directly, that is superior.

There are many other text manipulation functions. The online help provides a listing of commands by functional category, including text functions. You should inspect the list to acquaint yourself with some of the other choices. You will see functions for stripping off blanks, counting numbers of characters, converting to upper case, and so on.

Labels in More than One Language

Suppose you wanted to create descriptions in more than one language. You could simply create an additional label variable for each language, for example:

```
DEFINE PRODUCT_LONG_DESCRIPTION2 VARIABLE TEXT <PRODUCT>
```

…and use this variable to hold, say, Spanish language labels.

But it would be better to use the organizing capabilities of dimensions. Start by creating a "language dimension" whose purpose is to contain a value for each language you intend to include. Then define a two-dimensional variable: one dimension tells which product you're referring to and the other dimension tells which language.

First you need to delete your old PRODUCT_LONG_DESCRIPTION so you can create a new one with the new dimensionality:

```
DELETE PRODUCT_LONG_DESCRIPTION
```

Now define your new objects:
```
DEFINE ALL_LANGUAGES DIMENSION TEXT
MAINTAIN ALL_LANGUAGES ADD 'AMERICAN' 'SPANISH'
DEFINE PRODUCT_LONG_DESCRIPTION VARIABLE TEXT -
<PRODUCT ALL_LANGUAGES>
```

PRODUCT_LONG_DESCRIPTION has two dimensions to "tie down" when you set the values using QDRs: the product dimension and the ALL_LANGUAGES dimension. You can do it with two-dimensional QDRs like this:

```
PRODUCT_LONG_DESCRIPTION(PRODUCT 'TP001' ALL_LANGUAGES -
'AMERICAN') = 'Healthy Pro Toothpaste, Clean Mint'
PRODUCT_LONG_DESCRIPTION(ALL_LANGUAGES 'AMERICAN' PRODUCT -
'TP002') = 'Children\'s Toothpaste, Glitter Mint'
PRODUCT_LONG_DESCRIPTION(ALL_LANGUAGES 'AMERICAN' PRODUCT -
'TP003') = 'Revitalizing Toothpaste, Vanilla'
```

And here's how you set the Spanish labels:
```
PRODUCT_LONG_DESCRIPTION(ALL_LANGUAGES 'SPANISH' PRODUCT -
'TP001') = 'Pasta dentífrica pro, sabor de menta pura'
PRODUCT_LONG_DESCRIPTION(ALL_LANGUAGES 'SPANISH' PRODUCT -
'TP002') = 'Pasta dentífrica para niños, sabor de menta'
PRODUCT_LONG_DESCRIPTION(ALL_LANGUAGES 'SPANISH' PRODUCT -
'TP003') = 'Pasta dentífrica revitalizante sabor de -
vainilla'
```

Or you can group the assignments by language and do the QDR on the remaining dimension:
```
LIMIT ALL_LANGUAGES TO 'AMERICAN'
PRODUCT_LONG_DESCRIPTION(PRODUCT 'TP001') = -
'Healthy Pro Toothpaste, Clean Mint'
PRODUCT_LONG_DESCRIPTION(PRODUCT 'TP002') = -
'Children\'s Toothpaste, Glitter Mint'
PRODUCT_LONG_DESCRIPTION(PRODUCT 'TP003') = -
'Revitalizing Toothpaste, Vanilla'

LIMIT ALL_LANGUAGES TO 'SPANISH'
PRODUCT_LONG_DESCRIPTION(PRODUCT 'TP001') = -
'Pasta dentífrica pro, sabor de menta pura'
PRODUCT_LONG_DESCRIPTION(PRODUCT 'TP002') = -
'Pasta dentífrica para niños, sabor de menta'
PRODUCT_LONG_DESCRIPTION(PRODUCT 'TP003') = -
'Pasta dentífrica revitalizante sabor de vainilla'
```

Numerical Descriptions

In addition to text descriptions for the dimension values, you sometimes want to describe the objects they represent with numerical data. For example, you may want to tell how much the product weighs or what it costs. This can be done in much the same way as creating labels, except that the variables created to capture the information would be numerical values rather than textual. For instance:

```
DEFINE PRODUCT_WEIGHT VARIABLE DECIMAL <PRODUCT>
```

...to which you can give values like this:
```
PRODUCT_WEIGHT(PRODUCT 'TP001') = 3.4
PRODUCT_WEIGHT(PRODUCT 'TP002') = 4.6
PRODUCT_WEIGHT(PRODUCT 'TP003') = 3.4
PRODUCT_WEIGHT(PRODUCT 'TP004') = 4.8
PRODUCT_WEIGHT(PRODUCT 'TP005') = 4.8
PRODUCT_WEIGHT(PRODUCT 'TP006') = 4.0
PRODUCT_WEIGHT(PRODUCT 'TP007') = 3.7
```

Using Properties to Describe the Dimension Itself

You've seen how text variables can be used to create descriptions of what the dimension members refer to, but what about describing the dimension itself? It's done in the DML through the use of properties. It's possible to create and set properties for most objects in the DML. Since properties are associated with the object itself (rather than its values), they can be used for creating object descriptions.

Properties are created and set using the PROPERTY command:
```
CONSIDER PRODUCT
PROPERTY 'LONG_DESCRIPTION' 'Product'
```

The CONSIDER statement is used to designate which object you're working with and the second statement defines and sets the LONG_DESCRIPTION property. You can create any property you want; you just need to give it a name and a value as was done in the statement above.

In order to see the properties that have been defined, you need to use the FULLDSC command.

```
->FULLDSC PRODUCT
DEFINE PRODUCT DIMENSION TEXT
PROPERTY 'LONG_DESCRIPTION' -
'Product'
```

Or, if you know a property is there, you can see its value using the OBJ function, like this:
```
->SHOW OBJ(PROPERTY 'LONG_DESCRIPTION' 'PRODUCT')
Product
```

Sorting Dimension Members

Let's see how to do a temporary sort of dimension values. You may want, for example, to REPORT a set of values in a particular order. The method you are about to see will produce a temporary sort. It won't change the default order (which is determined by how the values were originally stored).

Sorts are done according to a criterion and can be in ascending or descending order. You can sort a given dimension by anything that is dimensioned by it. In the simplest case, you can sort a dimension by its own values. For example the statement:

```
SORT PRODUCT A PRODUCT
```

…sorts the product dimension values alphabetically, using the actual code in ascending order (hence the "A"). The statement:

```
SORT PRODUCT D PRODUCT
```

…sorts them in reverse alphabetical order ("D" for descending). More likely, you'll need to sort them alphabetically according to their labels:

```
SORT PRODUCT A PRODUCT_LONG_DESCRIPTION
```

I've left out a very important detail. If the label was set up for more than one language, you need to tell the system which language to use, either by using a LIMIT command:

```
LIMIT ALL_LANGUAGES TO 'AMERICAN'
SORT PRODUCT A PRODUCT_LONG_DESCRIPTION
```

...or by using a QDR:
```
SORT PRODUCT A PRODUCT_LONG_DESCRIPTION(ALL_LANGUAGES -
'AMERICAN')
```

If you fail to limit the language dimension to a single value, the system will simply use the first value of ALL_LANGUAGES in status. If it happened to be 'AMERICAN' that would be used; if it happened to be 'SPANISH' that would be used. To make sure you get what you want, make sure you set the status of ALL_LANGUAGES to your choice.

There is no concept of a default dimension member built directly into the DML, even though a user interface could be created that accommodates such a feature.

And incidentally, if you do want to save a particular sort permanently, so that it becomes the default order, you can do so with the MAINTAIN command, like this:

```
MAINTAIN PRODUCT MOVE VALUES(PRODUCT) FIRST
```

7 | Categorizing Dimension Members with Attributes

In this chapter you will see a simple but powerful building block of dimensional analysis, the technique of categorizing dimension members on the basis of similar characteristics, performance, or ways that you wish to interact with them. You will be introduced to the *relation* object type and explore its capabilities as an analytical tool. The discussion will delineate the difference in analytical power between associating attributes to dimension members via text-valued labels versus the more powerful technique of DML relations.

Base Dimensions Versus Related Dimensions

In their most basic use, dimensions represent descriptive, categorical information that goes with an event or transaction. A sale is made. You can capture (for example) what was sold, where it was sold, to whom it was sold, and when it was sold; giving rise to product, store, customer, and time dimensions. You can call product, store, customer, and time base dimensions.

The things represented by the members of base dimensions (products, stores, etc.) may have characteristics or *attributes* that are themselves interesting. A product has a flavor, texture, or packaging type; a customer has a gender and marital status. As you can see, these characteristics contain categorical information. Since they are categorical, they can be used as the basis for defining a dimension.

Imagine, for example, a flavor dimension with values like mint and vanilla. Clearly members of the flavor dimension can be used to categorize or classify the members of the product dimension. A dimension that is used to categorize another dimension will be called a *related dimension*. In other words, base dimensions are associated with data, related dimensions are associated with other dimensions. In this chapter, you will learn the process of setting relationships for modeling the attributes of the objects that are represented by a base dimension.

Object Attributes

If labels name the things represented by a dimension member, attributes (in the sense that I'm using the word here) classify them. Defining attributes for a dimension is a standard and powerful analytical technique. You often want to examine all elements with a given characteristic or get summarized data as a function of those characteristics. For example, you may want to know which toothpaste products come in a bottle. Or you may want to know how much toothpaste you sold in a tube versus how much you sold in a bottle. These questions can be answered with the help of attributes.

How do you use the DML to associate product characteristics with individual products? Take a look at the data in the table below.

Product Code	Flavor Code	Texture Code	Packaging Code
TP001	MINT	PASTE	LAYDOWNTUBE
TP002	MINT	GEL	LAYDOWNTUBE
TP003	VANILLA	LIQUIDGEL	SQUEEZEBOTTLE
TP004	MINT	PASTE	LAYDOWNTUBE
TP005	MINT	LIQUIDGEL	SQUEEZEBOTTLE
TP006	VANILLA	PASTE	STANDUPTUBE
TP007	TEATREE	PASTE	LAYDOWNTUBE

Survey the products and you'll see they can all be described by one of three different flavors: MINT, VANILLA, and TEATREE.

In the spirit of the labeling process from the last chapter, it is tempting to proceed like this:
```
DEFINE FLAVOR_LONG_DESCRIPTION VARIABLE TEXT <PRODUCT>
```

This would give you a text value that you could use to describe the flavor for each product. Those values could be populated with assignment statements like this:

```
FLAVOR_LONG_DESCRIPTION(PRODUCT 'TP001') = 'MINT'
FLAVOR_LONG_DESCRIPTION(PRODUCT 'TP002') = 'MINT'
FLAVOR_LONG_DESCRIPTION(PRODUCT 'TP003') = 'VANILLA'
```

This would certainly accomplish the basic purpose of getting each product described by a flavor. But it turns out that using text-valued variables to capture attribute information throws away some of the analytical power of the language. Let's look at a better way of accomplishing things.

You're dealing with a discrete set of flavors, so use them as the basis for defining a flavor dimension:

```
DEFINE FLAVOR DIMENSION TEXT
```

Use the MAINTAIN command to add dimension members:
```
MAINTAIN FLAVOR ADD 'MINT' 'VANILLA' 'TEATREE'
```

In the next section you will see the most powerful means for mapping each product to a flavor.

Using Relations

Now let's look at another object type found in the DML: the relation. The function of the relation is to relate the values of one dimension to those of another. You can define a relation that maps each PRODUCT value to a FLAVOR value, like this:

```
DEFINE R.FLAVOR.PRODUCT RELATION FLAVOR <PRODUCT>
```

You are free to choose any valid name for the relation. Here I followed a convention that's often used to make it easy to see the dimensions being mapped. It starts with "R" to signify that it is a relation, followed by the name of the two dimensions that are being related. This relation is dimensioned by PRODUCT and takes on values of FLAVOR. The relation has one value of FLAVOR for each value of PRODUCT.

One difference between using text variables and relations is that the text variables can take on *any* text value, but the relation can only take on values that are valid FLAVOR dimension members—so it forces mapping to one of the designated choices.

You can assign values to relations just as you do with variables:
```
R.FLAVOR.PRODUCT(PRODUCT 'TP001') = 'MINT'
R.FLAVOR.PRODUCT(PRODUCT 'TP002') = 'MINT'
R.FLAVOR.PRODUCT(PRODUCT 'TP003') = 'VANILLA'
```

Just as with dimensions and variables, you can report the relation:
```
->REPORT W 25 R.FLAVOR.PRODUCT

PRODUCT            R.FLAVOR.PRODUCT
--------------     ------------------------
TP001              MINT
TP002              MINT
TP003              VANILLA
TP004              MINT
TP005              MINT
TP006              VANILLA
TP007              TEATREE
```

…and as with variables, you can use these relations in filtering operations.

You could find all the mint-flavored items using the same approach as in the last chapter when you were finding a dimension member with a given label:

```
LIMIT PRODUCT TO R.FLAVOR.PRODUCT EQ 'MINT'
```

The system will search through the list of product values for the ones that were mapped to MINT.

But if you leave off the "EQ" as follows:
```
LIMIT PRODUCT TO R.FLAVOR.PRODUCT 'MINT'
```

…then the limit will take advantage of the automatic indexing that accompanies relations. Index-based limits can be dramatically faster when there are large numbers of dimension members. This dimension has only seven values, but in actual practice you may encounter dimensions with thousands (or even millions) of dimension values. The superior filtering performance is one good reason to use relations rather than variables to capture attribute information.

Conveniently, the following will also work:
```
LIMIT PRODUCT TO FLAVOR 'MINT'
```

The system knows there's a relation that's mapping products to flavors and it uses it.

It's possible to break the process out into two steps: identify the FLAVOR values desired using a limit statement and then find the products with those FLAVOR values:

```
LIMIT FLAVOR TO 'MINT'
LIMIT PRODUCT TO FLAVOR
```

You can find all products with any one of a number of FLAVORs. The following finds all teatree- and vanilla-flavored products:

```
LIMIT FLAVOR TO 'TEATREE' 'VANILLA'
LIMIT PRODUCT TO FLAVOR
```

Now imagine, in actual application, a scenario in which you execute a complex multistage filtering process to identify attribute values that satisfy a set of business rules. Suppose you now need to find the base dimension members that are mapped to them. A process like the one above can be used to get them.

By the way, there could be more than one relation between product and flavor. If that were the case, which one would it use? Find out like this:

```
->SHOW OBJ(RELATION ACTUAL 'PRODUCT' 'FLAVOR')
R.FLAVOR.PRODUCT
```

And set it like this:
```
RELATION PRODUCT R.FLAVOR.PRODUCT
```

Dimension Profilers

Now I will introduce the concept of a dimension profiler. A dimension profiler is an analytic device that profiles a set of dimension members on the basis of its attributes—it tallies the number of base dimension members as a function of its attribute values.

That's pretty abstract. I'll make things more concrete by doing it for the product dimension. We will generate the profile information using the COUNT function.

The COUNT function counts the number of true values of a Boolean expression. It breaks the result out by the dimension specified in its second argument. Count includes only the base and related dimension values that are in status.

To include all values, use a Boolean expression that always evaluates to yes, such as "PRODUCT EQ PRODUCT" as shown here:

```
->DECIMALS = 0
->LIMIT PRODUCT TO ALL
->LIMIT FLAVOR TO ALL
->REPORT COUNT(PRODUCT EQ PRODUCT, FLAVOR)
                   COUNT(PROD
                    UCT EQ
                   PRODUCT,
FLAVOR              FLAVOR)
--------------    ----------
MINT                      4
VANILLA                   2
TEATREE                   1
```

So you see there are four mint-flavored products, two vanilla-flavored products, and one teatree-flavored product. The ability to break out counts on the basis of related dimensions is another reason to use relations rather than text-valued variables.

What if you only want a count based on products that weigh at least 3.75 ounces? You could limit the product dimension to such products, or incorporate the condition in the COUNT function as follows (this is assuming you've populated the PRODUCT_WEIGHT numerical description as presented in the last chapter):

```
->REPORT NOHEAD COUNT(PRODUCT_WEIGHT GE 3.75, FLAVOR)
MINT                            3
VANILLA                         1
TEATREE                         0
```

Next, suppose you wanted to know what the product count is as a function of both flavor and texture.

```
->ALLSTAT
->REPORT COUNT(PRODUCT EQ PRODUCT, FLAVOR TEXTURE)
```

Chapter 7
Categorizing Dimension Members with Attributes

```
                COUNT(PRODUCT EQ PRODUCT, FLAVOR
                ------------TEXTURE)------------
                ------------TEXTURE------------
FLAVOR             PASTE         GEL        LIQUIDGEL
--------------  ----------  ----------  ----------
MINT                 2            1           1
VANILLA              1            0           1
TEATREE              1            0           0
```

Finally, take a look at it broken out by all three attributes:
```
->REPORT COUNT(PRODUCT EQ PRODUCT, FLAVOR TEXTURE PACKAGING)
FLAVOR: MINT
                COUNT(PRODUCT EQ PRODUCT, FLAVOR
                --------TEXTURE PACKAGING)-------
                -----------PACKAGING------------
                 LAYDOWN      SQUEEZE     STANDUP
TEXTURE           TUBE         BOTTLE      TUBE
--------------  ----------  ----------  ----------
PASTE                2            0           0
GEL                  1            0           0
LIQUIDGEL            0            1           0

FLAVOR: VANILLA
                COUNT(PRODUCT EQ PRODUCT, FLAVOR
                --------TEXTURE PACKAGING)-------
                -----------PACKAGING------------
                 LAYDOWN      SQUEEZE     STANDUP
TEXTURE           TUBE         BOTTLE      TUBE
--------------  ----------  ----------  ----------
PASTE                0            0           1
GEL                  0            0           0
LIQUIDGEL            0            1           0

FLAVOR: TEATREE
                COUNT(PRODUCT EQ PRODUCT, FLAVOR
                --------TEXTURE PACKAGING)-------
                -----------PACKAGING------------
                 LAYDOWN      SQUEEZE     STANDUP
TEXTURE           TUBE         BOTTLE      TUBE
--------------  ----------  ----------  ----------
PASTE                1            0           0
GEL                  0            0           0
LIQUIDGEL            0            0           0
```

You can see there is a data block for each value of flavor. These displays are examples of the multidimensional reporting style. Rows, columns, and data blocks map to functional categories. They are usually more helpful for doing analysis than the "relational style" display such as this:

```
PACKAGING        TEXTURE      FLAVOR      COUNT
-------------    ----------   ----------  -------
LAYDOWNTUBE      PASTE        MINT           2
LAYDOWNTUBE      PASTE        VANILLA        0
LAYDOWNTUBE      PASTE        TEATREE        1
LAYDOWNTUBE      GEL          MINT           1
LAYDOWNTUBE      GEL          VANILLA        0
LAYDOWNTUBE      GEL          TEATREE        0
LAYDOWNTUBE      LIQUIDGEL    MINT           0
LAYDOWNTUBE      LIQUIDGEL    VANILLA        0
LAYDOWNTUBE      LIQUIDGEL    TEATREE        0
SQUEEZEBOTTLE    PASTE        MINT           0
SQUEEZEBOTTLE    PASTE        VANILLA        0
SQUEEZEBOTTLE    PASTE        TEATREE        0
SQUEEZEBOTTLE    GEL          MINT           0
SQUEEZEBOTTLE    GEL          VANILLA        0
SQUEEZEBOTTLE    GEL          TEATREE        0
SQUEEZEBOTTLE    LIQUIDGEL    MINT           1
SQUEEZEBOTTLE    LIQUIDGEL    VANILLA        1
SQUEEZEBOTTLE    LIQUIDGEL    TEATREE        0
STANDUPTUBE      PASTE        MINT           0
STANDUPTUBE      PASTE        VANILLA        1
STANDUPTUBE      PASTE        TEATREE        0
STANDUPTUBE      GEL          MINT           0
STANDUPTUBE      GEL          VANILLA        0
STANDUPTUBE      GEL          TEATREE        0
STANDUPTUBE      LIQUIDGEL    MINT           0
STANDUPTUBE      LIQUIDGEL    VANILLA        0
STANDUPTUBE      LIQUIDGEL    TEATREE        0
```

A dimension profiler looks like any other application measure, with the notable difference that it says nothing about the business transactions that have taken place; it only describes the universe of objects. Seeing how many products in the system have a particular type of packaging, for example, says nothing about what any customer may have bought.

The classic example of profiling is customer profiling. You might break out the customer base on the basis of demographic factors (such as gender, marital status, and age) and/or possibly other factors. Customer profiling may say nothing about what anyone did, but it will tell something about who they are.

Other Uses of Relations

The related dimension has been used to capture values for some characteristic of an object. You'll now learn other ways that the association between two dimensions can be used.

Performance Attributes

In this example, the related dimension is used to denote a characteristic not of the object, but of its behavior. Consider, for example, a group of customers. We will assume the data is available so that each customer can be classified on the basis of their purchasing behavior. There are different aspects of purchasing behavior that you might want to capture. For example, you could classify each customer on the basis of the span of time since their last order, something we'll call *recency*.

Now suppose you have business rules that define categories of recency. The rules could be simple or complex, but you can assume they define a number of categories and what qualifies as membership into each one. For example, you might have three categories defined as in Table 7.1.

Table 7.1. Recency Categories

Code	Description
REC01	Within the past month
REC02	1–3 months ago
REC03	More than 3 months ago

You use the definitions to define a recency dimension. Next you define a relation that you will use to map the customers to those values:

```
DEFINE RECENCY DIMENSION TEXT
MAINTAIN RECENCY ADD 'REC01' 'REC02' 'REC03'
DEFINE R.RECENCY.CUST RELATION RECENCY <CUSTOMER>
```

You might have written a DML program that populates this relation. This would be a program that determines each customer's recency value by analyzing the historical sales data contained in a variable. (You'll be learning how to write DML programs in Chapter 18: *Writing DML Programs*.)

You can keep going, defining other behavioral characteristics. Let's consider the classic recency, frequency, and monetary designations that are used in a standard database marketing application called *RFM analysis*. This is a well-known and widely applied method for identifying high-response customers to marketing promotions.

With RFM analysis, each customer is classified on the basis of when the last order was, how frequently an order was placed, and the value of their orders. Each customer is placed into one of the three-dimensional data cells.

Now create a metric that looks like the dimension profiler for customer, based on these three attributes to produce the basic data used for RFM analysis:

```
REPORT COUNT(CUSTOMER EQ CUSTOMER, RECENCY FREQUENCY -
MONETARY)
```

Customers who fall into the cells with greatest recency, frequency, and monetary are generally the best candidates for repeat business.

This is distinct from a dimension profiler: the related dimensions here get their values on the basis of customer behavior, which is a business process output. Dimension profilers are based on static object characteristics.

TREATMENT ATTRIBUTES

Here's another variation on the use of related dimensions. In this example, the related dimension specifies treatments (or interventions) undertaken in order to affect an outcome. For example, you have a set of products. You can choose to promote some of them in one particular way and others in a different way.

So you define a promotion dimension to describe the set of promotions and a relation to map the promotions to products.

```
DEFINE PROMOTION DIMENSION TEXT
MAINTAIN PROMOTION ADD 'NONE' 'PROMO01' 'PROMO02'
DEFINE R.PROMOTION.PRODUCT RELATION PROMOTION <PRODUCT>
```

This related dimension is not a characteristic of the product or its behavior, but of your handling of them. You can probably imagine countless other examples in various application arenas: medical treatments, remedial programs offered by a school, steps in a manufacturing process, and so on.

ATTRIBUTES AS APPLICATION DATA

Application data is usually numerical, but there are some situations in which the transactions themselves are of a categorical nature.

Maybe you want to measure customer loyalty and the outcome options are "cancelled service" and "did not cancel," for example:

```
DEFINE OUTCOME DIMENSION TEXT
MAINTAIN OUTCOME ADD 'NOTCAN' 'CANCELLED'
DEFINE R.OUTCOME.CUST RELATION OUTCOME <CUSTOMER>
```

Or maybe you have data on students where the data is "promoted," "retained," and "dropped out." Relations are sometimes used to encode the *outcomes* that you're measuring.

Multidimensional Relations

There are situations in which the attribute information is mapped to members of more than one dimension simultaneously. Consider, for example, the performance attributes from above. Customer behavior can change over time, so any given customer will not necessarily *always* be in the same RFM cell. In fact, the point of the marketing program is undoubtedly to push the customers into the cells representing greater purchasing!

To represent this temporal aspect, map the attribute values onto values of customer and time: this customer is characterized in this way at this time. A two-dimensional relation that accommodates this situation is defined in the obvious way:

```
DEFINE R.RECENCY.CUST RELATION RECENCY <CUSTOMER TIME>
```

And, of course, a relation can have more than two dimensions, or even none.

The Versatility of Relations

Representing attributes with relations is versatile. To recap some of what you've just learned about attributes, you've seen that there are generally three ways attributes can be used in an analytical process and these are as follows:

- As part of a filtering criterion.
- As data in a report.
- As a breakout dimension for some aggregate metric.

The examples you've seen of these three uses are:
```
LIMIT PRODUCT TO R.PACKAGING.PRODUCT 'TUBE'
```

In this statement, you set the status of the product dimension to all the products that have the packaging called TUBE. Next you saw:

```
REPORT PRODUCT_LONG_DESCRIPTION R.PACKAGING.PRODUCT
```

While reports generally show numerical data, they can also show text-valued data, as this simple report does.

Finally, you were introduced to the COUNT function:
```
REPORT COUNT(PRODUCT EQ PRODUCT, R.PACKAGING.PRODUCT)
```

This creates a report of data broken out by the various values of the related dimension.

8 | Organizing Dimension Members into Hierarchies

Hierarchies are a fixture in the world of business intelligence systems. Hierarchical data representations provide the means for storing summary data at differing levels of detail. Graphical user interface elements provide clickable hierarchical displays that give the user a mechanism for navigating between those levels.

This is a basic operation analysts want to do: to see the big picture, then drill down into the details to see how the result was obtained. In this chapter, you're going to investigate hierarchies thoroughly, starting with very simple situations and building up from there.

Fortunately, hierarchies are familiar: everyone's seen organizational charts that show hierarchical arrangements of information. You can start your exploration with a simple organizational chart, such as the one shown in Figure 8.1.

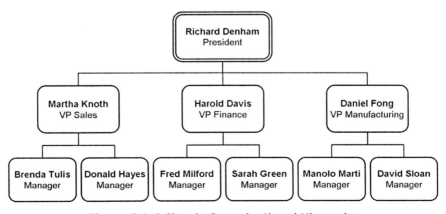

Figure 8.1. A Simple Organizational Hierarchy

77

Looking at this chart, you can infer that managers report to vice presidents, and vice presidents report to the president. It's easy to see the relationships, since hierarchies are graphical structures displaying the relationships among the various members in the hierarchy.

There are a few rules to which these relationships must conform. For instance, a given member can only **rep**ort to a single other member, and there's an element at the top that doesn't report to any member. On the other hand, a given member can have more than one element **repor**ting to it.

The members of a hierarchy constitute the nodes in the diagram. The nodes with no children at the bottom of this hierarchy (the managers, in this case) are called *leaf nodes*, and the node at the top that doesn't report to anyone (the president) is called the *root node*. The *depth of a node* is the number of links between it and the root node.

The term *level* is used as a logical designation that specifies what kind of object is being represented. In the hierarchy of Figure 8.1, there are three levels: president, vice president, and manager. In this hierarchy, all the nodes at the same depth are at the same level. So, for example, the vice presidents are all at depth one, the managers are all at depth two, and so on.

The relationship between a node and another node that reports to it is called a parent-child relationship. Notice that a child node has only one parent, not two.

The organizational chart can also be represented by a diagram as shown in Figure 8.2. You could also turn the diagram on its side.

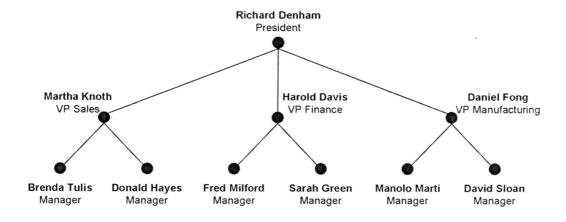

Figure 8.2. Alternate Representation of the Organizational Hierarchy

To represent a hierarchy in the DML, you need a unique dimension member to represent each node. In this example, there is 1 president, 3 vice presidents, and 6 managers for a total of 10 members.

Next, you need a way to represent the reporting relationships between the nodes in the hierarchy. This will be done with a relation, the same object type used to represent attributes in the last chapter. You'll be using it in a slightly different way here, though: rather than mapping the members of one dimension to those of another dimension, you'll have relations between the members of a single dimension. This usage is called a *self-relation*.

The hierarchy in this example represents the reporting relationships in an organization. It is a special case, in the sense that it is basically documenting something that's already there. In developing a business intelligence application; however, there is usually a certain amount of analysis and design required in order to identify the appropriate hierarchical structure that suits the needs of the application—they don't arrive preordained as they do with the organization.

In practice, the hierarchical design sometimes entails subtleties or complications that must be dealt with, so this chapter and the next will spend some time looking at both the straightforward use of the design and at some possible exceptional situations.

Developing a Customer Hierarchy

Let's start with a hierarchical illustration that is typical of what would be encountered in a business intelligence application. Suppose you want to analyze customer purchasing behavior. Imagine a customer loyalty program where at a given store outlet, the customers enroll in the program and provide some basic personal information.

As an analyst, you would be interested not so much in the behavior of individual customers, as in groups of customers. The goal would be to see patterns of activity—that entails looking at groups. Metaphorically, the story of what is going on is in the forests; not an individual tree.

Hierarchies are powerful tools that provide a mechanism for moving from one level of detail to another, making it easy to look at large groups for more general information and then easily switch over to smaller groups for more specific information.

Your design process should be guided by consideration of what kinds of questions you want to answer, what factors you think could be drivers in the performance of the business process, and what data are available. You might think in terms of what is likely to be an influencer or predictor of outcome behavior. Is it where the customer shops? Or is it where the customer lives?

Figure 8.3 and Figure 8.4 show a hierarchy based on where a given customer enrolled in the loyalty program. Although the figures show only a tiny subset of what real data might look like, the hierarchical structure itself is reflective of what might actually be used.

This hierarchy has four levels: the individual customer level, outlet level, division level and the "all customers" level. In Figure 8.3, you can see how a hierarchy like this might appear as an element in a GUI.

Hierarchies in a user interface are display elements that can be interacted with. There are drill icons that can be clicked to open or close a branch of the hierarchy. In Figure 8.3, all branches have been opened, and the small squares with the minus (-) sign in them can be clicked on to close up the corresponding branch.

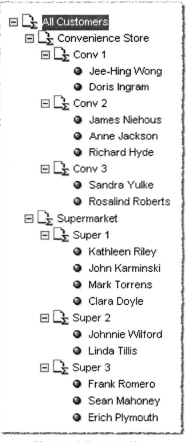

Figure 8.3. How the Hierarchy Looks From a Graphical Interface

Representing Hierarchy Information in a Tabular Format

Although inherently graphical, the information represented by a hierarchy can also be captured in tabular form. It will be useful to see how that is done because, eventually, you'll need to be able to load in hierarchy data from such formats.

Glancing at the hierarchy in Figure 8.4, it is easy to see that the same information is conveyed in Table 8.1.

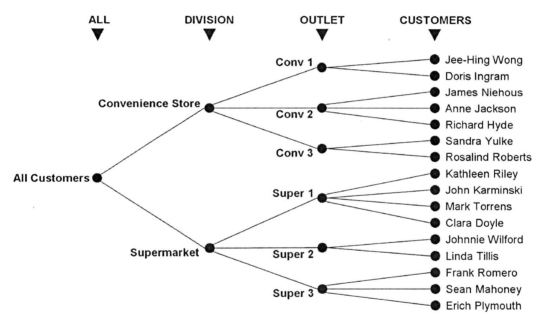

Figure 8.4. A Hierarchy Based on Where the Customer Enrolled in the Loyalty Program

Table 8.1. Documenting Hierarchy Information in a Tabular Format

Customer Label	Outlet Label	Division Label	All Customers Label
Jee-Hing Wong	Conv 1	Convenience Store	All Customers
Doris Ingram	Conv 1	Convenience Store	All Customers
James Niehous	Conv 2	Convenience Store	All Customers
Anne Jackson	Conv 2	Convenience Store	All Customers
Richard Hyde	Conv 2	Convenience Store	All Customers
Sandra Yulke	Conv 3	Convenience Store	All Customers
Rosalind Roberts	Conv 3	Convenience Store	All Customers
Kathleen Riley	Super 1	Supermarket	All Customers
John Karminski	Super 1	Supermarket	All Customers
Mark Torrens	Super 1	Supermarket	All Customers
Clara Doyle	Super 1	Supermarket	All Customers
Johnnie Wilford	Super 2	Supermarket	All Customers
Linda Tillis	Super 2	Supermarket	All Customers
Frank Romero	Super 3	Supermarket	All Customers
Sean Mahoney	Super 3	Supermarket	All Customers
Erich Plymouth	Super 3	Supermarket	All Customers

You can see in Table 8.1 that there's one row for each leaf node, the leafs being customers. Notice that each row in this table gives you the path you would traverse to get from any given leaf node to the root.

Understand that when you look at the hierarchy depictions, you're looking at the *labels* that go with the nodes. Normally, these labels would apply to an underlying code. A more complete table would include the codes corresponding to the values, and might look something like Table 8.2.

CHAPTER 8
Organizing Dimension Members into Hierarchies

Table 8.2. Hierarchy Information Including the Underlying Codes

Customer Code	Customer Label	Outlet Code	Outlet Label	Division Code	Division Label	All Code	All Label
CU001	Jee-Hing Wong	CNV001	CONV 1	DIVCNV	Convenience Store	ALL	All Customers
CU002	Doris Ingram	CNV001	CONV 1	DIVCNV	Convenience Store	ALL	All Customers
CU003	James Niehous	CNV002	CONV 2	DIVCNV	Convenience Store	ALL	All Customers
CU004	Anne Jackson	CNV002	CONV 2	DIVCNV	Convenience Store	ALL	All Customers
CU005	Richard Hyde	CNV002	CONV 2	DIVCNV	Convenience Store	ALL	All Customers
CU006	Sandra Yulke	CNV003	CONV 3	DIVCNV	Convenience Store	ALL	All Customers
CU007	Rosalind Roberts	CNV003	CONV 3	DIVCNV	Convenience Store	ALL	All Customers
CU008	Kathleen Riley	SUP001	SUPER 1	DIVSUP	Supermarket	ALL	All Customers
CU009	John Karminski	SUP001	SUPER 1	DIVSUP	Supermarket	ALL	All Customers
CU010	Mark Torrens	SUP001	SUPER 1	DIVSUP	Supermarket	ALL	All Customers
CU011	Clara Doyle	SUP001	SUPER 1	DIVSUP	Supermarket	ALL	All Customers
CU012	Johnnie Wilford	SUP002	SUPER 2	DIVSUP	Supermarket	ALL	All Customers
CU013	Linda Tillis	SUP002	SUPER 2	DIVSUP	Supermarket	ALL	All Customers
CU014	Frank Romero	SUP003	SUPER 3	DIVSUP	Supermarket	ALL	All Customers
CU015	Sean Mahoney	SUP003	SUPER 3	DIVSUP	Supermarket	ALL	All Customers
CU016	Erich Plymouth	SUP003	SUPER 3	DIVSUP	Supermarket	ALL	All Customers

Let me point out something new here. For the dimensions without hierarchies, there was a homogeneity in the type of objects represented by dimension members. For example, in the PRODUCT dimension we worked with, all the dimension values represented products; all values of FLAVOR represented flavors. But in the CUSTOMER dimension, only *some* of the dimension members represent customers: others represent outlets and divisions, and one member represents the "all customers" value. So even though you call it the CUSTOMER dimension, some of its values will represent things that are not customers.

Often, as is the case here, the type of object being represented can be determined by the depth of the node. (Depth-zero node is ALL, depth-one nodes are store types, depth-two nodes are individual stores, and depth-three nodes are customers.)

The DML Representation of a Hierarchy

Now let's see the exact DML language elements for representing a hierarchy. The steps for implementing the example hierarchy are as follows:

- STEP 1: Create the CUSTOMER dimension.

- STEP 2: Add dimension values to represent the customers and other members of the hierarchy.

- STEP 3: Create the RELATION to map child nodes to their parent.

- STEP 4: Populate the relation with values representing those links.

So the first step is:
```
DEFINE CUSTOMER DIMENSION TEXT
```

Next add the dimension values:
```
MAINTAIN CUSTOMER ADD 'CU001' 'CU002'...'CNV001'...'DIVCNV'... -
'ALL'
```

I didn't show all 25 values, but they are all the customer codes, outlet codes, division codes, and 'ALL.' In the production application, the values would undoubtedly be read values from a table or file (the procedure for doing this will be shown in Chapter 16: *The Star Schema and Beyond* and Chapter 19: *Getting Data In and Out of Analytic Workspaces*.)

To represent the parent-child relationships, define a relation like this:
```
DEFINE CUSTOMER_PARENTREL RELATION CUSTOMER <CUSTOMER>
```

What you see here is the mechanism for mapping CUSTOMER dimension members onto other CUSTOMER dimension members. Let's look at some of these mappings.

CUSTOMER-OUTLET links look like this (you'd do this for all 16 customers):
```
CUSTOMER_PARENTREL(CUSTOMER 'CU001') = 'CNV001'
```

OUTLET-DIVISION links look like this (you'd do this for the six stores):
```
CUSTOMER_PARENTREL(CUSTOMER 'CNV001') = 'DIVCNV'
```

DIVISION-ALL links look like this (you'd do this for both divisions):
```
CUSTOMER_PARENTREL(CUSTOMER 'DIVCNV') = 'ALL'
```

The ALL value of CUSTOMER is at the root of the hierarchy. Make sure you have:
`CUSTOMER_PARENTREL(CUSTOMER 'ALL') = NA`

Having added all the dimension values and assigned all the values of the customer parent relation, you have now modeled this hierarchy. Operationally what this means is that you could inspect all the parent relation values and from them alone could draw the complete hierarchy.

Notice that in the sample data of Table 8.2, I followed the suggestion made in Chapter 5: *Creating Dimensions* and chose codes that tell you something about what they represent. One can easily deduce, for instance, that DIVCNV is a division and is for convenience stores or that CU004 is a customer.

As mentioned in Chapter 5, if you have the leeway to use an informative coding scheme like this, it can be a great convenience for doing work within the OLAP Worksheet. It would be naive to assume that a developer's information would come exclusively from the GUI, or that one would never have occasion to do some kind of analysis or exploration directly with the command-line interface. In such situations, meaningful codes are a great help.

Representing Multiple Hierarchies

It's common to have more than one way of organizing dimension members. For example, you might also want to analyze the data on the basis of the location of the customer's residence. To do this you would want to create a geographical hierarchy.

Figure 8.5 shows a hierarchy that might be created.

To represent this additional hierarchy, you need to add dimension members for each of the new nodes. The customers, outlets, divisions, and the 'ALL' value are already there from the prior hierarchy, but cities and zip codes are new and must be added.

To establish the parent-child links in this second hierarchy, you might be tempted to proceed by creating a new relation to capture the new relationships:

`DEFINE CUSTOMER_PARENTREL2 RELATION CUSTOMER <CUSTOMER>`

And then set the values to reflect the new relationships:
`CUSTOMER_PARENTREL2(CUSTOMER 'CU001') = '33634'`

This situation is analogous to the one in Chapter 6: *Describing Dimension Members with Labels* where we wanted labels in multiple languages. Just as there you created a dimension to enumerate each *language*, here you'll create a dimension to enumerate each *hierarchy*. This will give you flexibility and a tremendous advantage from the viewpoint of system maintainability. It's going to make adding hierarchies like adding data, rather than adding objects to the AW. This will mean a standard data load process can be used to add hierarchies.

Let's do it. First create the hierarchy-enumerating dimension:
```
DEFINE CUSTOMER_HIERDIM DIMENSION TEXT
```

Then add a dimension value for each hierarchy you want. In the example you have two:
```
MAINTAIN CUSTOMER_HIERDIM ADD 'DIVISIONHIER' 'GEOHIER'
```

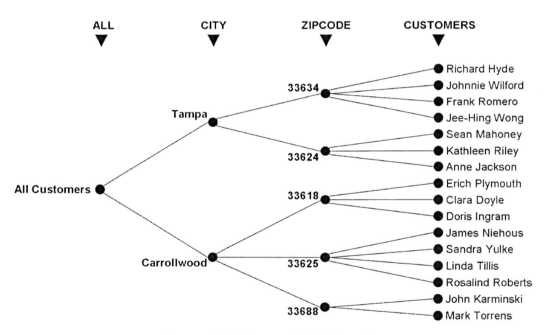

Figure 8.5. A Geographical Hierarchy

Now discard your prior customer-parent relationship:
```
DELETE CUSTOMER_PARENTREL
```

...and define a new parent relationship with two dimensions, CUSTOMER_HIERDIM and CUSTOMER:

```
DEFINE CUSTOMER_PARENTREL RELATION CUSTOMER <CUSTOMER – CUSTOMER_HIERDIM >
```

Populate the data by limiting the CUSTOMER_HIERDIM dim to the hierarchy you wish to set up and assign the parent-child relationship values. (I won't show all the assignment statements!)

First do the division hierarchy:
```
LIMIT CUSTOMER_HIERDIM TO 'DIVISIONHIER'
CUSTOMER_PARENTREL(CUSTOMER 'CU001') = 'CNV001'
```

Then do the geography hierarchy:
```
LIMIT CUSTOMER_HIERDIM TO 'GEOHIER'
CUSTOMER_PARENTREL(CUSTOMER 'CU001') = '33634'
```

You can have as many hierarchies as you want by continuing to add values to the CUSTOMER_HIERDIM dimension. No new objects need to be defined; you're doing a MAINTAIN instead of a DEFINE.

If you have experience working with the relational database, you might think of a task in the relational world in which you can accomplish something by adding a new row of data to a table rather than by creating a new table. This is similar to that.

Not All Self-Relations Define Hierarchies

Self-relations are not exclusively tied to defining hierarchies. As an example, the rules of the game Rock, Paper, Scissors can be described using a relation. (If you are not familiar with this game, you can Google "rock, paper, scissors" to find out about it.)

```
DEFINE PLAYING_PIECE DIMENSION TEXT
MAINTAIN PLAYING_PIECE 'ROCK' 'PAPER' 'SCISSORS'
DEFINE BEATS RELATION PLAYING_PIECE <PLAYING_PIECE>
BEATS(PLAYING_PIECE 'ROCK') = 'SCISSORS'
BEATS(PLAYING_PIECE 'SCISSORS') = 'PAPER'
BEATS(PLAYING_PIECE 'PAPER') = 'ROCK'
```

The AW can play the game by secretly making its move:
```
LIMIT PLAYING_PIECE TO INTPART(RANDOM(1,4))
```

Don't cheat! But you could command the AW to:
```
SHOW PLAYING_PIECE
```

The expression INTPART(RANDOM(1,4)) returns either 1, 2, or 3. This is used in selecting either the rock, paper, or scissors.

Now you make your move. Let's say you chose to throw "scissors." To see if the AW won, type the expression below:

```
->SHOW BEATS eq 'SCISSORS'
YES
```

This relation describes a circular relationship among the three dimension members; there's no hierarchy described.

Hierarchically Based Filtering

Hierarchies are created on the basis of the relationship between one member of a dimension and another of the same dimension. Two members may have a parent-child relationship, they may be siblings, one may be an ancestor of another, and so on. There exist numerous filtering choices where the filtering criterion is based on specifying members in terms of these kinds of relationships. Let's examine those.

CHILDREN

All children of zip code 33634:
```
LIMIT CUSTOMER_HIERDIM TO 'GEOHIER'
LIMIT CUSTOMER TO CHILDREN '33634' USING CUSTOMER_PARENTREL
```

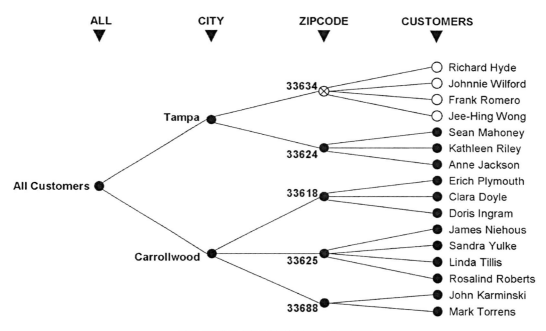

Figure 8.6. The Children of 33634

DESCENDANTS

Moving toward the leaf node includes children, and their children, as far as it can go gives descendants. Depicted below are all descendants of Carrollwood:

```
LIMIT CUSTOMER_HIERDIM TO 'GEOHIER'
LIMIT CUSTOMER TO DESCENDANTS 'Carrollwood' USING -
CUSTOMER_PARENTREL
```

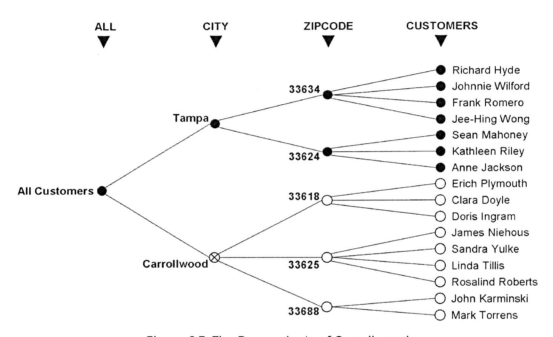

Figure 8.7. The Descendants of Carrollwood

Parents

The parents of Tampa (note the plural "parents" even though there is only one):
```
LIMIT CUSTOMER_HIERDIM TO 'GEOHIER'
LIMIT CUSTOMER TO PARENTS 'CTYTPA' USING CUSTOMER_PARENTREL
```

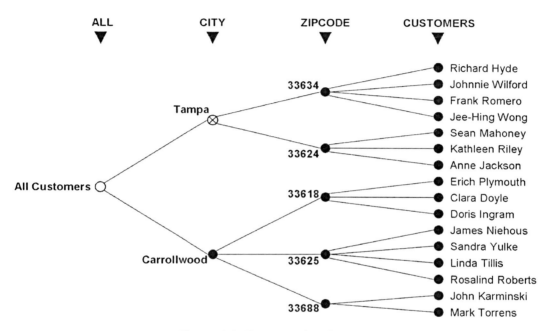

Figure 8.8. The Parents of Tampa

ANCESTORS

Moving toward the root, including parents and their parents, as far as it can go, gives ancestors. Below are the ancestors of Kathleen Riley:

```
LIMIT CUSTOMER_HIERDIM TO 'GEOHIER'
LIMIT CUSTOMER TO ANCESTORS 'CU008' USING CUSTOMER_PARENTREL
```

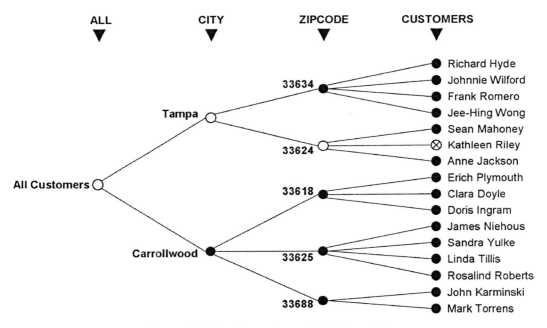

Figure 8.9. The Ancestors of Kathleen Riley

Working with Levels

Unlike the simple dimensions you saw in the previous chapters, the members of a hierarchical dimension represent different kinds of objects. The CUSTOMER dimension has some members that represent customers, but others represent outlets, zip codes, and cities. You may want to select dimension members on the basis of the type of object they represent. For instance, you may want to select all the zip code values in the CUSTOMER dimension.

To accommodate this situation, you will create an attribute whose job is to associate an object type with each dimension member. Following the process described in the last chapter, there is a base dimension (in this case CUSTOMER) and a related dimension (specifying the object type). A relation associates each base dimension member with a related dimension member.

Rather than thinking in terms of object type, you can equivalently think in terms of hierarchy levels, since in this hierarchy, there is an exact correspondence between the hierarchy level and type of object type represented. We will do that because that is the most common way of modeling this kind of information.

The CUSTOMER dimension is already there, but you need to create a dimension that has one value for every level of every hierarchy:

```
DEFINE CUSTOMER_LEVELDIM DIMENSION TEXT
```

Next, add a dimension member to represent each possible level:
```
MAINTAIN CUSTOMER_LEVELDIM ADD 'CUSTOMER_LEV' 'OUTLET_LEV' -
'DIVISION_LEV' 'ZIP5_LEV' 'CITY_LEV' 'ALL_LEV'
```

Create a relation with which you will map each CUSTOMER dimension member to its level in the hierarchy:

```
DEFINE CUSTOMER_LEVELREL RELATION CUSTOMER_LEVELDIM -
<CUSTOMER>
```

Next populate this relation, which can be done with a series of assignment statements.

Just to get a little more practice working with text manipulation, take advantage of the fact that all dimension members representing customers, and those only, start with the letters CU. You can populate the level relation for all those levels like this:

```
LIMIT CUSTOMER TO EXTCHARS(CUSTOMER, 1, 2) EQ 'CU'
CUSTOMER_LEVELREL = 'CUSTOMER_LEV'
```

EXTCHARS is another character-manipulation function. Here it is being used to extract the first two characters of the customer dimension values.

The relation, CUSTOMER_LEVELREL, would need to be populated for all values of the CUSTOMER dimension.

Level-Based Filtering

The members at the zip code level are shown in Figure 8.10.

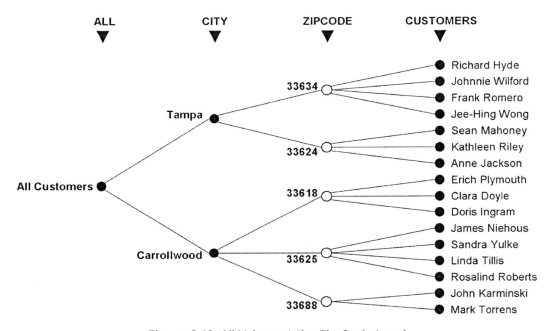

Figure 8.10. All Values at the Zip Code Level

Level-based filtering works exactly like any other attribute; you limit the dimension to its attribute value. To get all the zip codes, for instance, you would issue this statement:

```
LIMIT CUSTOMER TO CUSTOMER_LEVELREL 'ZIP5_LEV'
```

The examples in *Hierarchically Based Filtering* above were based on relative position and depended on the hierarchy. Unlike those examples, in level filtering it is not necessary to specify the hierarchy by limiting the CUSTOMER_HIERDIM dimension.

Reporting Hierarchy Information

You've seen the DML statements that will populate the hierarchy descriptions from data in a table. Now let's go the other way. Assume that the objects describing a hierarchy have been populated and let's see how to generate a tabular report of that information.

Table 8.2 gives the hierarchy information for the division hierarchy. Let's see how to generate some of the columns for that table of data. The first column has the code for each leaf node (the customers). To find those values:

```
LIMIT CUSTOMER TO CUSTOMER_LEVELREL 'CUSTOMER_LEV'
```

Now sort them:
```
SORT CUSTOMER A CUSTOMER
```

You could generate the CUSTOMER CODE column by:
```
REPORT CUSTOMER
```

Next, let's generate the other columns that have codes. The OUTLET CODE column contains the parents in DIVISIONHIER hierarchy. Tell the system which hierarchy you want to work with:

```
LIMIT CUSTOMER_HIERLIST TO 'DIVISIONHIER'
```

The OUTLET CODE column is given by:
```
REPORT CUSTOMER_PARENTREL
```

The DIVISION CODE column is given by:
```
REPORT CUSTOMER_PARENTREL(CUSTOMER CUSTOMER_PARENTREL)
```

The ALL CODE column is given by:
```
REPORT CUSTOMER_PARENTREL(CUSTOMER -
CUSTOMER_PARENTREL(CUSTOMER CUSTOMER_PARENTREL))
```

These columns could all be displayed side-by-side:
```
REPORT DOWN CUSTOMER CUSTOMER_PARENTREL -
CUSTOMER_PARENTREL(CUSTOMER CUSTOMER_PARENTREL) -
CUSTOMER_PARENTREL(CUSTOMER CUSTOMER_PARENTREL -
(CUSTOMER CUSTOMER_PARENTREL))
```

Generating the columns with the label data is straightforward. Here are a few examples:

The CUSTOMER LABEL column is given by:
```
RPR DOWN CUSTOMER CUSTOMER_LONG_DESCRIPTION
```

The OUTLET LABEL column is given by:
```
REPORT CUSTOMER_LONG_DESCRIPTION(CUSTOMER CUSTOMER_PARENTREL)
```

9 | Representing Unnatural, Ragged, and Other Hierarchy Variations

The hierarchy examples from the last chapter were, in a sense, well behaved. They organized nicely into levels that had clear meanings. The leaf-level nodes all represented the same sorts of things; the levels themselves had a hierarchical character to them. In practice, hierarchies often follow this nice structure, but there are also situations where they depart in some way from this simplicity. In this chapter, I will show you different kinds of departures from "normalcy" that arise. Knowing how to deal with them is important; being able to do so makes you a true *"hierarchaeologist."*

Natural Versus Unnatural Hierarchies

By now, you have seen a few examples of hierarchies. These examples illustrate how hierarchies provide a framework for moving among different levels of detail. A customer's home occupies a certain piece of land, a customer's zip code encompasses an even larger tract (that may include other customers), and the city even larger still. The outlet where a customer enrolled in the loyalty program encompasses other customers who enrolled there, as well. The outlet's division encompasses those customers as well as customers from the other outlets that report to it.

The essential feature of these hierarchies is that they provide a facility for looking at some characteristic of the thing represented by the leaf node in broader and broader categories. A hierarchy with this feature is called a *natural hierarchy.* Time yields a good example of a natural hierarchy, with months, quarters, and years each representing larger chunks of time. Another example would be items, brands, and manufacturers where each level represents broader and broader categories of products.

It is possible to create hierarchies that do not possess this feature; they will be called *unnatural hierarchies.* I'm going to show you an example in this section and show you why it's important to be able to recognize these two different cases. As you'll see, there are subtleties involved in creating and interpreting hierarchies. Being familiar with them and the accompanying design points will help you chart the best course of action.

Now let's lay the groundwork for creating an unnatural hierarchy using the customer dimension. Start by assuming that when a customer enrolls in the loyalty program, they provide marital status and gender information. You will recognize these two as fitting into the concept of attributes as presented in Chapter 7: *Categorizing Dimension Members with Attributes.* Following the methodology outlined there, you could define a marital status dimension and a gender dimension, and then model attributes by mapping the leaf values of the customer dimension (i.e., the customers) to values of the attribute dimensions (marital status and gender) with relations.

Now let's look at a different way this information could be handled. Rather than create marital status and gender attributes, you could use marital status and gender to define levels in a hierarchy and create a hierarchy such as the one shown in Figure 9.1 and Figure 9.2. Notice in Figure 9.2 that as you go up in the hierarchy from leaf to root, you are not following a single characteristic of the leaf in broader and broader categories. You're actually going from one characteristic to a fundamentally different one.

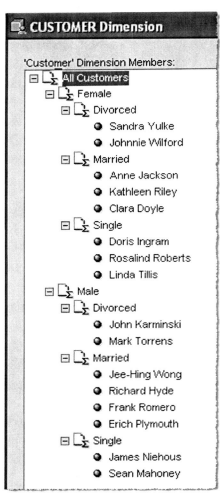

Figure 9.1. Hierarchy of Figure 9.2 Displayed from AWM

These characteristics (gender and marital status) are not structurally related, as were zip code and city. That's what makes this an unnatural hierarchy.

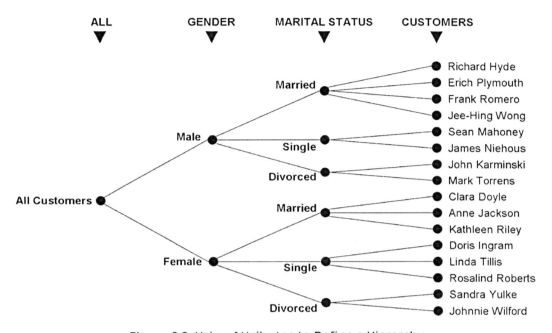

Figure 9.2. Using Attributes to Define a Hierarchy

I've seen situations where a client has asked for hierarchies like this, so let's take a closer look at it. Figure 9.1 is how the hierarchy might be displayed in a graphical interface. Already you can see one potential source of confusion: there are multiple nodes with the same label and that could lead to confusion. The interface does not necessarily have to show the entire hierarchy, and if it only showed a segment, from say, married down to leaf, you might not be able to tell if you were looking at male married or female married. In this example you could probably figure it out from the names, but you could surely imagine other examples where it would not be possible to sort things out like that from the leaf nodes.

Qualitative Differences Between Natural and Unnatural Hierarchies

The mechanics of creating an unnatural hierarchy are essentially the same as for the natural hierarchy: make sure there is a dimension member for each node in the hierarchy and establish the parent-child links by populating a self-relation. There are, however, three significant qualitative differences between natural and unnatural hierarchies as follows:

- STRUCTURAL RELATIONSHIP BETWEEN LEVELS—In a natural hierarchy, knowing the value at one level means you can determine the value in the next level up. For instance, if you know the zip code, you can determine the city; if you know the outlet, you can determine the division. On the other hand, if you know the marital status of a customer, you don't necessarily know that customer's gender, and vice versa. In other words, there is a structural relationship between the logical levels of a natural hierarchy, but not for an unnatural hierarchy.

- INTERCHANGEABILITY OF LEVELS—The levels in a natural hierarchy cannot be interchanged. If you tried to interchange the city and zip code levels in the geography hierarchy, you wouldn't be able to make a meaningful hierarchy. You couldn't have, for example, a customer report to a city and then the city report to a zip code; it only works one way. On the other hand, in an unnatural hierarchy, you could interchange levels and still get a valid hierarchy. For example, you could interchange marital status and gender to get the hierarchy shown in Figure 9.3.

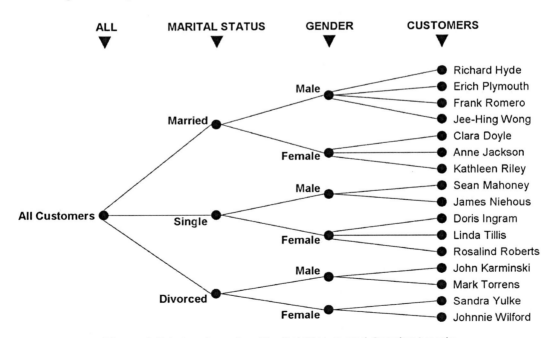

Figure 9.3. Interchanging Marital Status and Gender Levels

- **LEVELS AS SENSIBLE BREAKOUT DIMENSIONS**—It would be perfectly sensible to create a report of summarized data broken out by marital status, gender, product, and time. But it would be a bad design to create a report giving summaries broken out by zip code, city, product, and time. Since the zip code determines the city, including both a zip code and city dimension in a report would be redundant. On the other hand, marital status and gender are independent; one does not determine the other. There is no redundancy by including both as dimensions in a report. In general, the levels of an unnatural hierarchy are sensible, logical choices as breakout dimensions in a report, while those of a natural hierarchy are not.

So why does it matter if it's an unnatural or a natural hierarchy, if the process for creating it is essentially the same? If you are proposing to create an unnatural hierarchy, you have an additional choice that doesn't come with a natural hierarchy. Because the levels correspond to independent pieces of information, you could use them as breakout dimensions as an *alternative* to using them to define a hierarchy.

In the case of the current example, this means rather than breaking out the data by product, time, and customer, you could break it out by product, time, gender, and marital status. This would create a more logical display of the data, since it doesn't imply a hierarchical relationship between gender and marital status. You do lose, however, the ability to drill all the way to the customer level.

It would be fair to say that natural hierarchies are more logically coherent than unnatural hierarchies. If you can recognize the difference, when a user asks for an unnatural hierarchy, you might suggest the alternative representation so that you can use the attributes as breakout dimensions instead.

We have been looking at the issues and merits of using attributes to define a hierarchy. Conversely, any hierarchy level could be used as the basis for creating an attribute. For example, you could have a zip code attribute that maps each customer to a member in a separate zip code dimension. In some situations, it makes sense to do both, to have a level in a hierarchy *also* represented as a separate attribute.

Creating an Unnatural Hierarchy

Encoding an unnatural hierarchy follows the same process as encoding any hierarchy: represent the nodes and set the parent-child relation values. It is instructive to see how the data is used to set up the hierarchy. Let's show the data for this hierarchy in a table format, such as Table 9.1.

Table 9.1. Hierarchy Data for Creating the Hierarchy of Figure 9.2

Customer Code	Customer Label	Marital Status Code	Marital Label	Gender Code	Gender Label	All Code	All Label
CU001	Jee-Hing Wong	MMAR	Married	M	Male	ALL	All Customers
CU002	Doris Ingram	FSGL	Single	F	Female	ALL	All Customers
CU003	James Niehous	MSGL	Single	M	Male	ALL	All Customers
CU004	Anne Jackson	FMAR	Married	F	Female	ALL	All Customers
CU005	Richard Hyde	MMAR	Married	M	Male	ALL	All Customers
CU006	Sandra Yulke	FDIV	Divorced	F	Female	ALL	All Customers
CU007	Rosalind Roberts	FSGL	Single	F	Female	ALL	All Customers
CU008	Kathleen Riley	FMAR	Married	F	Female	ALL	All Customers
CU009	John Karminski	MDIV	Divorced	M	Male	ALL	All Customers
CU010	Mark Torrens	MDIV	Divorced	M	Male	ALL	All Customers
CU011	Clara Doyle	FMAR	Married	F	Female	ALL	All Customers
CU012	Johnnie Wilford	FDIV	Divorced	F	Female	ALL	All Customers
CU013	Linda Tillis	FSGL	Single	F	Female	ALL	All Customers
CU014	Frank Romero	MMAR	Married	M	Male	ALL	All Customers
CU015	Sean Mahoney	MSGL	Single	M	Male	ALL	All Customers
CU016	Erich Plymouth	MMAR	Married	M	Male	ALL	All Customers

The codes for the parent-level labels have a first letter that identifies gender, followed by three letters identifying marital status. That's because even though the label you see may read Single, the system knows whether it is Male-Single or Female-Single, as these separate nodes in the hierarchy must all have distinct identities among the dimension values.

Balanced Hierarchies Versus Ragged Hierarchies

A balanced hierarchy is one in which the parent of each member comes from the level immediately above the member. The unnatural hierarchy in Figure 9.3 is balanced: if you look at any customer node and move up one link, you'll always arrive at a gender node.

Equivalently, balanced means that the depth of a node determines its object type. So if you know how many links you need to follow to get from the root to a given node, you can say what the object type of the given node will be. (In the organization hierarchy of the last chapter you know that if you go two levels down from the president, you'll arrive at a manager.) If you further add the requirement that the depth of all leaf nodes is the same, then you can call it a *regular* balanced hierarchy.

Every hierarchy illustrated thus far has been a regular balanced hierarchy. Let's look at some exceptions.

Figure 9.4 shows an example of a hierarchy that is balanced but not regular.

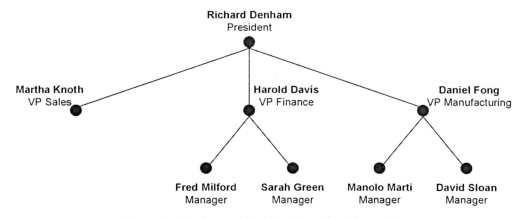

Figure 9.4. Balanced but Not Regular Hierarchy

In this hierarchy, you retain the property that the parent of each member comes from the level immediately above the member. You can determine the level of the member by its depth. However, the vice president of sales has no one reporting to her, so it is a leaf node. The distance from the president to that leaf is one, whereas the distance from the president to the leaf at Fred Milford is two. Since the depth of all leaf nodes is not the same, the hierarchy is not regular.

A ragged hierarchy is one in which the parent for some member does not come from the level immediately above it. Figure 9.5 gives an example of a ragged hierarchy.

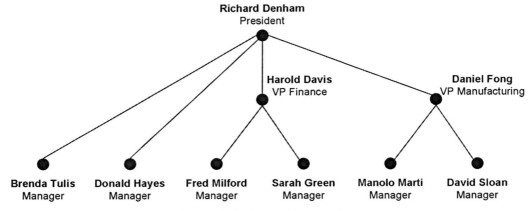

Figure 9.5. Ragged Hierarchy

Here you have two managers who report directly to the president. In this hierarchy, you lose the property that the parent of each member comes from the level immediately above that member, because the level above manager is vice president. Also, you cannot determine the level of a member by its depth in this hierarchy.

Representing a Ragged Hierarchy in the DML

Representing a ragged hierarchy is easy, since it involves the same process of specifying parent-child relationships that was used with the balanced hierarchy. But there's a twist: the tabular data format you've been using to specify the hierarchy will no longer work!

To see why, take a look at Table 8.1. Its format implies a regular, balanced hierarchy. Each row of data is the path from leaf to root and that path has the same number of links in all cases. The level of a particular node can be determined from what column it is found in, which is equivalent to the number of links traversed to get there.

But with a ragged hierarchy, the parent isn't necessarily from the level immediately above it; the parent isn't necessarily from the column next to it. So a different format for the data for a ragged hierarchy is needed.

Table 9.2 presents a flexible data format for representing parent-child relationships. Where the format of Table 8.1 had a row for every leaf node, this format has a row for every node. Where the other format had a column for every level, this has a column for every hierarchy. There's an (optional) column for specifying the level. Take a look at the data in Table 9.2 for the ragged hierarchy of Figure 9.5. Since this data has the parent for every node, it fully specifies the hierarchy. Multiple hierarchies are accommodated by using multiple columns. Indeed, the specification for any hierarchy can be accomplished in this format.

Table 9.2. Data for the Ragged Hierarchy of Figure 9.5

Code	Label	Parent for Hierarchy 1	Level
P01	Richard Denham	NA	PRES
P02	Harold Davis	P01	VP
P03	Daniel Fong	P01	VP
P04	Brenda Tulis	P01	MAN
P05	Donald Hayes	P01	MAN
P06	Fred Milford	P02	MAN
P07	Sarah Green	P02	MAN
P08	Manolo Marti	P03	MAN
P09	David Sloan	P03	MAN

Table 9.3 compares the two data file formats: balanced hierarchy only versus any hierarchy.

Table 9.3. Comparison of the Two Formats: Balanced Hierarchy Only vs. Any Hierarchy

Balanced Hierarchy Only	Any Hierarchy
One row for each leaf node.	One row for every node.
One column for code, label, every hierarchy level, every hierarchy level label, and for each attribute.	One column for code, label, every hierarchy (to show the parents for that hierarchy), and for each attribute.
Hierarchy levels are identified by the column.	Hierarchy levels are represented explicitly in a dedicated column.
Star schema.	Not star schema.

As you will see in Chapter 19: *Getting Data In and Out of Analytic Workspaces,* data in the "Balanced Hierarchy Only" format can be directly related to a dimension table in a star schema data warehouse. The other, more flexible format of any hierarchy does not.

Finally, let me point out that if a dimension has multiple hierarchies, it would be possible for them to be of mixed types. You could have one hierarchy that is balanced, one that is ragged, and so on. There is no restriction by the DML on the type of hierarchies that can be modeled for a given dimension, though a user interface layer may impose restrictions.

Part III:
Designing Multidimensional Data

10 | Storing Data in Analytic Workspaces

Now that you have a good handle on dimensions, we'll turn our attention to the application data itself. Application data are measurements of the business process of interest. These measurements could be a measure of intensity (how many dollars, how much product, how many ounces, how much time) or a count of something (how many customers, how many cities, how many occurrences of some particular type of event). So you need to understand how such data is stored in the AW and how to work with it, which brings us to variables.

Variables are the primary data storage elements in the DML. Variables are designed specifically to hold data in a multidimensional format. *Variables have a data type and a dimensionality.* The text-valued variables used to store dimension member descriptions have one or two dimensions, but data variables generally have more, typically three to eight.

You first saw variables in Chapter 6: *Describing Dimension Members with Labels* when they were used to store descriptions of dimension values. In this chapter, you'll be looking at the essential function of variables, which is to store the application data. You will also see some physical design considerations that can have an impact on performance.

Although variables are overwhelmingly the most common means for storing application data, other object types are used in some situations. In Chapter 7: *Categorizing Dimension Members with Attributes,* you saw how relations were used to capture customer behavior. In subsequent chapters you will see a few more examples of application data stored in other DML object types, but variables constitute the normal case.

Determining Dimensionality

Choice of dimensions is obvious in some situations; it requires considerable thought in others. To see an example of a choice, consider a situation in which you wish to store historical data on the number of units of product that have been purchased. It might be reasonable to use three dimensions: one to capture the customer, one for the product, and one for time. But other choices might make more sense, depending on the specifics of the situation. For instance, four dimensions: customer, store, product, and time. Or maybe you don't know the customer, so you use store, product, and time. Or maybe you want to see the data as a function of payment method so you use store, payment method, product, and time. You may even want the data displayed in more than one way with different dimensionalities. The point is, don't be surprised if in the design of a given application, some time is devoted in determining the dimensionality of the various data elements.

Defining Variables

Assume you choose to break out a variable containing the units of product sold by customer, product, and time. Then define a variable to hold this information like this:

```
DEFINE UNITS VARIABLE DECIMAL <CUSTOMER PRODUCT TIME>
```

The variable called UNITS will be used to store the number of units of a given product that was purchased by a given customer at a given time. Suppose you also wanted to record the revenue generated by the products, then you could define a second variable called REVENUE to store that data:

```
DEFINE REVENUE VARIABLE DECIMAL <CUSTOMER PRODUCT TIME>
```

Having created two variables—REVENUE and UNITS—that use the same dimensions a question might arise: Is there a copy made of a given dimension for each variable that uses it or do these variables somehow all share that same dimension? The answer is that they share that same dimension and all its dimension values—there is no separate copy of the dimension made for each object that uses it.

This has two consequences of note. First, a storage economy is realized. Even though a thousand objects may use a dimension, it is represented only *once* in the system.

Second, if a dimension member is added or deleted, the effect will be seen in every object that is dimensioned by it.

Think of the dimension as a resource, created once and available to be used in the creation of any object. Because it is a shared resource, if a dimension member is deleted (using MAINTAIN DELETE), it deletes the corresponding data from every object that uses the dimension.

For example, if you do this:
```
MAINTAIN DELETE PRODUCT 'TP001'
```

…then every object that is dimensioned by product will no longer have data for product TP001, which is now out of the system.

If several multidimensional variables use the same set of dimensions, you should list them in the DEFINE statement in the same order for all of those variables. This is because the AW creates supporting structures for the dimensionality itself. Keeping the dimensions in the same order prevents unnecessary redundancy, which keeps storage requirements down.

Getting Information About Variables

The OBJ function can be used to retrieve specific information about the variables you create. The following are a few examples.

You can get the data type of an object like this:
```
->SHOW OBJ(DATA 'UNITS')
DECIMAL
```

You can display the dimensionality of UNITS:
```
->SHOW OBJ(DIMS 'UNITS')
CUSTOMER
PRODUCT
TIME
```

Of course you can find out the above information by **simply** describing UNITS, with a DESCRIBE UNITS command. The OBJ function is **often** used in programs that need to access such information in an explicit way.

Here's how to get a list of every object that has the same dimensionality as UNITS:
```
->SHOW VALUES(LIMIT(NAME TO OBJ(DIMS NAME) EQ -
OBJ(DIMS 'UNITS')))
UNITS
REVENUE
```

You can see the total number of memory pages used to store the object:
```
->SHOW OBJ(DISKSIZE 'UNITS')
1
```

The page size of the AW:
```
->SHOW AW(PAGESIZE)
8128
```

So that the total storage requirement in bytes is:
```
->SHOW OBJ(DISKSIZE 'UNITS')*AW(PAGESIZE)
8128
```

Multicube Approach

Not all variables need to have the same dimensionality. The AW can have hundreds of dimensions, but a given variable may use only a few of them. Typically data variables have from three to eight dimensions. (If a variable has many more than eight, there may well be something wrong or confused about how it was defined.) The ability to create different variables with different dimensionalities is sometimes called the multicube approach.

A three-dimensional variable can be depicted with a cube-like representation: one dimension representing the x-axis, another the y-axis, and another the z-axis. Other dimensionalities can be thought of as "hypercubes," borrowing from the mathematical concept generalizing a cube to more than three dimensions. Even when there are more than three dimensions, the prefix "hyper" is usually left off and the variable simply referred to as a "cube."

Data Storage Order

When a variable is created, the system creates a place to store a data value for every combination of members of its dimensions. To visualize this, think of a variable as being a hotel for storing data. In fact, let's create a variable called HOTEL dimensioned by ROOM, LEVEL, and BUILDING. Assuming these dimensions have been defined, you can proceed:

```
DEFINE HOTEL VARIABLE INTEGER <ROOM LEVEL BUILDING>
```

You could use a variable like this for storing the number of days the room has been vacant, or anything else that suits your fancy. We're using it as a "specimen" with which to explore physical storage issues.

When the HOTEL variable is defined, the system creates a storage cell for every combination of room, level, and building. Assume that you created dimension members to represent two buildings, each with two levels and four rooms per level. Then there would be a total of 2 x 2 x 4 = 16 places for storing numbers. Assume you stored consecutive integers in those places. Now report on the HOTEL variable:

```
->REPORT HOTEL
BUILDING: BLD1
                       -------------------HOTEL------------------
                       -------------------ROOM-------------------
LEVEL             ROOM1         ROOM2         ROOM3         ROOM4
--------------    ----------    ----------    ----------    ----------
LEVEL1                1             2             3             4
LEVEL2                5             6             7             8

BUILDING: BLD2
                       -------------------HOTEL------------------
                       -------------------ROOM-------------------
LEVEL             ROOM1         ROOM2         ROOM3         ROOM4
--------------    ----------    ----------    ----------    ----------
LEVEL1                9            10            11            12
LEVEL2               13            14            15            16
```

Looking at the output above, you'll notice that the report comes in two pieces: one for BLD1 and one for BLD2. Think of this as two groups of data, or since they are sometimes put on two separate pages, as two pages of data. Also note that each number has three dimension members associated with it. For example, the number 13 has BLD2, LEVEL2, and ROOM1 associated with it. The dimension members associated with a piece of data can be called a *tuple*. You can think of a tuple as the number's address.

The default display order takes the first dimension and uses it for the headings *across,* the second dimension is used for the rows *down,* and the remaining dimensions become the groups or *pages.* It's easy to remember: the words across, down, and page are in alphabetical order.

Now let's think about performance considerations. Consider the physical process of storing the data. To get the best performance, you want to know what data is stored in contiguous storage compartments on the disk. The reason you care is because if the data is retrieved in the same order that it is stored, it will be accessed in the fastest possible order, since physical movement of the read head will be minimized. If a large amount of data is being read (consider cases where there are many, perhaps millions of dimension values), this kind of efficiency can make a significant difference!

The sample data shown in the report above (the numbers from 1 to 16) were chosen to illustrate the storage order: the consecutive integers were stored in consecutive spaces. The storage process works this way: When a variable is defined, the first dimension (in this case, ROOM) in the dimension list becomes the fastest varying. The second dimension (here, LEVEL) is the next fastest varying, until the last dimension in the list, which is the slowest to vary.

Think of your car odometer, with the one's place cycling through all values, zero through nine, before the ten's value moves once; the ten's value cycles through all values before the hundred's value moves once. The one's place is the fastest to vary.

In the hotel example, reading the data in the order that it is stored, you'll cycle through all the rooms for a given level and building, then switch the level and cycle through all the rooms for that level, until you've gone through all levels; then you'll switch buildings and continue the process. ROOM is the fastest-varying dimension, LEVEL is the second-fastest-varying dimension, and BUILDING is the slowest-varying dimension.

Assuming that we have all dimension values in status, note that doing a simple REPORT command will display the data in the order that it is stored. The column headings are values of the first dimension, the row headings are values of the second dimension, and all subsequent dimensions result in new groups of data. So the default display retrieves the data using the fastest ordering.

Using the Random Number Generator to Create Test Data

There are situations in which you may want to generate test data; you need numbers with which to work but the real data isn't available yet. This is easily accomplished with the RANDOM function, which generates pseudorandom numbers from a uniform distribution. Here's how to completely populate the REVENUE variable with random numbers between 0 and 1,500:

```
ALLSTAT
REVENUE = RANDOM(0,1500)
```

Value-Based Filtering

In this section we are going to look at examples of filtering based on the numerical values of a data variable. The examples shown here are a representative sample of all the possibilities. Many other variations can be found in the online help and the user's guide.

Let's find all customers that generated revenue greater than $1,000 during March 2009.

```
LIMIT PRODUCT TO 'ALL'
LIMIT TIME TO 'MAR09'
LIMIT CUSTOMER TO REVENUE GT 1000
```

When filtering with a multidimensional object, there is normally one dimension whose values are being searched (call it the *filtering dimension*), while the values of all other dimensions are fixed to a single specified value. Here, the product and time dimensions are fixed to one value and the customer dimension is being searched.

Here's another example. Let's find the top-10 customers on the basis of revenue for March 2009:

```
LIMIT PRODUCT TO 'ALL'
LIMIT TIME TO 'MAR09'
LIMIT CUSTOMER TO TOP 10 BASEDON REVENUE
```

In the above example, you have a three-dimensional variable. You set two of the dimensions to a single value and search the third for values that satisfy the criterion. More generally, if you're filtering on an N-dimensional variable, you'll set the status of N-1 dimensions to one value, then limit on the remaining dimension.

What happens if you forget to explicitly "lock down" all of the non-filter dimensions to a single value? If only a single dimension value happens to be in status for a non-filter dimension, that value is used. If there is more than one in status, the first value that happens to be in the status list is used. You generally do not want this to happen!

As has been mentioned, the DML doesn't have a "default value" construct that fills in missing values for such situations. The moral of the story is, if you're getting unexpected or inconsistent results with a LIMIT command, check to make sure you are properly managing the status of all non-filtering dimensions.

What if you don't want to lock down one of the dimensions to a single value? Suppose, for example, you want to find the customers who generated revenue greater than $1,000 during *any* month.

Use the following statements:
```
LIMIT PRODUCT TO 'ALL'
LIMIT TIME TO TIME_LEVELREL 'MONTH'
LIMIT CUSTOMER TO ANY(REVENUE GT 1000, TIME)
```

How about the ability to search more than one dimension at a time? You may want to know all customer-time combinations where the revenue was greater than $1,000. The solution to this kind of problem will be dealt with in Chapter 12 in the *Counting and Selecting with Combinations* section.

Choosing Dimension Order to Maximize Performance

As described above, the order of the dimensions in the DEFINE statement affects how the data is stored, which in turn can affect system performance. What we've looked at so far is the interaction between dimension ordering and performance in the context of data retrieval.

Let's dig a little deeper into the issue of performance. What are the kinds of data operations, and who is impacted by the performance level in them? Nearly all data manipulations can be classified into one of four categories: load, build, filtering, and reporting.

- LOAD—Reading data from an external source into the AW.

- BUILD—Calculating quantities derived from the loaded data. This includes computing the summary data values.

- FILTERING—Determining which dimension values meet a criterion.

- REPORTING—Retrieving data to generate a tabular display of data. This may include calculating values on-the-fly.

Load and build are normally transparent to the user. There will be a time window within which these functions must be completed, but given that the data is made available for the scheduled times, the user is not impacted by performance with these functions. On the other hand, the user is impacted by performance in filtering and reporting.

System administrators and others responsible for creating the system and making it work, in contrast, are very directly concerned with performance in the first two categories. They may or may not be impacted by filtering and reporting performance, depending on whether the build step includes those types of operations.

Another factor to consider in strategizing for performance is that the load and build steps are carried out by programs whose design can be conscientiously designed to maximize performance. User interactions, on the other hand, are more difficult to control or influence and may be more varied in nature.

These observations should guide your design strategy. If there's likely to be a challenge meeting the load and build time window, then that constraint should drive the design. If the load/build process occurs comfortably within the time window, end-user performance can drive the design. Although optimizing for one type of performance need not compromise performance in another, these objectives oftentimes do contradict—a win for one is a loss for the other.

So now you have a starting point for what is generally a complex issue that may require a certain amount of experimentation. A common situation in a basic data variable is that there is a large disparity in the number of dimension values. For instance, you might have 500,000 customers, 5,000 products, and 500 time frames. If it's known that the user would do frequent filtering on the large dimension (customers), that would motivate you to put it first in the dimension list, so that for fixed values of the other two, the system would cycle through the large dimension as efficiently as possible.

If the user does not make frequent filters on the large dimension, but does frequent large time-trend reports, you may want to put the time dimension first.

Measure Dimensions

So far you've been using dimensions to create multidimensional breakouts of data. You also used them to classify dimension members for a base dimension. Finally, you saw how they could be used in a data management capacity: enumerating languages and hierarchies. You will now see another important use of dimensions.

Measure dimensions are a data modeling technique that makes it possible to store a number of different measurements in a single variable.

Consider the UNITS and REVENUE variables. Each has the same dimensionality (CUSTOMER, PRODUCT, and TIME) and the same data type (decimal). This similar structure makes it possible to apply the next technique.

The first step is to define a measure dimension, a dimension that will have one value for each different measure you want to store:

```
DEFINE MEASURE_DIM DIMENSION TEXT
```

Then populate the dimension members, one value for UNITS and one for REVENUE:
```
MAINTAIN MEASURE_DIM ADD 'UNITS' 'REVENUE'
```

Finally, define a variable that has the original breakout dimensions plus the measure dimension:

```
DEFINE APP_DATA VARIABLE DECIMAL <CUSTOMER PRODUCT TIME -
MEASURE_DIM>
```

This new variable can hold all the data of both of the original variables. You can populate APP_DATA with the data in the UNITS and REVENUE variables like this:

```
ALLSTAT
LIMIT MEASURE_DIM TO 'UNITS'
APP_DATA = UNITS
LIMIT MEASURE_DIM TO 'REVENUE'
APP_DATA = REVENUE
```

Clearly, MEASURE_DIM is an ordinary text-valued dimension. It's called a measure dimension solely by virtue of how it is used. You can continue to add dimension members to it and thusly, add as many different measures as needed.

Measure Dimensions Don't Add Detail

If you examine the data stored in UNITS, you can identify the most detailed data available from the system. Your dimensions (CUSTOMER, PRODUCT, and TIME) all presumably have a hierarchy defined for them. The most detailed data is the data at leaf-level values for all three dimensions. This most detailed data defines the *grain* of the data.

Now suppose you had data broken out by an additional dimension, say store:
```
DEFINE UNITS_DETAILED VARIABLE DECIMAL <CUSTOMER STORE -
PRODUCT TIME>
```

The variable UNITS_DETAILED tells you everything that UNITS told you, *plus* it tells you in which store the product was purchased. This is more detailed and UNITS_DETAILED would have a different grain.

So more dimensions usually means more specificity. *Measure dimensions are an exception to this rule*. Although APP_DATA is broken out by four dimensions and UNITS is broken out by three dimensions, the data from APP_DATA is not more detailed than that of UNITS. If you need to make the distinction, you can call CUSTOMER, STORE, and TIME data breakout dimensions, because the data is actually broken out into those three dimensions.

So if you're using APP_DATA for reporting and someone asks the dimensionality of your data, three would probably be the most meaningful answer; saying "four" may give a false impression.

Display Dimensions

There's a useful concept in thinking about reports, the idea of a *display dimension*. You can conceptualize three display dimensions: column, row, and group, or equivalently, across, down, and page. These three dimensions constitute the three *edges* of a report.

Data dimensions, in contrast, are the actual dimensions by which the variable you want to display is broken out. Since the data, ultimately, will be displayed on a flat, two-dimensional report, the data dimensions are, in effect, assigned to display dimensions before the system can determine how to render it.

The REPORT command has many options for configuring the display produced. Some of those options have to do with how the data dimensions translate into the display dimensions. Let's see how they work. Suppose you want to see the hotel data with one room per row rather than one level per row. You can specify that you want the ROOM dimension to be the rows using the DOWN keyword:

```
->REPORT DOWN ROOM HOTEL
BUILDING: BLD1
                      --------HOTEL--------
                      --------LEVEL--------
ROOM                     LEVEL1       LEVEL2
--------------        ----------   ----------
ROOM1                         1            5
ROOM2                         2            6
ROOM3                         3            7
ROOM4                         4            8
```

```
BUILDING: BLD2
                --------HOTEL--------
                --------LEVEL--------
ROOM              LEVEL1      LEVEL2
--------------  ----------  ----------
ROOM1                    9          13
ROOM2                   10          14
ROOM3                   11          15
ROOM4                   12          16
```

Unlike the original report, in the above report, the order in which you see the data (1, 5, 2, 6, etc.) is not the order in which it is physically stored.

As another variation, you can specify that you want the rooms going down and the buildings going across (note the colon due to the "across" specification after the word *building*!).

```
->report down room across building: hotel
LEVEL: LEVEL1
                --------HOTEL--------
                ------BUILDING-------
ROOM               BLD1        BLD2
--------------  ----------  ----------
ROOM1                    1           9
ROOM2                    2          10
ROOM3                    3          11
ROOM4                    4          12

LEVEL: LEVEL2
                --------HOTEL--------
                ------BUILDING-------
ROOM               BLD1        BLD2
--------------  ----------  ----------
ROOM1                    5          13
ROOM2                    6          14
ROOM3                    7          15
ROOM4                    8          16
```

Sparsity Happens

When a variable is created, a storage cell is created for every combination of its dimension members. Consider the UNITS variable. Suppose there are 500,000 customers, 5,000 products, and 500 time periods amounting to 500,000 x 5,000 x 500 = 1.25 x 10^{12} data cells. Intuitively you know you couldn't possibly have so much data! Logically, it would be unbelievable that every customer would buy some of every product in every time period. In actual application, a customer buys a small fraction of the possible products and in many time frames may buy nothing, so most of the data cells are empty. The manner in which the number of possible data cells expands dramatically as the number of base dimensions or base dimension values increases is an example of the phenomenon of *combinatorial explosion*. The phenomenon of a *high vacancy rate* that typically accompanies situations with a very large number of dimension combinations is referred to as *sparsity*—a very important issue in any multidimensional system. Sparsity can lead to inefficient use of space and performance degradations in other ways as well; fortunately, there are techniques for coping with it.

The primary mechanism that Oracle OLAP provides for reducing sparsity is a construct called a *composite*. When a composite is defined, the user specifies dimensions for which a small percentage of the total number of possible combinations will have data. The composite is incorporated into the definition of the variable to trigger its use. Using the composite, only cells for combinations for which there is data will have space reserved.

As you might guess, using composites where they are not needed can result in performance losses. But using composites where they do fit not only results in storage savings, it can actually result in performance (speed) gains as well.

Proper use of composites is a big topic for which there is a wealth of information online. Since it mainly concerns physical design and not analysis techniques, I'm only touching upon it here.

Suppose you want to accommodate the fact that any given customer will buy only a few of the possible products. Then you can specify CUSTOMER and PRODUCT to be sparse as follows:

```
DEFINE UNITS VARIABLE DECIMAL <TIME SPARSE<CUSTOMER -
PRODUCT>>
```

Anytime there is data for a customer-product combination, a space is made to save it, and there is one such space for every time value. The SPARSE keyword in the define statement will cause a separate object, a customer-product composite, to be created. The system will generate a cryptic name for it, but if you issue:

```
LISTNAMES COMPOSITE
```

…it will be there. With composites, you're effectively mixing relational-style data storage with multidimensional storage to get the best of both worlds.

Now suppose you define your revenue variable in a similar manner:
```
DEFINE REVENUE VARIABLE DECIMAL <TIME SPARSE<CUSTOMER -
PRODUCT>>
```

This will work, but it is better to use a named composite. Named composites give you more control. They give you the ability to force variables that have similar sparsity patterns to use the same composite. This can result in more efficient use of disk storage.

To this end:
```
DEFINE CP COMPOSITE <CUSTOMER PRODUCT>
```

And the syntax for creating UNITS and REVENUE variables that share it is:
```
DEFINE UNITS VARIABLE DECIMAL <TIME CP<CUSTOMER PRODUCT>>
DEFINE REVENUE VARIABLE DECIMAL <TIME CP<CUSTOMER PRODUCT>>
```

Notice that in the DEFINE statement you use the name of the composite instead of the SPARSE keyword.

There is one more option available, the use of compressed composites:
```
DEFINE CP COMPOSITE <CUSTOMER PRODUCT> COMPRESSED
```

Compressed composites have numerous additional advantages, along with some restrictions. In some situations, they can decrease storage requirements even further and can result in dramatically faster aggregations.

Use of composites affects the rules of optimum dimension ordering, so make sure you consult the Oracle documentation for those guidelines.

11 | Calculating Data On-the-Fly

In this chapter, you will learn how to calculate data at the time it is requested—on-the-fly. Precalculating derived data makes system performance fast, but does so at the expense of the build time used to perform the calculations and requires additional storage. For situations in which the economics do not justify the investment in build time and/or storage, DML *formulas* can be used to calculate data at the time it is requested.

Calc This, Not That

Here are situations where precalculating a derived quantity in a build step may not make sense:

- ■ The calculation required is so trivial that the performance boost from doing it in advance is negligible.

- ■ Precalculating gives an appreciable boost in performance, but it's not possible to do the calculations in the available time window.

■ Precalculation gives an appreciable boost in performance and can be performed in the required time window, but the data is very rarely accessed by the user so it's not worth the expenditure in resources.

The first case is a clear fit for the application of formulas. The second is more complex and may benefit from clever computational or caching strategies. You may choose to calculate only some aggregate values. The third case may be dealt with like the second—perhaps tolerating occasional disappointing performance. In all three cases, formulas play a part.

Defining a Formula

A formula definition consists of two parts. The "define" part has the same form as a variable definition, except that the word "formula" is used instead of "variable." The second part (the "EQ") contains the expression that is evaluated and returned by the formula. Let's see an example. Here is a formula that returns the ratio of revenue to the number of units:

```
DEFINE F.REV_PROD FORMULA DECIMAL <CUSTOMER PRODUCT TIME>
EQ REVENUE/UNIT
```

The formula F.REV_PROD doesn't cause any calculation to occur until it's triggered either through a reporting statement or an assignment statement.

The statement:
```
REPORT F.REV_PROD
```

…would cause the EQ expression to be evaluated for every combination of customer, product, and time in status. This is basically equivalent to doing:

```
REPORT REVENUE/UNIT
```

The formula gives a "handle" to the calculation and assigns a dimensionality and data type to it.

The other way to trigger a formula evaluation is through an assignment statement. The following example illustrates this by showing how to store a formula's calculations into a variable.

Start by defining a variable to hold the results:
```
DEFINE V.AVG_REV_PROD VARIABLE DECIMAL <CUSTOMER PRODUCT -
TIME>
```

Then set status and use an assignment statement to store the results. Note the implicit looping!

```
ALLSTAT
V.AVG_REV_PROD = F.REV_PROD
```

The values that were computed by the formula are now stored in the variable.

Changing a Formula's EQ

You can change the EQ expression of a formula by "considering" the formula, then re-executing the EQ command:

```
CONSIDER F.REV_PROD
EQ REVENUE
```

Now you have:
```
->DESCRIBE F.REV_PROD
DEFINE F.REV_PROD FORMULA DECIMAL <CUSTOMER PRODUCT TIME>
EQ REVENUE
```

This modified definition F.REV_PROD would simply return the value of REVENUE.

I've observed that people sometimes think an EQ has to have a calculation, so they multiply by 1 (i.e., REVENUE*1). That's not necessary!

By the same token, if you need the negative of something, you can just use −REVENUE, there's no need for −1*REVENUE.

Formulas for Common Calculations

FORMULA 1: REVENUE INDEX

Suppose you want to index revenue to a value it had at a certain point in time. This formula indexes revenue to its JAN09 value:

```
DEFINE F.REV_INDEX FORMULA DECIMAL <CUSTOMER PRODUCT TIME>
EQ 100*REVENUE/REVENUE(TIME 'JAN09')
```

When this formula evaluates, the numerator uses the values for customer, product, and time that are passed in and the denominator uses customer and product, but time is pegged at JAN09.

FORMULA 2: PERCENT OF REVENUE (CUSTOMER)

What percent of the revenue does this customer account for, at this time, for this product?

```
DEFINE F.REV_INDEX FORMULA DECIMAL <CUSTOMER PRODUCT TIME>
EQ 100*REVENUE/REVENUE(CUSTOMER 'ALL')
```

Keep in mind dimensions are typically organized in a hierarchy, where different dimension members are different types of objects depending on their level. So if you evaluate the expression for a leaf-level customer member, the formula gives the percent of the total revenue from that customer. At the zip code level, the formula gives the percent of total revenue attributable to that zip code, and so on.

FORMULA 3: PERCENT OF REVENUE (PRODUCT)

What percent of the revenue does this product account for, for this customer, at this time?

```
DEFINE F.REV_INDEX FORMULA DECIMAL <CUSTOMER PRODUCT TIME>
EQ 100*REVENUE/REVENUE(PRODUCT 'ALL')
```

FORMULA 4: PERCENT OF REVENUE (CATEGORY)

Suppose you have an attribute on products called category. You want to know what percent of the product category's revenue is attributable to a given product in the category.

This calculation has a couple of twists to it:

- The formula evaluates for all dimension values, yet the category attribute might only be defined for the lowest levels of the product hierarchy.

- The denominator needs to be revenue broken out by category and since category is an attribute and not a hierarchy level (by presumption), you can't simply QDR on a product member like in the previous example.

I will show the formula and then explain it:
```
DEFINE F.REV_CAT FORMULA DECIMAL <CUSTOMER PRODUCT TIME>
EQ 100*REVENUE/REVCAT(CATEGORY R.CATEGORY.PRODUCT)
```

The numerator is just REVENUE; nothing new there. The denominator has a variable called REVCAT and a QDR that uses a relation. The job of that relation is to translate the product value it sees into its category. REVCAT is evaluated at that category value. REVCAT is revenue, but as a function of category, not product.

The REVCAT variable will have a definition like this:
```
DEFINE REVCAT VARIABLE DECIMAL <CUSTOMER CATEGORY TIME>
```

As you can see, there is a CATEGORY dimension (not a product dimension!). So now the question is this: how do you get the data for REVCAT? In Chapter 14 on aggregations, I'll show you how to populate REVCAT from REVENUE. So for now, just assume the data is there.

Translating a product into its category is a straightforward application of relations, just like you've already seen. The category relation has the definition you'd probably expect:
```
DEFINE R.CATEGORY.PRODUCT RELATION CATEGORY <PRODUCT>
```

Of course, this relation needs to be populated for things to work. This would be done by a series of assignment statements or by a data load as will be shown in Chapter 19: *Getting Data In and Out of Analytic Workspaces*.

If a given product is not mapped to a category, the relation returns NA, and the entire expression will return NA. And by the way, you can alter this behavior by using the NAFILL function, which you'll see in Formula 6: *Substituting a Forecast Value for a Missing Actual*.

Formula 5: Ampersand Substitution

Suppose you have a particular calculation sequence that can be applied to a variety of different variables. You could define a separate formula for each of the many variable choices, but it is possible to create a single formula that handles all the choices and this may give you a system that is easier to manage. One way is using a DML feature called ampersand substitution. Ampersand substitution gives a way of dynamically assigning the variable to be used.

To illustrate this feature, you'll need to create text variables whose purpose will be to hold the names of the numerical variables that will actually be involved in the calculations. Then create an EQ expression using the ampersand operator in front of the text variables.

The ampersand operator in effect says "don't use this variable, evaluate the variable to find out the variable to use." Let's take a look at an example. Start by defining two text variables:

```
DEFINE NUMERATOR VARIABLE TEXT
DEFINE DENOMINATOR VARIABLE TEXT
```

Now define the formula in terms of them, using the ampersand operator like this:
```
DEFINE F.RATIO FORMULA DECIMAL <CUSTOMER PRODUCT TIME>
EQ 100*&NUMERATOR/&DENOMINATOR
```

The value of text variables could be assigned to the name of any variable in the AW. For example, if you could make this assignment:

```
NUMERATOR = 'REVENUE'
DENOMINATOR = 'UNITS'
```

…then the formula F.RATIO returns revenue divided by units. If, on the other hand, you assign:

```
NUMERATOR = 'UNITS'
DENOMINATOR = 'REVENUE'
```

…then the formula would return the reverse: units divided by revenue.

Formula 6: Substituting a Forecast Value for a Missing Actual

Imagine a situation where a revenue value is sometimes missing or not available, but where a forecast value exists. You want a formula that gives that revenue value when it is available and the forecast otherwise. This can be accomplished with the NAFILL function. NAFILL returns its first argument if it is not NA and its second argument otherwise. Here's a formula that does it:

```
DEFINE REVENUE_FILL FORMULA DECIMAL <CUSTOMER PRODUCT TIME>
EQ NAFILL(REVENUE, FORECAST)
```

FORMULA 7: RELATIVE TIME

Normally the dimension members in a time dimension correspond to specific periods of time. For instance, the code MAR2009 refers to the date March 2009.

Sometimes, however, you'll want to use *relative* demarcations of time, such as "the current month" or "last month" or "this month a year ago." In situations like this, the time period represented by the dimension member changes over time. "This month" could be January 2009; later, it would signify February 2009, and so on.

Let's see how to make a formula that provides data denominated in relative time values. This is done with the use of a variable to translate relative time values to absolute time values.

For example, create a variable:

```
DEFINE ABSOLUTE_TIME VARIABLE TEXT <TIME>
```

…with the understanding that TIME contains members to represent both absolute (such as 'MAR2009') and relative (such as 'CURRMONTH') values.

You will need to populate ABSOLUTE_TIME with the appropriate values for all time dimension members. Absolute time values get mapped to themselves:

```
ABSOLUTE_TIME(TIME 'MAR2009') = 'MAR2009'
```

But relative time values get mapped to their corresponding absolute time values, for example:
```
ABSOLUTE_TIME(TIME 'CURRMONTH') = 'OCT2009'
```

Be careful: when the mappings change—like at the start of a new month—the variable must be repopulated to reflect the new mappings for the relative times! Here is a formula that works for both absolute and relative times:

```
DEFINE F1.REVENUE FORMULA DECIMAL <CUSTOMER PRODUCT TIME>
EQ REVENUE(TIME ABSOLUTE_TIME)
```

I'd like to show you another way to accomplish this that shows a few other features of the DML. With this other approach, you only need to populate the ABSOLUTE_TIME variable for relative time codes; you don't need to map the absolute values to themselves. It is based on the ability to determine if a code corresponds to a relative time period or not. It uses an IF statement in the EQ to determine the appropriate response.

Assume you defined a relative time hierarchy for the relative time values. And let's say you have a valueset called TIME_INHIER that tells for each hierarchy what dimension members belong to it. Such a valueset might look like this:

```
DEFINE TIME_INHIER VALUESET <TIME_HIERLIST>
```

The following formula tests to see if the time dimension member is in the relative time hierarchy value, doing the time translation if it is, and simply returning REVENUE without translation otherwise.

```
DEFINE F2.REVENUE FORMULA DECIMAL <CUSTOMER PRODUCT TIME>
EQ IF INSTAT(TIME_INHIER(TIME_HIERLIST 'REL_HIER')TIME) -
THEN REVENUE(TIME ABSOLUTE_TIME) ELSE REVENUE
```

As you see, the EQ uses an IF-THEN-ELSE. If the time dimension member seen is in the REL_HIER hierarchy, it is a relative time value and REVENUE(TIME ABSOLUTE_TIME) is returned. Otherwise it returns REVENUE straight, with no transformations.

FORMULA 8: REVENUE A YEAR AGO

Suppose you want to compare revenue to its value a year ago. One thing you could do would be to simply set status to the base time value and to the time value a year before and do the report. But there are situations in which it's more convenient to have a version of data that has the time lag built into it.

You can do it with a formula and the LAG function:
```
DEFINE F.REV_YAGO FORMULA DECIMAL <CUSTOMER PRODUCT TIME>
EQ LAG(REVENUE, 12, TIME, TIME_LEVELREL)
```

Formula 9: Revenue Delta

This formula computes the difference between the current value and the value 12 months previous.

```
DEFINE F.REV_DELTA FORMULA DECIMAL <CUSTOMER PRODUCT TIME>
EQ REVENUE - LAG(REVENUE, 12, TIME, TIME_LEVELREL)
```

Or:
```
CONSIDER F.REV_DELTA
EQ REVENUE - REVENUE_YAGO
```

It's perfectly legal for a formula to call another formula. This is one way of achieving complex calculations that have multiple steps. But exercise caution. I have seen a number of systems where one formula calls another, which calls another, and so on, numerous levels deep. The result is a constellation of many, in some cases thousands, of formulas. This "cascading formula architecture" can become unwieldy and difficult to maintain, debug, and optimize. If you find yourself drowning in a sea of "spaghetti calcs," you might consider packing all the logic associated with a given computation into a single program and set the EQ property to that program.

Uh oh Joey, looks like Daddy's having another software maintenance nightmare

Formula 10: Hiding a Dimension from a Measure

You have a revenue variable broken out by customer, product, and time. Now suppose you have an application where you want the data broken out by product and time only; you don't need the data as a function of customer. You can create such a thing from the REVENUE variable using a formula. Here's how:

```
DEFINE REVENUE_PT FORMULA DECIMAL <PRODUCT TIME>
EQ REVENUE(CUSTOMER 'ALL')
```

REVENUE_PT effectively removes the CUSTOMER dimension from the REVENUE variable. Notice that you didn't need to store an additional two-dimensional variable to get the two dimensional object you wanted. This formula is an example of an important use of formulas: to restructure data. Don't think of formulas as solely for performing calculations; they are also used to restructure output. They can be likened to a "view" in the relational world.

Formula 11: Stitching Variables Together

Assume you've stored the revenue data in two separate variables, using one variable for each year. Let's say the variables are called REV2009 and REV2010. The formula below stitches them together into a single object.

```
DEFINE FSTITCH.REVENUE FORMULA DECIMAL <CUSTOMER PRODUCT -
TIME>
EQ IF R.YEAR.TIME EQ '2009' THEN REV2009
ELSE IF R.YEAR.TIME EQ '2010' THEN REV2010
ELSE NA
```

Breaking something big into smaller parts, then putting them back together is often done for performance reasons. For example, you could have put REV2009 and REV2010 into separate AWs and load them concurrently, perhaps on different machines. Then you would want a way to tie them together again so they could be used as a single object; this formula illustrates the basic technique.

Using formulas to stitch together data from multiple pieces forms the basis of a technique known as *capstoning*. Oracle 10g has a partitioning feature that, in effect, does this automatically for you.

FORMULA 12: SMOOTHING A TIME SERIES WITH MOVING AVERAGES

This and the next example are concerned with the manipulation of time series data. Often these kinds of calculations are done for the leaf time levels only. To simplify your life, you may want to consider using a separate time dimension that only contains leaf-level values, stored in order. That is what I assume here. (You can always tie the data you create at leaf level into other objects that use a complete time dimension using the "stitching" technique that was shown in Formula 11.)

Moving averages is one of the simplest and most popular ways of smoothing a data time series in order to make trends easy to spot. A simple moving average is computed by averaging the data from the last N time periods relative to a given time period, for example the last seven days or the last three months.

I think it will be helpful to express the computation using standard mathematical notation in order to see exactly what the MOVINGAVERAGE function does. To this end, suppose you have a raw data series, x(t) where t represents time. You want to smooth this series out by averaging, say, three data values. You will average the data for any time "t," time t minus 1, and time t minus 2. The moving average calculation adds the three values and divides by three to produce the values for a smoothed time series "y(t)."

In sigma notation this is written:

$$y(t) = \frac{1}{3}\sum_{i=1}^{3} x(t-i+1)$$

Figure 11.1. Equation 1: Moving Average with Three Data Values

How would you create a DML built-in function to perform this computation? There is a built-in function for doing it: MOVINGAVERAGE.

This formula averages the current month and the prior two to get a moving monthly average based on a quarter's worth of data.

```
DEFINE F.REV_MA FORMULA DECIMAL <CUSTOMER PRODUCT TIME>
EQ MOVINGAVERAGE(REVENUE, -2, 0, 1, TIME)
```

I think the MOVINGAVERAGE function's arguments speak for themselves; please take a look at the documentation for a complete explanation. Our goal is to move beyond this and see how to do more sophisticated kinds of filtering (shown in the next section).

The values that get averaged are based on the default ordering of the dimension members, so the TIME dimension members need to be stored in chronological order with all the values of the same level together. Only non-NA values are averaged, so if there are only two data values to work with; it adds them and divides by two.

Before we leave, let's relate the DML objects to the mathematical equations. Since the data coming in is from REVENUE and the data produced is F.REV_MA, you have the correspondences: x(t) = REVENUE and y(t) = F.REV_MA. But take note, the DML objects are actually dimensioned by more than just time! The other dimensions, CUSTOMER and PRODUCT, are not expressed explicitly in Equation 1, so the DML really gives you the framework for an array of time series.

Formula 13: Implementing Finite Impulse Response Digital Filters

There are actually other mathematical operations on time series that have greatly superior smoothing characteristics over moving averages, including some digital filters. One class of such computations is known as finite impulse response (FIR) digital filters. (Don't confuse this usage of the word "filter" with the one associated with limiting a dimension!) Moving averages are a special case of an FIR filter.

There is a huge literature available on the design of FIR filters, so I'm not going to take it on here. But for the reader familiar with such filters, I want to illustrate how easy it is to implement them in the DML and at the same time demonstrate the technique of using an integer-valued dimension as a counter.

The operation of FIR filters is given by a weighted sum defined in the equation:

$$y(t) = \sum_{i=1}^{N} w(i) * x(t-i+1)$$

Figure 11.2. Equation 2: FIR Filter with N Weights

If you think of x(t) as the input time series, y(t) as the output time series, N as the number of weights in the filter, and w as the set of weights that define the filtering action, you'll recognize the moving average example to be the case in this equation with all weights equal to one-third and N = 3.

To evaluate this expression, cycle over the set of integers represented by the subscript i.

To get such a set of numbers, define an integer-valued dimension:
```
DEFINE I DIMENSION INTEGER
```

Add one dimension member for each weight; if you have three:
```
MAINTAIN I ADD 3
```

Now, define a variable to store the weights:
```
DEFINE W VARIABLE DECIMAL <I>
```

The summation can be carried out with the TOTAL function:
```
DEFINE SMOOTH_REV FORMULA DECIMAL <CUSTOMER PRODUCT TIME>
EQ TOTAL(W*REVENUE(TIME TIME-I+1), CUSTOMER PRODUCT TIME)
```

To use the formula, values for the weights (i.e., w) must be set. To get the moving average example from the above section, you would use:

```
W = .3333
```

The astute reader will recognize that for some time dimension values, the formula will "fall off the edge," producing an error. This happens when either TIME-I+1 is less than one or greater than the number of dimension values, OBJ(DIMMAX 'TIME'). This can be fixed by testing within the formula and returning NA for such cases. The following modification to the formula fixes the problem. It uses the STATRANK function, which gives the position of the dimension member being worked with.

```
CONSIDER SMOOTH_REV
EQ IF (STATRANK(TIME TIME) - I GT 0) AND -
(STATRANK(PRODUCT -PRODUCT)-I LE OBJ(DIMMAX 'TIME'))-
THEN TOTAL(W*REVENUE(TIME -TIME-I+1), CUSTOMER PRODUCT -
TIME) ELSE NA
```

12 | Filtering, Relationships, and Combinations

In this chapter, we are going to extend the foundations of OLAP technology that we've laid. You have already seen a wealth of data modeling techniques. You have seen different ways to use dimensions, how to create relationships between dimensions, filtering operations, and different types of metrics. Armed with this knowledge, you are well prepared to take the ideas and techniques further still. In this chapter, you will see how to build advanced multistage filters, gain a deeper understanding of how objects can be connected together, and see how to work with combinations of dimension values.

The techniques you will see will be invaluable for creating measures based on counting. Such measures can be very relevant and highly actionable. You may want to identify and report on customers (businesses, clients, etc.) with special characteristics or that have exhibited designated behaviors, or find time frames where events of interest either happened or know the number of occurrences. The techniques you will learn will serve you well for that.

The powerful, practical techniques you will see here demonstrate OLAP's potential, showing applications that go beyond the basic operations of aggregating dimensional data.

Limit Types

Filtering is the process of identifying which dimension members satisfy a criterion (or set of criteria). In the DML, as you now well know, this identification process is the job of the LIMIT command.

Each LIMIT command contains a selection criterion. For example, the statement:
`LIMIT PRODUCT TO R.PRODUCT.FLAVOR 'TEATREE'`

...contains a criterion specifying that the product flavor must be teatree.

In addition to the selection criterion, you have a choice for determining how to handle the qualifying dimension members. So far, you've been setting status *to* those members. This is your way of saying, "these are the members I want to work with." Here are other choices:

- ADD the qualifying members to the members currently in status.
- REMOVE the members from the ones in status.
- KEEP only the members that meet the criterion and that are currently in status.

The choices TO, ADD, REMOVE, and KEEP are called *limit types*. They correspond to the basic set operations often illustrated with Venn diagrams.

"Add" corresponds to the union of two sets, namely, the set of values in status and the set of values meeting the filtering criterion. This is illustrated in Figure 12.1.

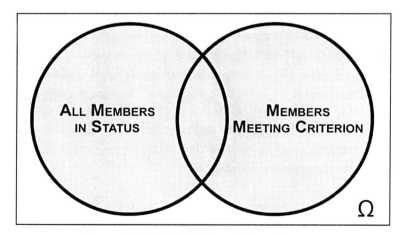

Figure 12.1. LIMIT ADD as a Venn Diagram

Remove and Keep are opposites. Remove says take the values meeting the criterion out of status; keep says retain only the values in status that also meet the criterion. In set theory nomenclature, "remove" corresponds to set subtraction, and "keep" corresponds to set intersection.

The syntax for such choices is exactly as you might expect:
```
LIMIT PRODUCT ADD R.PRODUCT.TEXTURE 'PASTE'
LIMIT PRODUCT REMOVE R.PRODUCT.TEXTURE 'PASTE'
LIMIT PRODUCT KEEP R.PRODUCT.TEXTURE 'PASTE'
```

The various limit types clearly add flexibility to the LIMIT command. They also make it possible to define meaningful multistep filters. You issue a series of LIMIT commands, normally with the first one using the "to" limit type, then add, remove, or keep from the initial set to get what you want.

For example, suppose you want all products in a squeeze bottle except those with a mintflavor:

```
LIMIT PRODUCT TO R.PRODUCT.PACKAGING 'SQUEEZEBOTTLE'
LIMIT PRODUCT REMOVE R.PRODUCT.FLAVOR 'MINT'
```

Of course, you can add as many conditions as needed.

By the way, there is an additional limit type: *complement*. Complement inverts status: the values that used to be in status are now out and the ones that were out are now in. It looks like this:

```
LIMIT PRODUCT COMPLEMENT
```

The Three Different Types of Relationships

In Part II: *Mastering Dimensions,* you have seen a number of different kinds of relationships between objects. You've seen the simple association of a text-valued label to a code, relationships between the members of two distinct dimensions, and relationships between the members of a single dimension.

I want to take a few moments to consider relationships in a more formal way; to show how all relationships can be classified into one of three different types. Once you learn to recognize a relationship's type, you will be able to quickly identify which DML construct will work for modeling it.

To assist in the discussion, think in terms of working with two collections of values: a *source* set and a *destination* set. Let's look at the possible scenarios for mapping values of the source set to values of the destination set. There are three cases: one-to-one, one-to-many, and many-to-many.

One-to-One Relationships

In one-to-one relationships, every value in the destination set is mapped to one value in the source set and vice versa. This is usually the case with labels: every dimension member gets a label, and a given label only applies to one member. In this situation there are two different ways of denoting the same thing. With codes and labels, you have one identification for the computer and one for the end user.

Another situation where one-to-one relationships are used is in working with "relative time" codes. For instance, you may have a code that signifies last month ('LASTMONTH'), and a mapping that tells which absolute time period ('JUN2010') the relative time code is associated with. Usually, variables are used to capture one-to-one relationships.

One-to-Many Relationships

In one-to-many relationships, the values in the destination set can map to more than one value in the source set, but each value in the source set gets mapped to only one value in the destination set. For example, you have many products with the same packaging type, but every product has only one packaging type. In these situations, the source set is "less aggregate," while the destination set is "more aggregate." In general, relations are used to capture relationships like this.

As you have seen, variables can also capture the information, but at the expense of lost analytical power. If you're certain you will never want that analytical power (faster, more-flexible filtering; the ability to aggregate on the related dimension), you may choose to use variables for their greater simplicity (simpler because it uses only one object, the variable; whereas, the relation needs two: the related dimension and the relation itself).

Many-to-Many Relationships

In many-to-many relationships, values in the destination set can map to more than one value in the source set and values in the source set can map to more than one value in the destination set. We haven't used any relationships of this type yet. Let's look at them now.

Consider, a collection of students and of classes. A student can take more than one class and each class can have more than one student. Or, consider musicians and albums. Each album can feature more than one musician and each musician can be on more than one album. As a final example, consider orders and items. An order can have more than one item and an item can be in more than one order. Capturing many-to-many relationships like this can be accomplished by working with combinations of dimension members.

There is a way to define a dimension whose members are combinations of the members of other dimensions. These dimensions are called *conjoint dimensions*. Conjoint dimensions give an easy way to capture many-to-many relationships. In the next chapter you will see another way to do it using DML valuesets.

Working with Combinations

Suppose you're developing an analytical application concerned with students, courses, professors, and semesters. The elements of this domain can be used as the basis for creating four dimensions. You might capture the information "student S1 took course C1 from professor P1 in semester M1" with an ordered set of the form <S1, C1, P1, M1>, where the first element specifies the student, the second the course, the third the professor, and the fourth the semester.

Assuming the base dimensions—student, course, professor, and semester—are available, a conjoint dimension that stores combinations of these dimension members can be defined like this:

```
DEFINE ENROLLMENT_INFO DIMENSION <STUDENT COURSE PROFESSOR -
SEMESTER>
```

The data type for the ENROLLMENT_INFO dimension is not text, it is a list of dimensions. And note the object type is dimension—there is no special object type for conjoint dimensions. Conjoint dimensions are dimensions like any other. They can be limited and variables can be dimensioned by them.

You will use one member of ENROLLMENT_INFO for a piece of student information. The information from the sample statement above would be captured like this:

```
MAINTAIN ENROLLMENT_INFO ADD <S1, C1, P1, M1>
```

Storing information as combinations of dimension values without accompanying quantitative data is analogous to a "factless fact table" in relational data warehousing.

Even without measuring any quantitative aspect of the process (for example, the final grade), you can use information like this to compute interesting analytics. For example, you could determine the number of students broken out by course and semester:

```
REPORT COUNT(ENROLLMENT_INFO EQ ENROLLMENT_INFO, COURSE -
SEMESTER)
```

If a student can only take a course one time, then there is an alternate approach to setting up the model you could consider. First define a conjoint dimension consisting of only student and course:

```
DEFINE ENROLLMENT_INFO DIMENSION <STUDENT COURSE>
```

Then define relations that map the professor and semester to each student-course combination:

```
DEFINE R.PROFESSOR.EI RELATION PROFESSOR <ENROLLMENT_INFO>
DEFINE R.SEMESTER.EI RELATION SEMESTER <ENROLLMENT_INFO>
MAINTAIN ENROLLMENT_INFO ADD <S1, C1>
R.PROFESSOR.EI = 'P1'
R.SEMESTER.EI = 'M1'
```

This would be considered a superior solution, because the total number of dimension values of ENROLLMENT_INFO used to accomplish the model would be far fewer. Although the DML will support very large numbers of dimension values, if it is possible to accomplish the same thing with fewer rather than more dimension members, the approach with fewer members would probably be superior since large numbers of dimension members puts the system under more stress.

With the alternative formulation, the same exact report statement:
```
REPORT COUNT(ENROLLMENT_INFO EQ ENROLLMENT_INFO, COURSE -
SEMESTER)
```

…would still work!

Some Practice Working with Counting and Combinations

Just as in the example above, when I speak of combinations, I'll be meaning combinations of dimension members from multiple dimensions. Let's look at another example, a simple order application. We will assume:

- a customer places an order that consists of items;
- the data will consist of the list of the items contained in each order; and
- each order will be identified by a distinct code and each item by a distinct code.

You would define an ITEM dimension and an ORDER dimension, then define a conjoint dimension consisting of these two base dimensions. The conjoint dimension will be used to store ITEM-ORDER combinations.

Now imagine a situation where you have three orders. ORDER1 consists of items ITEM1, ITEM2 and ITEM3; ORDER2 consists of items ITEM2 and ITEM3; and ORDER3 consists of items ITEM2 and ITEM4. This information could be captured in the following way:

Order1:
<ORDER1, ITEM1>
<ORDER1, ITEM2>
<ORDER1, ITEM3>

Order2:
<ORDER2, ITEM2>
<ORDER2, ITEM3>

Order3:
<ORDER3, ITEM2>
<ORDER3, ITEM4>

This set of combinations is an example of a many-to-many relationship. You can think of orders as comprising the source set and items comprising the destination set. In this data, you see ORDER1 has three items including ITEM2; ITEM2 is in three different orders, clearly a many-to-many relationship.

How to represent it using DML? First define the base dimensions:
```
DEFINE ORDER DIMENSION TEXT
MAINTAIN ORDER ADD 'ORDER1' 'ORDER2' 'ORDER3'
DEFINE ITEM DIMENSION TEXT
MAINTAIN ITEM ADD 'ITEM1' 'ITEM2' 'ITEM3' 'ITEM4'
```

Now define a conjoint dimension consisting of the two base dimensions:
```
DEFINE ORDER_ITEM_COMBO DIMENSION <ORDER ITEM>
```

Store the combinations into the conjoint dimension with the MAINTAIN command:
```
MAINTAIN ORDER_ITEM_COMBO ADD '<ORDER1, ITEM1>' -
'<ORDER1, ITEM2>' '<ORDER1, ITEM3>' '<ORDER2, ITEM2>' -
'<ORDER2, ITEM3>' '<ORDER3, ITEM2>' '<ORDER3, ITEM4>'
```

Let's report on the conjoint dimension ORDER_ITEM_COMBO to see all the values:
```
->REPORT ORDER_ITEM_COMBO

--ORDER_ITEM_COMBO---
   ORDER         ITEM
   ----------    ----------
   ORDER1        ITEM1
   ORDER1        ITEM2
   ORDER1        ITEM3
   ORDER2        ITEM2
   ORDER2        ITEM3
   ORDER3        ITEM2
   ORDER3        ITEM4
```

Counting and Selecting with Combinations

With this small collection of data on orders and items established, let's run through some examples of the common types of calculations.

EXAMPLE 1. FIND THE DISTINCT ITEMS IN A GIVEN ORDER

Specify the order you want to work with:
```
LIMIT ORDER TO 'ORDER1'
```

Find the order-item combinations that contain the specified order:
```
LIMIT ORDER_ITEM_COMBO TO ORDER
```

Now find all the items in those combinations:
```
LIMIT ITEM TO ORDER_ITEM_COMBO
```

When a conjoint dimension is defined, implicit relations between the conjoint values and their base dimension values are automatically created. These relations are what make the above statements work; the fact that they are indexed makes them very fast.

You can now report on ITEM to see all the items of ORDER1:
```
->REPORT ITEM

ITEM
--------------
ITEM1
ITEM2
ITEM3
```

Or just see how many there are:
```
->REPORT STATLEN(ITEM)

STATLEN(ITEM)
----------
        3
```

You can inspect the order-item combinations if you wish:
```
->REPORT ORDER_ITEM_COMBO

--ORDER_ITEM_COMBO---
   ORDER         ITEM
---------- ----------
ORDER1     ITEM1
ORDER1     ITEM2
ORDER1     ITEM3
```

By the way, you actually have the ability to control what kind of indexing is used in the implicit relations that are created when the conjoint dimension is defined. The choices are BTREE, NOHASH, and HASH. Here's the recommended choice:

```
DEFINE ORDER_ITEM_COMBO DIMENSION <ORDER ITEM> BTREE
```

Example 2. Find the Distinct Items Contained in Any (of More than One) Specified Orders

The only difference between this and Example 1 is that you limit it to the orders in which you're interested. In a real application, a multistep filter might be run to identify the orders of interest or they might be read in from a file. For the sake of the example, just set status with a limit statement to grab the last two orders:

```
LIMIT ORDER TO LAST 2
```

So now, find all items that were in either of the last two orders:
```
->LIMIT ORDER_ITEM_COMBO TO ORDER
->LIMIT ITEM TO ORDER_ITEM_COMBO
->REPORT ITEM

ITEM
--------------
ITEM2
ITEM3
ITEM4
```

Example 3. Find Which Orders Contain at Least One of the Specified Items

Just reverse the roles of item and order from above. Here you'll find the orders that contain ITEM1 or ITEM3:

```
->LIMIT ITEM TO 1 3
->LIMIT ORDER_ITEM_COMBO TO ITEM
->LIMIT ORDER TO ORDER_ITEM_COMBO
->REPORT ORDER

ORDER
--------------
ORDER1
ORDER2
```

Here are the order-item combinations found:
```
->RPR ORDER_ITEM_COMBO

--ORDER_ITEM_COMBO---
   ORDER         ITEM
 ----------   ----------
  ORDER1       ITEM1
  ORDER1       ITEM3
  ORDER2       ITEM3
```

EXAMPLE 4. A FORMULA THAT TELLS IF AN ITEM IS IN AN ORDER

Here's a formula that tells, for all combinations, if a given item was present in the given order:
```
->DEFINE ITEMS_IN_ORDER_BOOL FORMULA BOOLEAN <ORDER ITEM>
->EQ ISVALUE(ORDER_ITEM_COMBO <ORDER, ITEM>)
->RPR ITEMS_IN_ORDER_BOOL

                 ------ITEMS_IN_ORDER_BOOL-------
                 -------------ORDER--------------
  ITEM             ORDER1      ORDER2      ORDER3
 --------------  ----------  ----------  ----------
  ITEM1              yes         no          no
  ITEM2              yes         yes         yes
  ITEM3              yes         yes         no
  ITEM4              no          no          yes
```

This report tells, for instance, that ORDER1 contained ITEM 1, but ORDER 2 did not.

EXAMPLE 5. CALCULATE THE NUMBER OF DISTINCT ITEMS PER ORDER

Make a report that shows the number of distinct items as a function of the order:
```
->ALLSTAT
->DECIMALS = 0
->REPORT HEADING 'ITEMS PER ORDER' -
 COUNT(ORDER_ITEM_COMBO EQ ORDER_ITEM_COMBO, ORDER)

                   ITEMS PER
  ORDER             ORDER
 --------------   ----------
  ORDER1               3
  ORDER2               2
  ORDER3               2
```

EXAMPLE 6. TREND REPORT ON THE NUMBER OF DISTINCT ITEMS ORDERED

Now suppose you want the number of distinct items, ordered by anybody, per month. To get this, you need a relation that tells when each order occurred.

Create a time dimension:
```
DEFINE TIME DIMENSION TEXT
```

Populate it with values:
```
MAINTAIN TIME ADD 'JAN2009' 'FEB2009'
```

Create a relation to map orders to the times they were placed:
```
DEFINE ORDER_DATE RELATION TIME <ORDER>
```

Populate the relation:
```
ORDER_DATE(ORDER 1) = 'JAN2009'
ORDER_DATE(ORDER 2) = 'FEB2009'
ORDER_DATE(ORDER 3) = 'FEB2009'
```

Now use the same expression as in Example 5, but replace ORDER with TIME:
```
->REPORT HEADING 'TOTAL DISTINCT ITEMS PER MONTH' -
COUNT(ORDER_ITEM_COMBO EQ ORDER_ITEM_COMBO, TIME)
```

```
                 TOTAL
                 DISTINCT
                 ITEMS PER
TIME             MONTH
--------------   ----------
JAN2009                  3
FEB2009                  4
```

So here you defined a time attribute on the order, and you produced a report of the number of distinct items ordered per time period. You could have defined more than one attribute and broken out the report on all of them, or you could have defined some attributes for orders and other attributes for items.

EXAMPLE 7. TREND REPORT ON THE AVERAGE NUMBER OF ITEMS PER ORDER

The following uses the AVERAGE function to display the average number of items per order over time:

```
->DECIMALS = 2
->REPORT HEADING -
'AVERAGE NUMBER OF ITEMS PER ORDER OVER TIME' -
AVERAGE(COUNT(ORDER_ITEM_COMBO EQ ORDER_ITEM_COMBO, ORDER)-
TIME)
                        AVERAGE
                       NUMBER OF
                       ITEMS PER
                       ORDER OVER
TIME                     TIME
---------------        ----------
JAN2009                     3.00
FEB2009                     2.00
```

Switching Between Multidimensional and Relational Data Presentations

In the Chapter 7 discussion on dimension profilers, I showed two different types of reports. One was "dimensional style" where rows, columns, and blocks of data are associated with dimensions. Here's an example:

```
FLAVOR              PASTE        GEL       LIQUIDGEL
---------------   ----------  ----------  ----------
MINT                  2           1            1
VANILLA               1           0            1
TEATREE               1           0            0
```

The other type was "relational style" with data that looks like this:

```
PACKAGING      TEXTURE     FLAVOR      COUNT
------------   ---------   ---------   -------
LAYDOWNTUBE    PASTE       MINT          2
LAYDOWNTUBE    PASTE       VANILLA       0
LAYDOWNTUBE    PASTE       TEATREE       1
LAYDOWNTUBE    GEL         MINT          1
```

In this section, I'm going to show you how you can go from one type of display to the other. I also want to illustrate how the transformation that is used to switch between the two displays has analysis applications.

Suppose you have a basic RFM analysis framework consisting of the CUSTOMER dimension, the three related dimensions based on customer behavior, and the relations mapping each customer to each of these attributes. For the sake of making things concrete, assume there are three values of recency, three values of frequency, and two values of monetary. The system is described by the following statements:

```
DEFINE RECENCY DIMENSION TEXT
MAINTAIN RECENCY ADD 'REC01' 'REC02' 'REC03'
DEFINE R.RECENCY.CUST RELATION RECENCY <CUSTOMER>
DEFINE FREQUENCY DIMENSION TEXT
MAINTAIN FREQUENCY ADD 'FRQ01' 'FRQ02' 'FRQ03'
DEFINE R.FREQUENCY.CUST RELATION FREQUENCY <CUSTOMER>
DEFINE MONETARY DIMENSION TEXT
MAINTAIN MONETARY ADD 'MON01' 'MON02'
DEFINE R.MONETARY.CUST RELATION MONETARY <CUSTOMER>
```

The numbers that will be shown below will assume you have data on a set of customers and the relations have been populated (i.e., for each customer dimension member, a value of recency, frequency, and monetary have been assigned). With the populated relations you can report on the number of customers that fall into each cell:

```
REPORT COUNT(CUSTOMER EQ CUSTOMER, RECENCY -
FREQUENCY MONETARY)
```

In Chapter 11: *Calculating Data On-the-Fly* you learned how to save data from a calculation expression into a variable. Let's do that here, but we'll employ a programming "trick" that will make it possible to switch back and forth between the multidimensional and relational display formats.

Rather than define the variable that will hold the counts like this:
```
DEFINE RFM_CUST_COUNT VARIABLE INTEGER <RECENCY FREQUENCY -
MONETARY>
```

...first create a composite of the three dimensions:
```
DEFINE RFM_CELLS COMPOSITE <RECENCY FREQUENCY MONETARY>
```

...and then create the variable like this:
```
DEFINE RFM_CUST_COUNT VARIABLE DECIMAL <RFM_CELLS<RECENCY - FREQUENCY MONETARY>>
```

Now copy calculated values into the variable:
```
ALLSTAT
RFM_CUST_COUNT = COUNT(CUSTOMER EQ CUSTOMER, RECENCY - FREQUENCY MONETARY)
```

Look at the data in dimensional format (shown with hypothetical data):
```
->REPORT RFM_CUST_COUNT
MONETARY: MON01
                ---------RFM_CUST_COUNT---------
                ------------RECENCY-------------
FREQUENCY         REC01         REC02         REC03
--------------  ----------    ----------    ----------
FRQ01                  270           347           737
FRQ02                  524           681           648
FRQ03                  599           182           688

MONETARY: MON02
                ---------RFM_CUST_COUNT---------
                ------------RECENCY-------------
FREQUENCY         REC01         REC02         REC03
--------------  ----------    ----------    ----------
FRQ01                  521           997           246
FRQ02                  598           958           410
FRQ03                1,791           745         5,293
```

From this display you can easily see how the count varies as a function of the three coordinate dimension values. But now suppose you want a sorted list of the data cells so you can see which cells have the most customers down to the least number of customers. Then you'd need to work with the information as rows of data. Here's how you can do that.

Use the CHGDFN command to transform RFM_CELLS from a composite into a (conjoint) dimension:

```
CHGDFN RFM_CELLS DIMENSION
```

Now you can work with RFM_CELLS as with any dimension, including sorting:
```
SORT RFM_CELLS D RFM_CUST_COUNT
```

Display RFM_CUST_COUNT to see the sorted data:
```
->REPORT RFM_CUST_COUNT

          ----------RFM_CELLS------------
                                          RFM_CUST_C
MONETARY    FREQUENCY     RECENCY         OUNT
----------  ----------    ----------      ----------
MON02       FRQ03         REC03              5,293
MON02       FRQ03         REC01              1,791
MON02       FRQ01         REC02                997
MON02       FRQ02         REC02                958
MON02       FRQ03         REC02                745
MON01       FRQ01         REC03                737
MON01       FRQ03         REC03                688
MON01       FRQ02         REC02                681
MON01       FRQ02         REC03                648
MON01       FRQ03         REC01                599
MON02       FRQ02         REC01                598
MON01       FRQ02         REC01                524
MON02       FRQ01         REC01                521
MON02       FRQ02         REC03                410
MON01       FRQ01         REC02                347
MON01       FRQ01         REC01                270
MON02       FRQ01         REC03                246
MON01       FRQ03         REC02                182
```

To get back to the multidimensional display, you could change RFM_CELLS back into a composite (CHGDFN RFM_CELLS COMPOSITE); but suppose you want to be able to look at the data in either format at any given time without doing that.

This can be accomplished by using a formula to restructure the presentation of RFM_CUST_COUNT:

```
DEFINE F.RFM_CUST_COUNT INTEGER <RECENCY FREQUENCY MONETARY>
EQ RFM_CUST_COUNT
```

Report on this formula for the dimensional report:
```
->REPORT  F.RFM_CUST_COUNT

MONETARY: MON01
                --------F.RFM_CUST_COUNT--------
                ------------RECENCY------------
FREQUENCY         REC01         REC02         REC03
--------------  ----------    ----------    ----------
FRQ01                270           347           737
FRQ02                524           681           648
FRQ03                599           182           688

MONETARY: MON02
                --------F.RFM_CUST_COUNT--------
                ------------RECENCY------------
FREQUENCY         REC01         REC02         REC03
--------------  ----------    ----------    ----------
FRQ01                521           997           246
FRQ02                598           958           410
FRQ03              1,791           745         5,293
```

Report on F.RFM_CUST_COUNT to get the dimensional report, report on RFM_CUST_COUNT to get the relational-style report. Powerful!

13 | Working with Sets

The DML has a powerful facility for working with sets of dimension members. Called *valuesets,* they give a way of storing collections of dimension members into a named object. Valuesets correspond to the common mathematical concept of a set, with the difference that the mathematical concept defines a set by its contents without regard to order, whereas preserving order is an integral part of valuesets. *Thus, valuesets can be used not only for remembering members, but also for remembering orderings.*

In this chapter, you'll learn about the construction and application of valuesets.

Similarities Between Valuesets and Variables

It's possible to draw some comparisons between valuesets and variables. Think back to the HOTEL variable of Chapter 10: *Storing Data in Analytic Workspaces* that was used to illustrate how a variable was like a data hotel. Each combination of the variable's dimension members gives the address of a data cell that stores a single value, either a numeric value or a text value.

Similarly, with valuesets, each combination of the valueset's dimension members specifies a location for storing information, but that information is not just a single numerical or text value; it's an ordered list of dimension members. Whereas a variable can store the number of customers staying in the room, a valueset can store the members that represent them.

And just as you can define a scalar variable that holds only one data value, you can create a scalar valueset that stores only one set of dimension members. But whereas scalar variables are not so common, scalar valuesets are very common.

As you work with valuesets, please note that there are two places where dimensions enter. One is in the dimensionality of the valueset, and the other is with its data type. In variables, dimensions enter only in the dimensionality; the data type is either some kind of numerical value or a textual one, but not a dimension.

How Sets are Used in Business Intelligence Applications

There are many situations where the ability to save a set of dimension members offers significant value:

- The results of a filter are needed multiple times but status for the dimension gets changed between applications of those results and you don't want to have to rerun the filter to get them back.

- The status for a dimension must be set manually to a specific set of members. You want the ability to retrieve them multiple times without repeating the manual process.

- As a quality control mechanism you need to make sure the same exact members are referenced in multiple situations.

- Significant work is performed to put a set of dimension members into a particular order, and you wish to record that ordering.

- The members comprising some aggregate value are an arbitrary collection and you need a way of specifying that collection.

- The application data you are interested in consists of dimension members.

Saving the Results of a Filter into a Named Set

Suppose you have business rules that define the target audience for a given product. Your objective is to apply these rules to the data to identify the qualifying members. Then you want to store them away for convenient, fast retrieval.

Let's illustrate this process with an example.

Run the filter to identify the target group:
```
LIMIT CUSTOMER TO GENDER 'MALE'
LIMIT CUSTOMER REMOVE CHILDREN ZIP_CODE '33625'
LIMIT CUSTOMER KEEP MONETARY 'TOP20PCT'
SORT CUSTOMER A CUSTOMER_LONG_DESCRIPTION
```

Define a valueset to store customer dimension members:
```
DEFINE TARGET_GROUP VALUESET CUSTOMER
```

Finally, save the results into the valueset:
```
LIMIT TARGET_GROUP TO CUSTOMER
```

The valueset, TARGET_GROUP, stores the dimension values and it preserves the order.

Now suppose in the process of your work the status of CUSTOMER is altered with a LIMIT command, for example:

```
LIMIT CUSTOMER TO ALL
```

How do you get your target customers back? To reinstate the status of CUSTOMER to the filter results, simply reverse the role of the valueset and the dimension in the limit statement as follows:

```
LIMIT CUSTOMER TO TARGET_GROUP
```

The status of CUSTOMER is now set to the TARGET_GROUP. This limit statement is very fast, compared to re-executing the original set of commands making up the filter.

You can think of status as being an unnamed valueset that's automatically created by the system. Now you know how to save a status setting into a named set using valuesets.

A scalar valueset like TARGET_GROUP is sometimes called a *saved selection.*

Using a One-Dimensional Valueset to Store a Series of Filtering Results

Suppose you have a collection of products that you intend to promote. Assume you have, for each such product, a set of criteria that defines the target audience.

The criteria will translate into filters; applying the filters will yield sets of customers (the target audience). To prepare for the campaign, you'll identify the target audience for each product and store them for convenient and fast retrieval. How do you do this with valuesets?

Since the target audience varies as a function of product, you'll define a valueset dimensioned by product. Since you're storing customers, it has a customer data type.

```
DEFINE TARGET_AUD_PROD VALUESET CUSTOMER <PRODUCT>
```

So now you can run the filters and save the results. Run the filter for product TP001:
```
LIMIT CUSTOMER TO R.GENDER.CUST 'MALE'
LIMIT CUSTOMER REMOVE R.AGE.CUST '19TO25'
```

Save the customers into the valueset:
```
LIMIT TARGET_AUD_PROD(PRODUCT 'TP001') TO CUSTOMER
```

Run the filter for the next product, TP002:
```
LIMIT CUSTOMER TO R.MONETARY.CUST 'MON02'
LIMIT CUSTOMER REMOVE R.MARITAL.CUST 'SINGLE'
```

Save the customers into the valueset:
```
LIMIT TARGET_AUD_PROD(PRODUCT 'TP002') TO CUSTOMER
```

And so on, for all products for which a target audience has been defined. These are simple filters for illustration purposes only. In practice, they could be of any complexity and would probably be run from a DML program.

Once TARGET_AUD_PROD has been populated, the target audience for any product can be retrieved quickly and efficiently. Valuesets can be reported on directly, just like variables:

```
REPORT TARGET_AUD_PROD
```

Or maybe you only want to see how many members the valueset has:
```
REPORT STATLEN(TARGET_AUD_PROD)
```

Limiting the Valueset Directly

It's possible to limit the valueset directly without ever touching the status of the dimension whose members are being saved. You've been applying limit statements to a dimension, then saving the dimension members in a valueset. Alternatively, you could have applied all limit commands to the valueset itself. Observe:

```
LIMIT TARGET_AUD_PROD(PRODUCT 'TP001') TO R.GENDER.CUST -
'MALE'
LIMIT TARGET_AUD_PROD(PRODUCT 'TP001') REMOVE R.AGE.CUST -
'19TO25'
```

This populates the TARGET_AUD_PROD without disturbing the status of Customer.

Storing Information in Multidimensional Valuesets

In the last chapter, you worked with variables to save data from the RFM analysis. For example, we saw a variable that could store customer counts:

```
DEFINE CUST_COUNT VARIABLE INTEGER <RECENCY FREQUENCY -
MONETARY>
```

Now suppose you wanted to store, not the number of customers, but the customers themselves. This could be done with a three-dimensional valueset such as this:

```
DEFINE RFM_CUSTOMERS VALUESET CUSTOMER <RECENCY FREQUENCY -
MONETARY>
```

This three-dimensional valueset would be populated by a DML program. Once that has been accomplished, the customers corresponding to a particular cell can be quickly put into status, for example:

```
LIMIT CUSTOMER TO RFM_CUSTOMERS(RECENCY 'REC03' FREQUENCY -
'FRQ01' MONETARY 'MON01')
```

Now let's look at another application of multidimensional valuesets. Suppose you have a revenue variable in which you've stored revenue data:

```
DEFINE REVENUE VARIABLE DECIMAL <CUSTOMER PRODUCT TIME>
```

You can create a valueset that stores for each product and time period of interest the top customers.

Create a valueset to store customers as a function of product and time:
```
DEFINE HI_VAL_CUST VALUESET CUSTOMER <PRODUCT TIME>
```

Set the scenario you are interested in:
```
LIMIT PRODUCT TO 'TP001'
LIMIT TIME TO 'JAN09'
```

Run the filter to find the top-10 customers for the selected scenario:
```
LIMIT CUSTOMER TO CUSTOMER_LEVELREL 'CUSTOMER'
LIMIT CUSTOMER KEEP TOP 10 BASEDON REVENUE
```

Store the results in the valueset:
```
LIMIT HI_VAL_CUST TO CUSTOMER
```

You'd probably want to employ a DML program to cycle through all the product and time combinations of interest.

Thus, while variables are multidimensional arrays of numbers, valuesets are multidimensional arrays of sets.

Many-to-Many Relationships with Valuesets: A Healthcare Example

In Chapter 12: *Filtering, Relationships, and Combinations,* you saw the use of conjoint dimensions to encode many-to-many relationships. Valuesets can also be used to encode such relationships.

Consider a healthcare application consisting of patients and diagnoses. A patient can have more than one diagnosis and a diagnosis can belong to more than one patient, so this is a many-to-many relationship.

```
DEFINE PATIENT DIMENSION TEXT
DEFINE DIAGNOSIS DIMENSION TEXT
```

Let's create some patients (identified by social security numbers) and some diagnoses (identified by diagnostic codes):

```
MAINTAIN PATIENT ADD 'SS4321' 'SS7644' 'SS7752'
MAINTAIN DIAGNOSIS ADD '718.81' '716.90' '847.1'
```

Now, create a valueset that contains the diagnoses that apply to each patient:
```
DEFINE PATIENT_DIAGNOSIS VALUESET DIAGNOSIS <PATIENT>
```

Populate each patient with their diagnoses.

Patient 1 has nothing wrong:
```
LIMIT PATIENT_DIAGNOSIS(PATIENT 1) TO NA
```

Patient 2 has one diagnosis:
```
LIMIT PATIENT_DIAGNOSIS(PATIENT 2) TO '718.81'
```

Patient 3 has two diagnoses:
```
LIMIT PATIENT_DIAGNOSIS(PATIENT 3) TO '718.81' '847.1'
```

Although you can report directly on valuesets, let's create a formula for doing it:
```
DEFINE PATIENT_DIAGNOSES FORMULA TEXT <PATIENT>
EQ VALUES(PATIENT_DIAGNOSIS)
```

Or one to get the number of diagnoses per patient:
```
DEFINE PATIENT_DIAGNOSES FORMULA INTEGER <PATIENT>
EQ STATLEN(PATIENT_DIAGNOSIS)
```

Another Way to Save a Status List: The Push-Down Stack

The DML features a push-down stack that provides a convenient way to store, then retrieve, the status list for a dimension. (It also works to do the same for scalar variables and option values.) A push-down stack is a facility consisting of a list (or stack) in which the next item to be removed is the item most recently stored. Items are added to the list through a "push" operation and removed by a "pop" operation.

To use this feature, push the dimension whose status you wish to preserve onto the stack, run the limit statements you want, then pop the value off the stack to return status to its original value. You can also solve multiple status settings by doing multiple pushes.

This sequence is illustrated in the example below:
```
PUSH CUSTOMER
LIMIT CUSTOMER TO R.GENDER.CUST 'MALE'
LIMIT CUSTOMER REMOVE R.AGE.CUST '19TO25'
LIMIT TARGET_AUD_PROD(PRODUCT 'TP001') TO CUSTOMER
POP CUSTOMER
```

Now the status of customer is set back to where it was before the three limit statements were run.

14 | Aggregation

Usually, a single data value provides little useful information about the overall patterns of activity for a business process— *it is the behavior of groups of values that is telling, interesting, and relevant.* We look at this group behavior through *aggregation*. Aggregation is the process of transforming a group of data values into a single value that summarizes or represents the group. Because of the great value of measuring and seeing group behavior, aggregation is one of the most important computing processes in business intelligence applications.

The most common form of aggregation is summing data values (in which case it is the process of computing totals and subtotals). There are a number of other meaningful statistics that could be used to represent a group of data values; for instance, the average, median, or maximum value, or even something specific to the application, such as a count of dimension members satisfying some criteria. Aggregation of multidimensional data is the calculation that typically comprises the bulk of the build process.

If you refer to the data presentations in Chapter 3 in *The 30,000-Foot View* section, you can see that virtually all the numbers shown in the displays are aggregate values. In that illustration, the source data was at leaf level (i.e., products, stores, payment methods, and months). If even one of the four dimension members associated with each data value is not a leaf-level value (e.g., a product category, a store type, a year, and so on), then the data value is an aggregate. (By the way, even the granular data loaded into a business intelligence system is actually already summarized to some extent, for example, over time.)

These organized summarizations computed in the aggregation process are one of the key benefits delivered by a business intelligence system. Given the importance of aggregation, it shouldn't be surprising that there are specific DML commands dedicated to supporting it. In fact, the language has a feature-rich set of commands and functions for performing aggregations. If you were to go through all the documentation associated with this process, you'd be reading hundreds of pages.

I'm not going to cover all of the nuances of aggregations, but I do want to take a look at the core principles—principles not explicitly articulated in the documentation, but that will complement the many examples found there. Along with these core principles, I will show you enough examples so that you are familiar with the application of the various types of aggregation commands.

In this chapter, I will also discuss *accumulations*. Accumulation is a process that shares some of the characteristics of aggregation, but is actually distinct from it in that the data is not numerical and the result is not a single summarizing value.

Core Principles of Aggregation

If you examine any aggregation process, you will see three core principles at play: group specification, calculation operation, and calculation timing.

- GROUP SPECIFICATION—Data values are referenced by their associated dimension values. Specifying a group of data values, then, becomes a matter of specifying groups of dimension values. In the DML, groups of dimension members can be specified by hierarchies, custom groupings, status lists, and attributes.

- CALCULATION OPERATION—The calculation operation used to obtain the single value that summarizes or represents the group. I've mentioned totals as the most common choice.

- CALCULATION TIMING—Does the calculation occur up front in a build process or when a user requests an aggregate data value, or is it some combination of these two? Computing aggregates takes time so you may want to precalculate heavily used aggregates and allow the others to be calculated on-the-fly.

Group Specification Methods

Let's look a little closer at the ways sets of dimension members can be specified in the DML. The many options of the LIMIT command lead to a rich set of choices for specifying sets of dimension members. In a nutshell, here's how they work:

- HIERARCHY—If a collection of dimension members shares the same parent, you can consider them to constitute a group. Since hierarchies provide such an intuitive way to specify groups of dimension members, it is not surprising that it is the most common aggregation grouping method. Hierarchies provide a very structured organization of the aggregate values.

- CUSTOM GROUPING—Sets (using valuesets) define groups of dimension members in a direct manner allowing you to declare any collection of dimension members to constitute a group. Sets are the most flexible way to specify groups of dimension members; indeed, they are more flexible than hierarchies because the members in different groups defined by a hierarchy are mutually exclusive and that's not necessarily so with valuesets. Use this to create any custom grouping.

- STATUS LIST—A status list is essentially a set without a name and handle.

- ATTRIBUTE—All dimension members that share the same attribute value can be considered to be members of the same group.

From these choices you can undoubtedly represent groups any way you might want. For example, you can get all the customers in this zip code (hierarchy), my favorite products and your favorite products (custom grouping or status list), the top-10 customers based on sales revenue for a given week (custom grouping or status list), or all the products with this kind of packaging (attribute).

Some of the examples in this section will use simple examples built around one-dimensional variables to illustrate the points; some multidimensional aggregations will also be shown. Consult the documentation for full details.

The first examples are constructed around the customer dimension of Chapter 8: *Organizing Dimension Members into Hierarchies*. Recall that we created two hierarchies for the customer dimension: one contained geographical information with values of zip code and city; the other was based on the store where the customer enrolled in the loyalty program and contained stores and type of store (i.e., convenience vs. supermarket).

Hierarchies

AGGREGATING OVER ALL HIERARCHIES

You can use a one-dimensional variable that stores revenue as a function of customer to illustrate things.

```
DEFINE CUST_REV VARIABLE DECIMAL <CUSTOMER>
```

Assume that you've loaded in data for the leaf level (i.e., for all the customers). You could simulate this condition by populating the variable with random data values for the leaf-level dimension members.

```
LIMIT CUSTOMER TO CUSTOMER_LEVELREL 'CUST_LEV'
CUST_REV = RANDOM(0,100)
```

Having done this, you can inspect the data:
```
->LIMIT CUSTOMER TO ALL
->REPORT CUST_REV
```

CUSTOMER	CUST_REV
ALLCUST	NA
FLTPA	NA
FLCWD	NA
33625	NA
33624	NA
33634	NA
33688	NA
33618	NA
CU001	67.17
CU003	54.00
CU015	97.93
CU005	68.65
CU013	25.76
CU014	74.68
CU004	23.31
CU012	56.45
CU002	74.97

```
CU006                   74.99
CU009                   44.14
CU016                   53.59
CU010                    3.76
CU007                    1.24
CU008                   29.33
CU011                   29.36
DIVCNV                     NA
DIVSUP                     NA
CNV002                     NA
SUP002                     NA
SUP003                     NA
CNV003                     NA
SUP001                     NA
CNV001                     NA
```

Zip codes implicitly define groups of customers: all customers having the same zip code are a group. You could calculate the total revenue for a single zip code using the commands you already know. Let's illustrate with zip code 33625. Here you'll use the TOTAL function to aggregate the data corresponding to all the dimension members in status, then copy the result into data associated with "customer" 33625.

Get the customers who report to zip code 33625:
```
LIMIT CUSTOMER TO CHILDREN '33625'
```

Total those figures up and store the result into the cell represented by the zip code:
```
CUST_REV(CUSTOMER '33625') = TOTAL(CUST_REV)
```

To precalculate all of the geography aggregates, you could repeat this procedure for all zip codes. Once you've done it for all zip codes, you could perform a similar process for cities and then finally for the "ALL" value. While this would work, in practice it would not be done this way. *There's a DML command that performs these operations for every aggregate dimension member in a single step: the AGGREGATE command.* So you'll be doing the aggregation for this hierarchy using the AGGREGATE command; first, though, you need a little background.

The AGGREGATE command by default will calculate the aggregate values for all hierarchies in status; however, it accommodates a wide variety of situations. For instance, you can tell it to only compute certain aggregate values or to perform skip-level aggregations (in which the values at every other level are computed). The aggregation process has an operator parameter that specifies what kind of calculation is performed by the AGGREGATE command. You can choose from a variety of calculation operators; the default calculation operator is SUM (which is what we will use in the examples below).

To accommodate the broad range of choices, the AGGREGATE command uses a device called an *aggmap*. An aggmap is a distinct object type in the DML and it serves as a container for the parameters that specify the aggregation choices. To use the AGGREGATE command, you must first set up an aggmap.

So now perform the aggregation from the example above. First, set up an aggmap to specify that you're aggregating over CUSTOMER_PARENTREL, which is the relation that gives the parent-child relationships for the hierarchy. Then perform the aggregation for the example above. The process looks like this:

Define the aggmap:
```
DEFINE CUSTOMER.AGG AGGMAP <CUSTOMER>
```

Set its "aggmap" property with the AGGMAP command:
```
AGGMAP 'RELATION CUSTOMER_PARENTREL'
```

You can describe an aggmap to inspect its AGGMAP property:
```
->DESCRIBE CUSTOMER.AGG

DEFINE CUSTOMER.AGG AGGMAP
AGGMAP
RELATION CUSTOMER_PARENTREL
END
```

Having defined the aggmap object, you're ready to run the AGGREGATE command.

Make sure you first set the status of all relevant dimensions so the members you want included are included:

```
LIMIT CUSTOMER TO ALL
LIMIT CUSTOMER_HIERLIST TO ALL
```

Now perform the aggregation with the AGGREGATE command:
```
AGGREGATE CUST_REV USING CUSTOMER.AGG
```

Reporting on the variable now gives:

```
->REPORT CUST_REV

CUSTOMER            CUST_REV
--------------    ----------
ALLCUST               779.32
FLTPA                 417.53
FLCWD                 361.80
33625                 155.99
33624                 217.75
33634                 199.78
33688                  47.89
33618                 157.92
CU001                  67.17
CU003                  54.00
CU015                  97.93
CU005                  68.65
CU013                  25.76
CU014                  74.68
CU004                  23.31
CU012                  56.45
CU002                  74.97
CU006                  74.99
CU009                  44.14
CU016                  53.59
CU010                   3.76
CU007                   1.24
CU008                  29.33
CU011                  29.36
DIVCNV                364.33
DIVSUP                414.99
CNV002                145.96
SUP002                 82.21
SUP003                226.20
CNV003                 76.22
SUP001                106.58
CNV001                142.15
```

A few observations are in order:

- Aggregate values and leaf-level values are stored in the same object. The CUST_REV variable contains data at both leaf and aggregate levels. If you're familiar with relational data warehousing practices, you know that aggregate data are normally stored in separate summary tables. However, in the DML aggregate values are normally together with the leaf-level values in the same object. Of course, if you're using the DML and storing aggregates in the AW (as you're doing here), there would be no need to also have aggregates stored in the data mart/warehouse. (For that matter, once you've loaded the data into the AW, the source tables aren't used when data is being accessed from the AW.)

- The AGGREGATE command performs implicit looping. In Chapter 6: *Describing Dimension Members with Labels* you looked at the process of implicit looping with the assignment statement. The AGGREGATE command also does implicit looping: it cycles over all aggregate dimension members, performs the summary calculation, and makes the value assignments to those aggregate members.

  If something in the DML can be done as an implicit calculation, it should be, as this will yield results in the fastest time. And not only are the computations performed more quickly, as you can see it's much more convenient. The manual method performed at the beginning of this section was good to illustrate the calculations, but not an efficacious way to perform them.

- An aggmap is associated with dimensions, not variables. The CUSTOMER.AGG aggmap, for instance, could be used with any variable dimensioned by customer, not just the CUST_REV variable used here to illustrate it.

Let's demonstrate how an aggmap is associated with dimensions and not variables by using the aggmap to guide aggregation over a different variable. Suppose you wanted to calculate the number of customers reporting to each geographical value: you would begin by assigning a value of 1 to each customer node. This just records the obvious fact that one dimension member at the customer level represents one customer. Then you can aggregate using the same aggmap as before.

Create the variable that will hold the results:
```
DEFINE CUST_COUNT VARIABLE DECIMAL <CUSTOMER>
```

Limit customer to the leaf-level values:
```
LIMIT CUSTOMER TO CUSTOMER_LEVELREL 'CUST_LEV'
```

Assign 1 to the leaf-level data:
```
CUST_COUNT = 1
```

Compute the aggregate values:
```
AGGREGATE CUST_COUNT USING CUSTOMER.AGG
```

The results for the non-customer levels are now available:
```
->LIMIT CUSTOMER TO CUSTOMER_LEVELREL NE 'CUST_LEV'
->REPORT CUST_COUNT

CUSTOMER              CUST_COUNT
--------------        ----------
ALLCUST                       16
FLTPA                          7
FLCWD                          9
33625                          4
33624                          4
33634                          3
33688                          2
33618                          3
DIVCNV                         7
DIVSUP                         9
CNV002                         3
SUP002                         2
SUP003                         3
CNV003                         2
SUP001                         4
CNV001                         2
CUSTOM_AGG01                   2
```

Now blank out all the aggregate values of CUST_REV to prepare for the next section. This is done like so:

```
LIMIT CUSTOMER TO ALL
CUST_REV = NA
```

AGGREGATING OVER SELECTED HIERARCHIES

By default, the AGGREGATE command calculates the aggregate values for all hierarchies in status; however, it's possible to specify that you only want to aggregate over certain hierarchies within the aggmap itself.

The customer dimension has two hierarchies, but let's only aggregate over the GEOGRAPHY hierarchy.

Create a valueset to contain values of the dimension used to specify the hierarchies:
```
DEFINE CUST_AGG_HIERS VALUESET CUSTOMER_HIERLIST
```

Limit that valueset to the hierarchies over which you wish to aggregate:
```
LIMIT CUST_AGG_HIERS TO 'GEO_HIER'
```

Set the value of the aggmap:
```
CNS CUSTOMER.AGG
AGGMAP 'RELATION CUSTOMER_PARENTREL(CUST_AGG_HIERS)'
```

With such an aggmap, the AGGREGATE command you executed earlier:
```
LIMIT CUSTOMER TO ALL
LIMIT CUSTOMER_HIERLIST TO ALL
AGGREGATE CUST_REV USING CUSTOMER.AGG
```

...will only compute the aggregates for the GEOGRAPHY hierarchy.

So you can see:
```
->LIMIT CUSTOMER TO CUSTOMER_LEVELREL NE 'CUST_LEV'
->REPORT CUST_REV
CUSTOMER            CUST_REV
--------------      ----------
ALLCUST               779.32
FLTPA                 417.53
FLCWD                 361.80
33625                 155.99
33624                 217.75
33634                 199.78
33688                  47.89
33618                 157.92
DIVCNV                    NA
DIVSUP                    NA
CNV002                    NA
SUP002                    NA
SUP003                    NA
CNV003                    NA
SUP001                    NA
CNV001                    NA
```

AGGREGATING SELECTED VALUES ONLY

Computing aggregates takes both time and disk space. Suppose you want to pick and choose which aggregates are calculated. You'll focus on the aggregates that are heavily used and let the others be done on-the-fly. Here's how.

Create a valueset to hold the aggregates that you wish to calculate:
```
DEFINE SPCL_CUST_AGGS VALUESET CUSTOMER
```

Populate the valueset with the aggregates you want:
```
LIMIT SPCL_CUST_AGGS TO '33625'
```

Define the aggmap:
```
CNS CUSTOMER.AGG
AGGMAP 'RELATION CUSTOMER_PARENTREL PRECOMPUTE -
(SPCL_CUST_AGGS)'
```

You know the drill:
```
->AGGREGATE CUST_REV USING CUSTOMER.AGG
->LIMIT CUSTOMER TO CUSTOMER_LEVELREL NE 'CUST_LEV'
->REPORT CUST_REV

CUSTOMER           CUST_REV
--------------     ----------
ALLCUST                  NA
FLTPA                    NA
FLCWD                    NA
33625                155.99
33624                    NA
33634                    NA
33688                    NA
33618                    NA
DIVCNV                   NA
DIVSUP                   NA
CNV002                   NA
SUP002                   NA
SUP003                   NA
CNV003                   NA
SUP001                   NA
CNV001                   NA
```

SPECIFYING A CALCULATION OPERATOR

Now we are going to change the summary calculation to the group maximum using MAX rather than the default value SUM. (Remember that the aggregation process has an operator parameter associated with it that specifies what kind of operation is performed by the AGGREGATE command. The default value is SUM and that is what you've been getting in the above examples.)

Using the MAX operator, the group (for example, all customers living in the 33625 zip code) will be represented by the value of the group member that has the greatest data value. Perhaps you're doing this because you need to know the greatest revenue of any customer per zip code or city.

Now set its value explicitly to override that default:
```
CNS CUSTOMER.AGG
AGGMAP 'RELATION CUSTOMER_PARENTREL OPERATOR MAX'
```

Reissue the command:
```
AGGREGATE CUST_REV USING CUSTOMER.AGG
```

Custom Groupings

Sometimes you'll want to work with arbitrary groups whose group of dimension members are not definable by position within a hierarchy or through an attribute. For example, you might want to specify a group from a list of customers who filled out a questionnaire in a store. In this section, you'll see how to use valuesets to work with unconstrained groupings like this.

Just as hierarchies have one dimension member to represent each aggregate value, there's a dimension member to represent the chosen arbitrary group; the difference is that it won't be part of a hierarchy. You'll also create a valueset to specify the group with which you're working:

```
MAINTAIN CUSTOMER ADD 'ARBITRARY_GRP'
```

For now, suppose the group consists of customers CU001 and CU013 (Jee-Hing Wong and Linda Tillis). These customers don't share a common parent in any hierarchy or a common attribute, but you want to deal with them as a group and you want their total revenue. Let's see a couple of ways of computing the aggregate.

For this very simple example, you could compute the aggregate by just adding the two values:
```
CUST_REV(CUSTOMER 'ARBITRARY_GRP') = -
CUST_REV(CUSTOMER 'CU001') + CUST_REV(CUSTOMER 'CU013')
```

But in a real application, you might have a universe of hundreds of thousands of customers and the groups might have thousands, so the above simple technique wouldn't be practical.

For a larger set it is preferable to use a valueset to specify the members. For instance:
```
DEFINE VS_ARBITRARY_GRP VALUESET CUSTOMER
```

Set the contents of the valueset to prepare it for use:
```
LIMIT VS_ARBITRARY_GRP TO 'CU001' 'CU013'
```

(Or load the valueset from an external source with a program, as illustrated in Chapter 19: *Getting Data In and Out of Analytic Workspaces*.)

Now compute the aggregate like this:
```
LIMIT CUSTOMER TO VS_ARBITRARY_GRP
CUST_REV(CUSTOMER 'ARBITRARY_GRP') = TOTAL(CUST_REV)
```

But there's another way that's even better. Let's take a look at a more sophisticated, "managed" process. To this end I will introduce another object type, the *model,* and a function called *AGGREGATION* (not to be mixed up with the AGGREGATE command). Setup for the model is similar to that of the aggmap.

Create the model:
```
DEFINE MDL_ARBITRARY_GRP MODEL
```

Set the model contents using the model command:
```
MODEL JOINLINES('DIMENSION CUSTOMER' -
'ARBITRARY_GRP = AGGREGATION(VS_ARBITRARY_GRP)')
```

Now you have a model called MDL_ARBITRARY_GRP that you'll use to aggregate the CUST_REV variable for this group. Execute the model like this:

```
MDL_ARBITRARY_GRP CUST_REV
```

What are the advantages of using a model? Like the aggmap, using a model casts the aggregation instructions in terms of the dimension, not the object being aggregated and is thus more versatile. In addition, models can be appended to an aggmap so that the AGGREGATE command performs both hierarchical and non-hierarchical aggregations.

To stem potential confusion, I'm going to point out a few ways in which models and aggmaps are similar and ways in which they are different.

MODELS AND AGGMAPS: SIMILARITIES

- A model is a DML object type and an aggmap is a DML object type.

- Both models and aggmaps let you specify a calculation in terms of a dimension, independent of the variable to which it will be applied.

MODELS AND AGGMAPS: DIFFERENCES

- Once you define a model, you run it to perform the aggregation. An aggmap, however, is not run to perform the aggregation—it cannot be run. An aggmap is a container of aggregation setup information that is supplied as an argument to the AGGREGATE command, which actually performs the calculations.

- Models can be used for calculations other than aggregations. Models can be used more generally to compute the data corresponding to one dimension member in terms of the data associated with other dimension members. They are heavily used in financial applications to compute line-item data. Models can even solve simultaneous systems of linear equations!

Attributes

You will often start with data broken out by dimensions for which a number of attributes have been defined. Now suppose you want to see how the data changes as a function of those attributes rather than the underlying base dimension—that's the motivation for aggregating by attributes. You have already seen this situation several times: dimension profilers, RFM analysis, unnatural hierarchies, and the "percent of category" formula.

We will now look at this kind of an aggregation process. It won't involve aggmaps or models, but other built-in functions in the OLAP DML.

Percent of Category Formula

In Chapter 11: *Calculating Data On-the-Fly* you created a formula that calculated the revenue of a given product as a percent of its category by dividing the product revenue by the product category revenue. But you didn't have revenue broken out by category; there was no category level in the product hierarchy, so that information wasn't available from the REVENUE variable.

To get the needed information, you created a revenue variable broken out by category:
DEFINE REVCAT VARIABLE DECIMAL <CUSTOMER CATEGORY TIME>

That's easy enough to define, but how do you get the numbers in? There are a number of aggregation functions in the DML that work with relations, TOTAL is one of them.

```
ALLSTAT
LIMIT PRODUCT TO PRODUCT_LEVELREL 'PRODUCT_LEV'
REVCAT = TOTAL(REVENUE, CUSTOMER CATEGORY TIME)
```

Of course, you don't have to store the aggregated data. The aggregation can be done on-the-fly by using the aggregation expression as the EQ of a formula:

```
DEFINE F.REVCAT FORMULA DECIMAL <CUSTOMER CATEGORY TIME>
EQ TOTAL(REVENUE, CUSTOMER CATEGORY TIME)
```

Be careful! The TOTAL function is responsive to status settings and the F.REVCAT formula does nothing to set status.

Both REVCAT and F.REVCAT give revenue data broken out not by product, but by one of product's attributes (its category).

You may notice one novel feature of aggregation by attribute. In the case of hierarchies and sets, the result of the aggregation has the same dimensionality as the source information. With attributes, the result has a different dimensionality. In the example above, you aggregated REVENUE, broken out by customer, product, and time, and got REVCAT, broken out by customer, category, and time.

Sometimes confusion arises because the same term is being used in two different ways. On the one hand, category is an attribute that can be used, for example, to filter on the product dimension; on the other hand it is a dimension, in this case a base dimension of REVCAT. So is "category" a dimension or an attribute? To be precise, R.CATEGORY.PRODUCT is the attribute (that you may refer to as category), whereas CATEGORY is a dimension (that's also called category). So what you are referring to depends on the context. Using some categorical entity both as a dimension and as an attribute is a standard data-modeling construct, so don't let it be a point of confusion.

Before leaving this simple application of aggregation by attributes, I want to mention that there are a variety of other functions besides TOTAL by which one may aggregate. There are several other calculation operations possible; for instance, AVERAGE, MEDIAN, and MAX. They work in a similar way to what you've already seen: to get the average revenue by customer, category, and time (averaging over product) we could have used:

```
REVCAT = AVERAGE(REVENUE, CUSTOMER CATEGORY TIME)
```

MULTI-ATTRIBUTE BREAKOUTS AND PIVOT TABLES

Not only is the result of aggregation by attribute different in dimensionality from the input data source, in some cases it can even have a different number of dimensions. Any given dimension can have more than one attribute, and there's nothing to stop you from aggregating over more than one attribute at once; however, a caveat is in order. If you slice and dice the data into enough attributes, you'll start getting high levels of sparsity and data that can become hard to work with. If data is broken out by too many attributes, you'll start to get see page after page of blank data when reporting. You may even have to hunt to find a page that has some data on it.

Let's see some examples of aggregation based on multi-attribute breakouts. You have attributes defined for product: flavor, texture, and packaging type. Suppose you want to see revenue data broken out by customer, flavor, texture, packaging type, and time. You could get this by:

```
DEFINE REVCAT2 VARIABLE DECIMAL <CUSTOMER FLAVOR TEXTURE -
PACKAGING TIME>
REVCAT2 = TOTAL(REVENUE, CUSTOMER FLAVOR TEXTURE PACKAGING -
TIME)
```

Let's keep going. Not only can you break a dimension out into more than one attribute, you can do it for more than one dimension. So suppose you have two attributes defined for customer: gender and marital status. Let's get a revenue variable that breaks out the data by the two customer attributes, three product attributes, and time.

```
DEFINE REVCAT3 VARIABLE DECIMAL <GENDER MARITAL FLAVOR -
TEXTURE PACKAGING TIME>
```

Assuming you have relations populated with definitions like these:
```
DEFINE R.GENDER.CUST RELATION GENDER <CUSTOMER>
DEFINE R.MARITAL.CUST RELATION MARITAL <CUSTOMER>
```

You could populate the variable:
```
ALLSTAT
LIMIT PRODUCT TO PRODUCT_LEVELREL 'PRODUCT_LEV'
LIMIT CUSTOMER TO CUSTOMER_LEVELREL 'CUSTOMER_LEV'
REVCAT3 = TOTAL(REVENUE, GENDER MARITAL FLAVOR TEXTURE -
PACKAGING TIME)
```

What you're doing here is basically the command-line equivalent of what is called a *pivot table*. A pivot table is a graphical interface that lets you drag and drop attributes into a table to select which ones you want the data broken out by. Being a graphical tool, the pivot table is not a part of the DML, but I'm just pointing out that you're accomplishing something similar here.

Finally, I want to point out something curious: the aggregates thus produced have *more* dimensions than the source data! Usually, data broken out by more dimensions is more detailed than data broken out by fewer dimensions. In this case, however, it is not.

UNNATURAL HIERARCHIES

In Chapter 9: *Representing Unnatural, Ragged, and Other Hierarchy Variations,* I illustrated an unnatural hierarchy by organizing customer into a hierarchy with a gender and marital status level. I argued that with unnatural hierarchies, the levels themselves are meaningful breakout dimensions. So let's see that in action.

In the above section, we created a gender and marital status relation. Make use of those relations to create and populate a variable broken out by marital status and gender (but not customer):

```
DEFINE UNITS_MG VARIABLE DECIMAL <MARITAL_STATUS GENDER -
PRODUCT TIME>
LIMIT CUSTOMER TO CUSTOMER_LEVELREL 'CUSTOMER_LEV'
UNITS_MG = TOTAL(UNITS, MARITAL_STATUS GENDER PRODUCT TIME)
```

As noted in Chapter 9, it would generally not make sense to break out data by both a base dimension and one or more of its related dimensions. This would embody an inherent redundancy and would introduce unnecessary sparsity.

Accumulations

Accumulation is a process that shares some of the characteristics of aggregation, but is actually distinct from it in that the data is not numerical and the result of the calculation operation is not a single value. I will illustrate accumulations through an example.

Imagine that you have two groups of customers A and B and you wish to create a new group C comprised of the customers that are in either of these two groups (i.e., set union). Assume you have a dimension with members that represent these three groups. Combining the members of A and B is similar to aggregating with a hierarchy in the following sense: A and B report to C and the data associated with C is calculated from the data associated with A and B.

Let's look at an application. Consider a promotion dimension. Suppose this dimension is organized into a hierarchy with a level for two types of promotions—loyalty programs and sales offers—and a leaf level corresponding to individual programs/offers. The data you wish to associate with each node in the hierarchy are the customers associated with it. There are two dimensions involved in this example, a promotion dimension and a customer dimension. The data is dimensioned by promotion; the data values—rather than being numbers—are sets of customer dimension members. Figure 14.1 illustrates such a hierarchy.

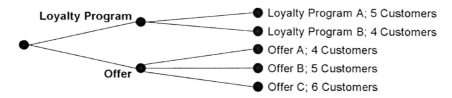

Figure 14.1. Promotion Dimension: Hierarchy

Assume Table 14.1 represents the data. Note in this data that the customer groups are not mutually exclusive; for example, you can see some customers in a loyalty program receiving more than one sales offer.

Table 14.1. Promotion Dimension: Sample Data with Non-mutually Exclusive Sets

Customer Label	Loyalty Program		Offer		
	A	B	A	B	C
Jee-Hing Wong			●		●
Doris Ingram	●				
James Niehous	●			●	
Anne Jackson					●
Richard Hyde	●	●			
Sandra Yulke					
Rosalind Roberts				●	
Kathleen Riley		●			●
John Karminski					
Mark Torrens	●	●		●	●
Clara Doyle			●		
Johnnie Wilford				●	
Linda Tillis	●		●		
Frank Romero		●			
Sean Mahoney			●	●	●
Erich Plymouth					●

The data in Table 14.1 is leaf-level data. The goal of this application is to determine which customers are associated with the aggregate nodes of the promotion hierarchy. How do you model this situation?

You set up this hierarchy in the usual manner:
```
DEFINE PROMOTION DIMENSION TEXT
MAINTAIN PROMOTION ADD 'ALL_PROMOS' 'LOYALTY_PRG' 'OFFERS' -
'LP_A' 'LP_B' 'OF_A' 'OF_B' 'OF_C'
DEFINE PROMOTION_LEVELLIST DIMENSION TEXT
MAINTAIN PROMOTION_LEVELLIST ADD 'L0' 'L1' 'L2'
DEFINE PROMOTION_LEVELREL RELATION PROMOTION <PROMOTION>
```

Assign the parent values:
```
PROMOTION_PARENTREL(PROMOTION 'LOYALTY_PRG') = 'ALL_PROMOS'
PROMOTION_PARENTREL(PROMOTION 'OFFERS') = 'ALL_PROMOS'
PROMOTION_PARENTREL(PROMOTION 'LP_A') = 'LOYALTY_PRG'
PROMOTION_PARENTREL(PROMOTION 'LP_B') = 'LOYALTY_PRG'
PROMOTION_PARENTREL(PROMOTION 'OF_A') = 'OFFERS'
PROMOTION_PARENTREL(PROMOTION 'OF_B') = 'OFFERS'
PROMOTION_PARENTREL(PROMOTION 'OF_C') = 'OFFERS'
```

Assign the level values:
```
PROMOTION_LEVELREL(PROMOTION 'ALL_PROMOS') = 'L0'
PROMOTION_LEVELREL(PROMOTION 'LOYALTY_PRG') = 'L1'
PROMOTION_LEVELREL(PROMOTION 'OFFERS') = 'L1'
PROMOTION_LEVELREL(PROMOTION 'LP_A') = 'L2'
PROMOTION_LEVELREL(PROMOTION 'LP_B') = 'L2'
PROMOTION_LEVELREL(PROMOTION 'OF_A') = 'L2'
PROMOTION_LEVELREL(PROMOTION 'OF_B') = 'L2'
PROMOTION_LEVELREL(PROMOTION 'OF_C') = 'L2'
```

Now you need a way to store the data of Table 14.1. Define a valueset dimensioned by promotion to store the customers:

```
DEFINE PROMO_CUSTS VALUESET CUSTOMER <PROMOTION>
```

Assume the leaf-level promotion members have been populated. Then you could generate the following report:

```
->RPR HEADING '#CUSTOMERS' STATLEN(PROMO_CUSTS)
PROMOTION         #CUSTOMERS
--------------    ----------
ALL_PROMOS                 0
LOYALTY_PRG                0
OFFERS                     0
LP_A                       5
LP_B                       4
OF_A                       4
OF_B                       5
OF_C                       6
```

Next you want to populate the non-leaf-level data values (these are the values where you see the zeros in the report). This could be done with a manual process like the one used to illustrate aggregation at the beginning of this chapter, for example:

```
LIMIT PROMOTION TO 'OFFERS'
LIMIT PROMO_CUSTS TO PROMO_CUSTS(PROMOTION 'OF_A')
LIMIT PROMO_CUSTS ADD PROMO_CUSTS(PROMOTION 'OF_B')
LIMIT PROMO_CUSTS ADD PROMO_CUSTS(PROMOTION 'OF_C')
```

These statements give the data you want for OFFERS.

Now the process needs to be continued for the other nodes. Unfortunately in this case you can't replace this tedious manual process with the AGGREGATE command because it is not a true aggregation process. How would you do this in an application environment dealing with a complex promotion hierarchy and hundreds of thousands of customers? You would write a program to perform these steps. Such a program is shown in Chapter 18: *Writing DML Programs*.

Part IV:
Graphical User Interfaces for OLAP

15 | Exploring Metadata

In this chapter and the next two, we're going to approach the Analytic Workspace Manager from a different perspective. We started our multidimensional journey in Chapter 4: *Pit Stop: Analytic Workspace Manager Administration Basics* by peeling back the product layers in order to expose the full power of the analytical core; we created analytic workspaces in *Object View*, we manipulated the workspace from the OLAP Worksheet, and we defined all the objects from the command line using DML instructions.

Enter the present metadata section. Here you are going to create an AW in *Model View*. You will define objects using AWM's graphical interface controls, and you'll use the OLAP Worksheet to explore the contents, not create them.

In this chapter and the next, you'll be using graphical interfaces to create what is known as a *standard-form* AW. Unlike the AWs you've been working in, the data you'll create here will be accessible from standard interface clients. The difference with the AW you're about to create can be summarized in one word: metadata.

As you'll soon see, the AW is going to become vastly more complex. There will be many more objects; the system will rely heavily on object properties. Fortunately, the additional complexity is handled automatically, for the most part.

By now, you know enough to design and build fairly complex analytical models. Moreover, since the same language you've learned to use to model data for analytical purposes is also used to model the user interface layer, you're also going to be able to understand *that* process, even if you don't create those elements directly yourself.

This section's material is going to be very practical. You'll get a good introduction to the mechanics of creating objects and loading data using the GUI. You're going to build, from scratch, *The 30,000-Foot View* "application" illustrated in Chapter 3 (referred to as the Demo Application). You're going to examine in some detail the graphical query builder and see how the various limit statements get translated into a graphical presentation. So now let's take a good look at metadata!

What is Metadata?

Entering into the world of business intelligence, be it through data warehousing, OLAP, or front-end user tools, you soon encounter the term *metadata*. Like so many terms in this field, the term metadata can have different meanings in different contexts. For our purposes, metadata essentially refers to the information used by the system to describe the program objects in order to make interactions through a GUI possible.

Metadata is all about building a bridge between the world of programming objects and the end user's conceptual world—it's where they meet. It lets the front-end application know that this variable is giving the labels for that dimension, this relation is being used to define that hierarchy, and so on. So metadata is concerned with modeling the world within which the user operates. That world consists of graphical reporting interfaces, data measures, attributes, and filtering and sorting tools for manipulating them.

Now let's get even more specific. Let's look at metadata as it is implemented in Oracle OLAP. This metadata is part of a standard known as CWM2 (Common Warehouse Metadata, version 2).

How can you create all those objects and properties so that you have compliant metadata? If you want to use the standard end-user client tools, you'll need compliance.

Actually, it's such a complex procedure that you don't do it directly: Oracle OLAP has a Java API that does it for you. But because you've been creating all your objects directly in the OLAP Worksheet in Object View, none of the routines that would have created the metadata were called. Now you'll trigger those routines by working in Model View and creating objects with the graphical interface.

Creating the Demo Application

So now it's time to build the Demo Application seen in *The 30,000-Foot View* section of Chapter 3, and you'll do it completely through interactions with AWM's graphical elements. Keep in mind that everything you do with the mouse has a programmatic equivalent using the Java API. Thus all the actions you take could be reenacted by a Java program.

Here are the steps you'll be taking:

- STEP 1: Create the dimensions along with their descriptions, hierarchies, and attributes.

- STEP 2: Create cubes and measures.

- STEP 3: Populate the data from a relational data warehouse.

Recall that when you first started creating DML objects in Chapter 4, you were asked to go into View and select Object View. This time, you're going to choose Model View.

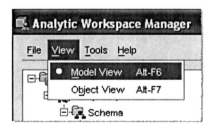

Figure 15.1. Choosing Model View as the Display Style

Next, right-click the "Analytic Workspaces" node and choose "Create Analytic Workspace," and create an AW called SALES_DEMO. Expanding the SALES_DEMO icon gives Figure 15.2.

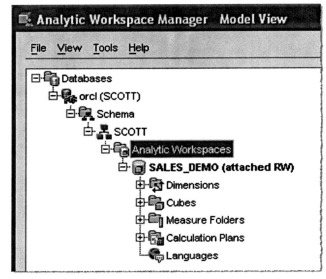

Figure 15.2. Expanding an Analytic Workspaces Node in Model View

In Figure 15.3, I will show the Analytic Workspaces node with the SALES_DEMO AW expanded in both Object View and Model View side-by-side so that you can compare the two views.

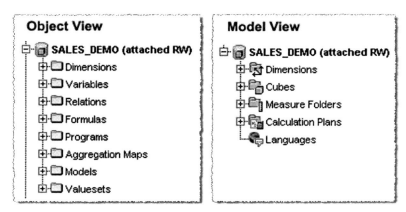

Figure 15.3. Expanding the Analytic Workspaces Node in Object View Versus Model View

So why are these two different, and why is one called "object" and the other "model"? Under Object View, you see the familiar DML object types you've worked with in previous chapters. Under Model View, you can see a different way of organizing an AW. Object View is denominated by the different object types in the programming language, while Model View is denominated in terms of the elements that make up the logical model presented to the user. In this chapter, you'll be exploring the most important elements in the Model View: Dimensions and Cubes.

CREATING DIMENSIONS AND THEIR DESCRIPTIONS

Start by creating the dimensions you'll need for the Demo Application. That application had four dimensions: store, product, payment method, and time. I'll only show product, but the other dimensions are done the same way.

Right-click "Dimensions" and the "Create Dimension" dialog box appears. On the "General" tab, in the "Name" box, type Product (the system will capitalize the word for you). Fill in the various labels if you don't want the defaults, but for the sake of this example, just keep them.

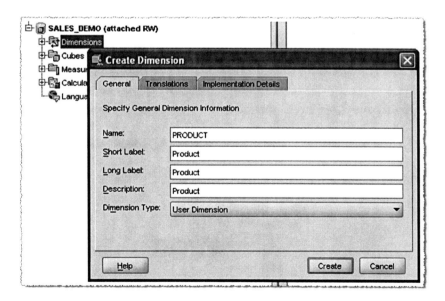

On the "Implementation Details" tab, select "Use Natural Keys from Data Source," since you're going to supply your own dimension member values, and then click "Create."

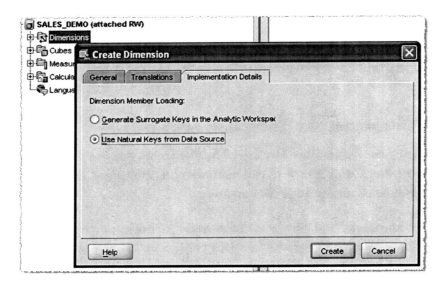

CREATING A HIERARCHY

Next you'll create a hierarchy for this dimension. If you expand the PRODUCT icon, you'll see Levels, Hierarchies, Attributes, and Mappings. Start the process by creating the levels. In this case you'll have three levels: product, category, and an "all products."

Right-click "Levels" and select "Create Level," and the "Create Level" dialog box appears.

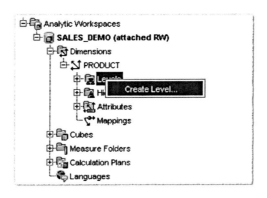

Chapter 15
Exploring Metadata

Create the three levels. Here is what it looks like as you create the first level:

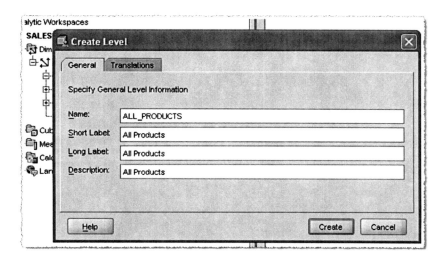

Once you've created all the levels the hierarchies require, you're ready to define the hierarchies. Right-click "Hierarchies" and select "Create Hierarchy," and the "Create Hierarchy" dialog box appears.

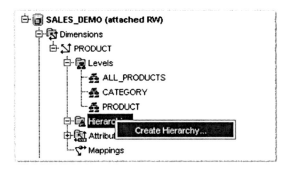

On the "General" tab, create one hierarchy called "PRODUCT_HIER." Enter the name of the hierarchy and select the levels that belong to the hierarchy, ordered from highest level to lowest. For this dimension, you only have one hierarchy, which uses all the defined levels. Then click "Create."

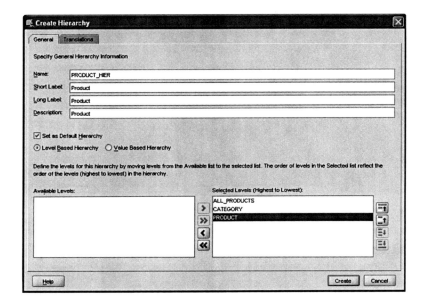

Next, create the attribute objects for the dimension. If you click the "Attributes" icon, you'll see that two are created by default: LONG_DESCRIPTION and SHORT_DESCRIPTION, which represent text-valued variables that will hold the labels for the dimension members.

Creating a Non-indexed Attribute

Now, let's suppose you want to create flavor and packaging attributes for the products. Right-click "Attributes," and select "Create Attribute," and the "Create Attribute" dialog box appears. On the "General" tab, name each attribute and set their labels and properties as shown below.

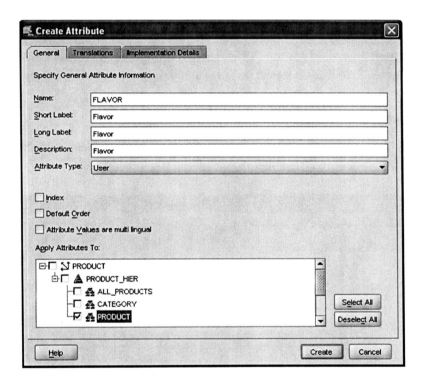

Recall that when you have a hierarchical dimension, dimension members at different levels correspond to different types of objects in the application realm, so a given attribute often pertains to only some levels.

In the bottom section of the dialog box, you can select the levels to which the attribute applies. In this application, flavor applies to the lowest level, corresponding to individual products. The next level up is the product category level, which may include products of various flavors, so the attribute does not apply. So uncheck the default (which specifies that the attribute applies to all dimension members) and then expand the icon, go down to the bottom, and check product only. You won't do anything under the "Translations" tab or the "Implementation Details" tab.

Before defining the next attribute, let me call your attention to the Index check box. If you check that box, the attribute will be created as a relation; if you don't check that box, it will be created as a text variable. Recall from Chapter 7: *Categorizing Dimension Members with Attributes* that the relation will generally be faster because a relation is indexed. If the base dimension has only a few values ("low cardinality") you won't see much difference, but for large numbers of values the difference can be significant. Don't check the box for this attribute; you'll do it for the next so we can make a comparison later on.

CREATING AN INDEXED ATTRIBUTE

So now create the packaging type attribute. Do it in the same way that you created the flavor attribute, with the exception that you should check the Index box.

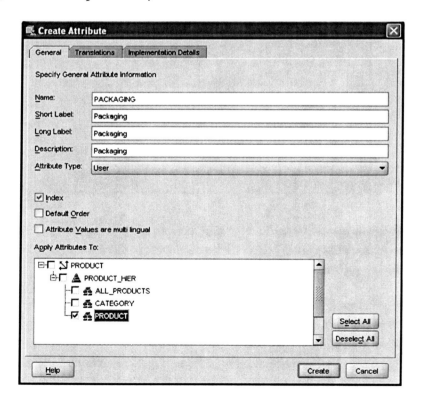

CREATING A DEFAULT ORDER ATTRIBUTE

You will create one last attribute, a "default order" attribute. This is a special attribute that makes it possible to specify the default ordering for dimension members. So if you need to see the dimension members in a particular order (for example, you want months displayed in chronological not alphabetical order), this is where you make it happen. So let's do that now.

Right-click "Attributes" and select "Create Attribute," and the "Create Attribute" dialog box appears. On the "General" tab, name the attribute and set its labels and properties as shown below. This time, check the box by "Default Order" to tell the system that the function of the attribute you are defining is to set the default order. For its name, type ORDER.

This attribute applies to all values of the members of the dimension, so leave the check box next to the product hierarchy icon checked in the "Apply Attributes To" section.

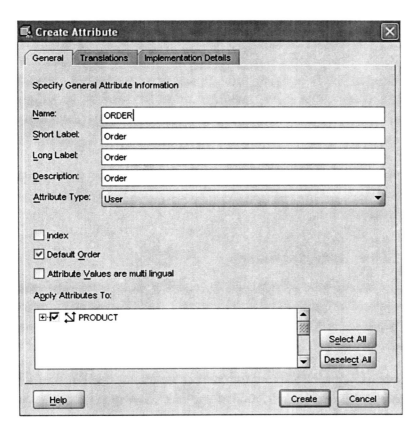

There's one extra step for this attribute. You need to go into the "Implementation Details" tab and tell the system that this attribute is integer-valued (if you did not take this step it would be defined as text-valued).

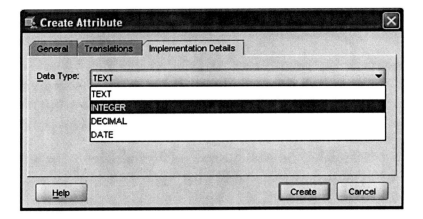

In Chapter 6: *Describing Dimension Members with Labels* there was a discussion of numerical-valued descriptions, using product weight as the example. You see something similar here. However, unlike the PRODUCT_WEIGHT variable containing data about the product itself, the product order variable created here contains data about the product's *position* in a graphical report—the difference between data and metadata.

I'm not going to show it, but the other three dimensions (time, customer, and payment method) could be created in the same way. Once the dimensions are there, the measures broken out by them can be created.

CREATING CUBES AND MEASURES

The term "cube" is used somewhat loosely in OLAP applications to refer to data variables, or sometimes formulas that display data, or even to refer to the entire AW. In any case, there is no "cube" object in the DML, just as there is no hierarchy, attribute, or measure object in the language.

However, the metadata specification *does* include an actual cube object. Let's take a little digression from building our application to explore it and some related concepts. Cubes are used to specify a measure's dimensionality. In other words, if you want a measure to be dimensioned by STORE, PRODUCT, PAYMENT_METHOD, and TIME, you'll first create a cube with that dimensionality.

Measures are the multidimensional data elements available to a graphical user. When a measure is created through the GUI, a formula is created in the DML. *If eyes are the windows of the soul, formulas are the windows of the AW*: all data that can be seen through a GUI is from a formula!

In the OLAP Worksheet you could report on variables, formulas, relations, and valuesets. Since the GUI will only display information through formulas, any information you wish to show in a GUI must be made presentable via a formula.

You've learned how to use formulas to show data from variables (Chapter 11: *Calculating Data On-the-Fly*; F.REV_PROD) and valuesets (Chapter 13: *Working with Sets*; PATIENT_DIAGNOSES). Displaying information from a relation uses the same basic approach: set the EQ of a formula to the relation.

With this understanding, let's return to building your application and create a cube for your measures, after which you'll be creating a measure. Right-click the "Cubes" icon and the "Create Cube" dialog box will appear.

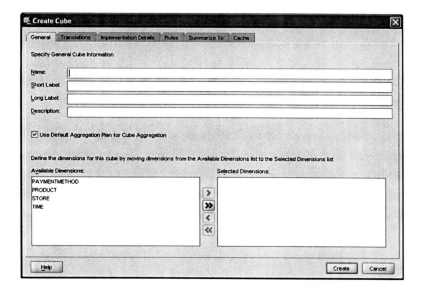

You only need to fill out the General tab information. Remember the discussion in Chapter 10: *Storing Data in Analytic Workspaces* about the importance of dimension ordering when defining a variable? Because creating a measure will result in the creation of a variable, the same principles apply here. The available dimensions will appear in alphabetical order, but you can move them over into the "Selected Dimensions" box in the order you want them to appear in the data variable. You're going to select all of the Available Dimensions *in this order:* STORE, PRODUCT, PAYMENTMETHOD, and TIME.

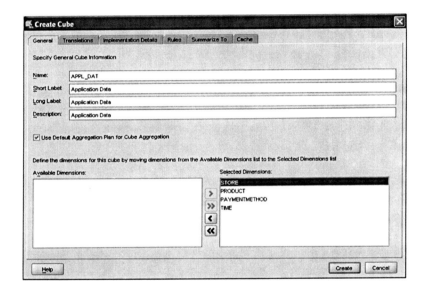

The more usual situation in a real application is that there would be many dimensions from which to select; any given cube would only use some of them.

The cube serves as a framework for defining measures. In it you specify a dimensionality as well as other properties having to do with things like aggregations and caching. Every measure belongs to a cube and it inherits the settings of that cube. The cube makes it possible to specify a dimensionality once, then create a multiplicity of measures without having to define a dimensionality for each.

Now create a UNITS measure. Right-click the "Measure" icon underneath "Cubes" and select "Create Measure," and the "Create Measure" dialog box will appear. Fill in the information on the "General" tab and click "Create."

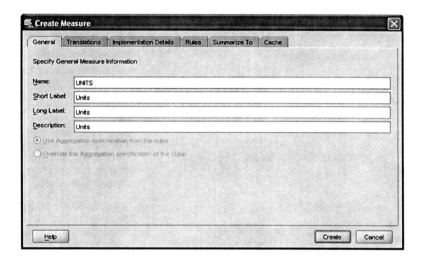

Exploring Objects Created from AWM's GUI

Your interactions with AWM's GUI has caused dimensions, formulas, and variables to be created. In this section let's look at the DML objects resulting from those interactions. This may seem a little bit tedious, but I think it's useful to examine what was created and relate it to similar objects you created in previous chapters using the OLAP Worksheet and see what the difference is. The comparison is shown in Table 15.1.

Keep in mind that the objects created by the system take care of creating the metadata; you'd normally have no reason to alter the values of any of those objects in the OLAP Worksheet, and should take great care if you decide to do so. On the other hand, I have found occasions where the objects created contained valuable information I needed and could make use of in a program.

Table 15.1. Object View Worksheet vs. Model View GUI

Created In	Statement	Comments
Object View Worksheet	->DESCRIBE PRODUCT DEFINE PRODUCT DIMENSION TEXT	Description of the product dimension created in Chapter 5 using the OLAP Worksheet.
Model View GUI	->DESCRIBE PRODUCT DEFINE PRODUCT DIMENSION TEXT	Description of the product dimension created in this chapter using the GUI. As you can see, it's the same description as above.
Object View Worksheet	->FULLDSC PRODUCT DEFINE PRODUCT DIMENSION TEXT	A full describe (FULLDSC) on the product dimension from Chapter 5 gives the same description as the "ordinary" description.
Model View GUI	->FULLDSC PRODUCT DEFINE PRODUCT DIMENSION TEXT PROPERTY 'AW$CLASS' 'IMPLEMENTATION' PROPERTY 'AW$CREATEDBY' 'AW$XML' PROPERTY 'AW$DIMDEF' NA PROPERTY 'AW$LASTMODIFIED' - '02DEC07_19:15:43' PROPERTY 'AW$LOGICAL_NAME' 'PRODUCT' PROPERTY 'AW$ROLE' 'DIMDEF' PROPERTY 'AW$STATE' 'VALID_MEMBER' PROPERTY 'AW$TYPE' NA PROPERTY 'COLUMN_NAME_ET' 'ET_COL_27' PROPERTY 'COLUMN_NAME_GID' 'GID_COL_29' PROPERTY 'COLUMN_NAME_PRNTET' - 'PET_COL_28' PROPERTY 'COLUMN_NAME_PRNTGID' - 'PGID_COL_30' PROPERTY 'DATA_TYPE' 'TEXT' PROPERTY 'DEFAULT_HIERARCHY' - 'PRODUCT_HIER' PROPERTY 'DESCRIPTION' - 'LANG=AMERICAN:Product' PROPERTY 'DISPLAYNAME' - 'LANG=AMERICAN:Product' PROPERTY 'PLURAL_DESCRIPTION' - 'LANG=AMERICAN:Product'	A full describe on the product dimension created from the GUI, however, reveals the many properties automatically generated by the system. These properties are part of compliance with the CWM2 metadata specification. The system knows how to interpret these properties; there is nothing you need to do with them.

Created In	Statement	Comments
Object View Worksheet	->FULLDSC PRODUCT_LONG_DESCRIPTION DEFINE PRODUCT_LONG_DESCRIPTION VARIABLE TEXT <PRODUCT ALL_LANGUAGES>	In Chapter 6, you created user-friendly labels for the dimension members. This was accomplished with a text-valued variable. You could have chosen any legal variable name for the variable, but I deliberately chose the name to match the metadata naming convention. The language dimension used to enable multiple languages could take any legal name, but I chose to use the same one the GUI uses when it creates them.
Model View GUI	->FULLDSC PRODUCT_LONG_DESCRIPTION DEFINE PRODUCT_LONG_DESCRIPTION VARIABLE TEXT <PRODUCT ALL_LANGUAGES> PROPERTY '$NATRIGGER' - 'if this_aw!ALL_LANGUAGES eq \'AMERICAN\' then NA else this_aw!PRODUCT_LONG_DES\ CRIPTION(this_aw!ALL_LANGUAGES \'AMERICAN\')' PROPERTY 'AW$ATTRDEF' NA PROPERTY 'AW$CLASS' 'IMPLEMENTATION' PROPERTY 'AW$CREATEDBY' 'AW$XML' PROPERTY 'AW$LASTMODIFIED' - '02DEC07_19:15:43' PROPERTY 'AW$LNG_ATTRIBUTE' yes PROPERTY 'AW$LOGICAL_NAME' - 'LONG_DESCRIPTION' PROPERTY 'AW$PARENT_NAME' 'PRODUCT' PROPERTY 'AW$ROLE' 'ATTRDEF' PROPERTY 'AW$STATE' 'VALID_MEMBER' PROPERTY 'AW$TYPE' - 'MEMBER_LONG_DESCRIPTION' PROPERTY 'COLUMN_NAME' 'ATTRIBUTE_31' PROPERTY 'DATA_TYPE' 'TEXT' PROPERTY 'DESCRIPTION' - 'LANG=AMERICAN:Long Description' PROPERTY 'DISPLAYNAME' - 'LANG=AMERICAN:Long Description'	When you create a dimension through the GUI in Model View, the system automatically creates variables for storing a long and short description for the dimension members. You don't create them as a separate action. The system creates these variables using a specific naming convention and it defines a number of properties for it as well (as seen here). The naming convention is to use the dimension name, followed by LONG_DESCRIPTION and for the other label, SHORT_DESCRIPTION.

Created In	Statement	Comments
Object View Worksheet	->DESCRIBE R.FLAVOR.PRODUCT DEFINE R.FLAVOR.PRODUCT RELATION FLAVOR <PRODUCT>	In Chapter 7, I said that attributes could be created as text variables, but argued that relations are superior in several ways. Here is the relation you created to model this attribute using a relation.
Model View GUI	->DESCRIBE PRODUCT_FLAVOR DEFINE PRODUCT_FLAVOR RELATION PRODUCT_FLAVOR_INDEX <PRODUCT>	Since you checked the "indexed" box in the dialog box, the system creates the attribute as a relation. It names the relation PRODUCT_FLAVOR and creates a related dimension named PRODUCT_FLAVOR_INDEX.
Model View GUI	->DESCRIBE PRODUCT_PACKAGING DEFINE PRODUCT_PACKAGING VARIABLE TEXT <PRODUCT>	By not checking "indexed" the system creates an ordinary text variable. A full describe would reveal its many properties.
Model View GUI	->DESCRIBE PRODUCT_ORDER DEFINE PRODUCT_ORDER VARIABLE INTEGER <PRODUCT>	In Chapter 6, the idea of numerical descriptions of a dimension member was introduced. Here we create a numerical description whose purpose is to show display order. It is similar to PRODUCT_WEIGHT in Chapter 6.

Created In	Statement	Comments
Object View Worksheet	DEFINE UNITS VARIABLE DECIMAL <STORE PRODUCT PAYMENTMETHOD TIME>	This is similar to the UNITS variable you created in Chapter 10, but you were working with a three-dimensional model there.
Model View GUI	->DESCRIBE APPL_DAT_UNITS DEFINE APPL_DAT_UNITS FORMULA NUMBER <STORE PRODUCT PAYMENTMETHOD TIME> EQ this_aw!APPL_DAT_PRT_TOPFRML(this_aw!APPL_DAT_PRT_MEASDIM 'UNITS') ->DSC APPL_DAT_PRT_TOPFRML DEFINE APPL_DAT_PRT_TOPFRML FORMULA NUMBER <APPL_DAT_PRT_MEASDIM STORE PRODUCT PAYMENTMETHOD TIME> EQ aggregate(this_aw!APPL_DAT_PRT_TOPVAR using this_aw!OBJ837621300) ->DSC APPL_DAT_PRT_TOPVAR DEFINE APPL_DAT_PRT_TOPVAR VARIABLE NUMBER WITH AGGCOUNT <APPL_DAT_PRT_MEASDIM APPL_DAT_COMPOSITE <STORE PRODUCT PAYMENTMETHOD TIME>>	You typed UNITS in the name field, but the system does not create a formula called UNITS. It actually creates a formula named APPL_DAT_UNITS, a concatenation of the cube name and name entered. The APPL_DAT_UNITS formula calls another formula, APPL_DAT_PRT_TOPFRML, which aggregates the data in the variable that ultimately contains the data. The amount of on-the-fly aggregation performed is guided by choices made in the "Summarize To" tab when the measure was defined. You've kept the default settings. Here the aggmap gets the name OBJ837621300. Remember when we talked about measure dimensions in Chapter 10? The system uses this technique to organize all the measures that belong to a given cube. The variable containing the data is dimensioned by our breakout dimensions as well as the measure dimension, APPL_DAT_PRT_MEASUREDIM.

Metadata Structures

In addition to all the objects created in response to the actions you took to build your application elements, there's a standard set of objects contained in any standard-form AW. Remember that in Chapter 4: Pit Stop: *Analytic Workspace Manager Administration Basics* when you created your first AW, it came into the world empty? When you issued the LISTNAMES command, you got this:

```
->LISTNAMES
There are no objects in the analytic workspace.
```

Immediately after creating your AW in Model View with the GUI, you would get this:
```
->LISTNAMES

LISTNAMES
 30 DIMENSIONs                          29 VARIABLEs
 ------------------------------         ------------------------------
  AGGREGATE_DIMENSION_PROP               AGGREGATE_DIMENSION_CATALOG
  AGGREGATE_GENERIC_PROP                 AGGREGATE_GENERIC_CATALOG
  ALLOCATE_DIMENSION_PROP                ALLOCATE_DIMENSION_CATALOG
  ALLOCATE_GENERIC_PROP                  ALLOCATE_GENERIC_CATALOG
  ALL_ATTRIBUTES                         ALL_DESCRIPTIONS
  ALL_ATTRTYPES                          ALL_TOOLS_PROP
  ALL_CALC_MEMBERS                       ATTR_DATA_MAP
  ALL_CUBES                              ATTR_VISIBLE
  ALL_DESCTYPES                          AW_NAMES
  ALL_DIMENSIONS                         CALC_MEMBER_CATALOG
  ALL_HIERARCHIES                        CUBE_CATALOG
  ALL_LANGUAGES                          DIMKEY_IS_UNIQUE
  ALL_LEVELS                             DIM_AW_OBJS
  ALL_MEASUREFOLDERS                     DIM_KEY_MAP
  ALL_MEASURES                           FORECAST_CATALOG
  ALL_MODELS                             GEN_AW_OBJS
  ALL_OBJECTS                            MEASURE_CATALOG
  ALL_SOLVEDFNS                          MEAS_DATA_MAP
  ALL_SOLVEGROUPS                        MEAS_KEY_MAP
  ALL_SOLVES                             MEAS_OPERATOR_MAP
  CALC_MEMBER_PROP                       OBJECT_LOADED
  COLUMN_DIM                             OBJ_CREATEDBY
  CUBE_PROP                              OBJ_ORIGINATOR
  DIM_OBJ_LIST                           PARENT_KEY_MAP
  FORECAST_PROP                          PARENT_LVL_MAP
  GEN_OBJ_ROLES                          SOLVEDFN_TYPE
  GID_DIMENSION                          SOLVE_MEMBER_SELECTION
```

IS_LOADED_DIMENSION   VISIBLE
MAPGROUP_DIM   ___XML_USER_AW_VERSION
MEASURE_PROP

1 PROGRAM   25 RELATIONs
-----------------------   -----------------------
ONATTACH   CALC_MEMBER_BASE_DIMENSION
                                    CUBE_AGGREGATION
                                    CUBE_DFLT_PARTITION_HIERARCHY
                                    CUBE_DFLT_PARTITION_LEVEL
                                    CUBE_MEASURES
                                    DEFAULT_HIER
                                    DIM_ATTRIBUTES
                                    DIM_HIERARCHIES
                                    DIM_LEVELS
                                    DYNAMIC_MEAS_AGGREGATION
                                    FOLDER_PARENTREL
                                    HIER_SORT_ATTR
                                    MAPGROUP_CUBEREL
                                    MAPGROUP_DIMREL
                                    MAPGROUP_HIERREL
                                    MAPGROUP_LVLREL
                                    MEAS_DOMAIN
                                    MEAS_PARTITION_HIERARCHY
                                    MEAS_PARTITION_LEVEL
                                    MODEL_BASE_DIMENSION
                                    RELATIONAL_ATTRIBUTE_DATA
                                    RELATIONAL_MEASURE_DATA
                                    SOLVE_BASE_MEAS
                                    SOLVE_SOLVEDFN
                                    SOLVE_SOURCE_MEAS

4 COMPOSITEs   12 VALUESETs
-----------------------   -----------------------
ATTR_MAP_COMPOSITE   CALC_MEMBERS_IN_MODEL
HIERLVL_MAP_COMPOSITE   CALC_MEMBER_OTHER_DIMENSIONS
LVL_MAP_COMPOSITE   CUBE_COMPOSITE_BASES
MEAS_MAP_COMPOSITE   CUBE_DIMENSIONS
                                    DEPENDENT_MEASURES
                                    MEAS_COMPOSITE_BASES
                                    MEAS_IN_FOLDER
                                    MODEL_OTHER_DIMENSIONS
                                    SOLVEDFN_CALCULATION_ORDER
                                    SOLVEDFN_SOLVE_ORDER
                                    SOLVE_ORDER
                                    SOLVE_TARGET_MEAS

These are all elements the system uses in managing metadata information. With your knowledge of the DML, you could explore these and figure out what they do; there's no documentation available for them. Although some can be useful to read and use, there is rarely any reason to change the values of any of them and doing so could make it impossible to attach your AW in Model View, so be forewarned!

16 | The Star Schema and Beyond

In this chapter, you're going to complete the process of creating the Demo Application by loading the AW created in the last chapter. You'll continue to use the GUI in Model View. You'll use its facility for mapping DML objects to columns in a relational data table and populate the dimensions and measures with that data—all without writing programs. (In the next section on programming, you'll be learning how to write programs to load data from flat files or relational data tables and see how to populate all types of objects including relations, valuesets, and conjoint dimensions.)

The data will be assumed to be housed in relational data tables organized as a star schema. We'll start with a brief description of the organization of the input data. Then you'll load it in and see how to browse the data directly from AWM to produce reports shown in the Demo Application. Finally, we'll look at going beyond the basic model represented in this example.

What Is a Star Schema?

The source data is hosted in a data warehouse using a design known as a *star schema*, a simple database design that separates the application data from the dimensional information. It consists of two types of tables: a central fact table and a set of dimension lookup tables.

The data in the Demo Application is broken out into four base dimensions: product, store, payment type, and time. Accordingly, the star schema consists of a fact table and four dimension tables. It's depicted in Figure 16.1, with a fact table in the center called "Fact_Data"; all other tables are dimension lookup tables.

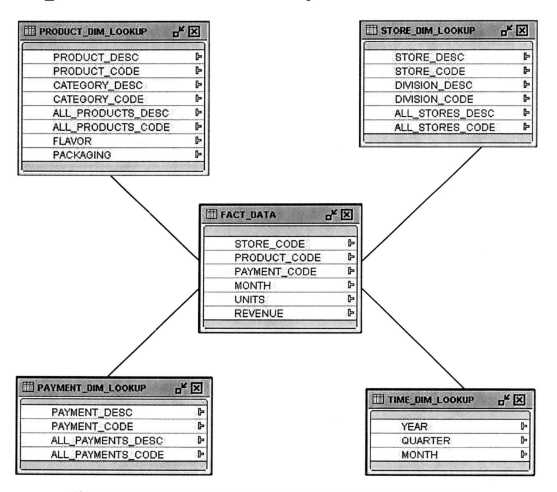

Figure 16.1. Star Schema Database Design for the Demo Application

(Depending on whether or not you have studied astronomy, Figure 16.1 may or may not look like a star to you!)

From Table 16.1 you can see that the fact table has one column for each of the four base dimensions and one column for each of the two measures, for a total of six.

The dimension lookup tables have a column for the dimension member and columns for each label, attribute, and hierarchy level.

The dimension columns in the fact table are foreign keys: every dimension member code in the fact table must be present in the dimension column of the corresponding dimension lookup table.

The Fact Table

A fact table contains leaf-level data only. It has one row for each combination of leaf-level dimension members for which there is data. In the Demo Application, this would be every combination of product, store, payment method, and month for which there are values of units and revenue.

Figure 16.2 shows the fact table as it is represented graphically in AWM.

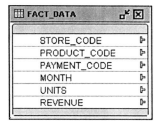

Figure 16.2. Graphical Representation of the Fact Table

The fact table contains the data that will be loaded into the AW. Aggregate values will be calculated within the AW, either when the "maintain" step is performed (shown later in this chapter) or at display time.

Before moving on to the dimension lookup tables, let's pause a moment to consider how a fact table resembles a DML variable. A fact table is like a multidimensional variable that has been presented in the row-oriented format.

In the *Switching Between Multidimensional and Relational Data Presentations* section of Chapter 12, you created a row-oriented report of the RFM customer count data.

The following report shows a few lines of this data:
```
->RPR RFM_CUST_COUNT
-----------RFM_CELLS------------
                                       RFM_CUST_C
  MONETARY    FREQUENCY    RECENCY        OUNT
-----------  -----------  ---------   ----------
  MON02        FRQ03        REC03        5,293
  MON02        FRQ03        REC01        1,791
  MON02        FRQ01        REC02          997
  MON02        FRQ02        REC02          958
  MON02        FRQ03        REC02          745
```

This data has three base dimensions and one fact, RFM_CUST_COUNT. You didn't create hierarchies for monetary, frequency, or recency, so this data is leaf level. The rows of data in this report are nothing more than the rows of a fact table! Figure 16.3 shows a representation of such a fact table.

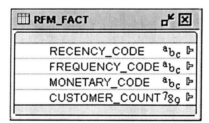

Figure 16.3. The RFM Displayed in Relational Format is Equivalent to the Rows of Data in a Fact Table

The essential difference between the data in a fact table and a DML variable is that all of the dimension members in the fact table are at the leaf level, but a DML dimension (usually) includes representation for non-leaf-level members as well.

It's perhaps even better to compare a fact table with the cube object seen in the last chapter. A fact table generally contains information for more than one measure, just as a cube specifies dimensionality for more than one measure. In building your data model in the AW, if you'd needed a measure with more than one distinct dimensionality, you would have created a cube to accommodate each different dimensionality. Likewise, in the data warehouse, you'd normally create an additional fact table to host the leaf-level data of each distinct dimensionality. (A design like that with multiple fact tables is called a *constellation schema*.)

Dimension Lookup Tables

Let's examine the dimension lookup tables. A dimension lookup table has one row for each leaf-level dimension member. The purpose of the columns in this table is to describe those members, their labels, attributes, and hierarchy parentage.

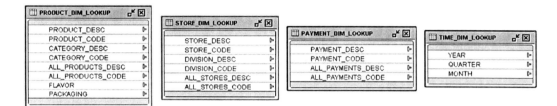

Figure 16.4. Dimension Lookup Tables

Hierarchy structure is encoded by providing, for each dimension member, the path from leaf to root. If a hierarchy has three levels, such as the product dimension above, there will usually be a total of six columns used. One column is for the dimension member, one for its parent, and one for the parent's parent, making three levels. Then there is a column for each of the descriptions for these three.

In the case of the time dimension, the codes themselves are appropriate display descriptions (assuming, for instance, the year code is 2009, and that is an acceptable display element), thus no columns for the descriptions are needed and the three level hierarchy uses only three columns.

If you refer back to Chapter 8: *Organizing Dimension Members into Hierarchies,* you'll observe that the data table of Figure 8.6 is in the form of a star-schema dimension lookup table for a customer dimension with a three-level hierarchy. That table contains information that's redundant in the following sense: there are dimension members who have the same parent, and because there is a column to describe the parents, the same parent label is in the table more than once. For example, the label for CNV001 (a parent value) is entered twice.

Placing such data into a relational table results in a *denormalized* table. Relational database design practices dictate that redundancies like this be removed by restructuring the data according to normalization rules. Doing so would result in the creation of additional tables, one for each hierarchy level. Table joins would then be used to associate the labels from these new tables.

In data warehousing practice, denormalized tables such as the dimension lookup tables are acceptable (if not advisable) because of the greater query performance realized by eliminating joins. This is relevant for some ROLAP solutions, but when hosting the data within the AW, the data warehouse is only used for loading AW data objects and does not impact query performance. Once loaded, the data queried from the AW does not access the data in relational tables. By loading the data into the AW, you're in effect creating an OLAP warehouse.

If the dimension lookup tables are normalized, the resulting design is called a *snowflake schema*. Both star and snowflake designs are acceptable formats for loading the AW from AWM's graphical tools, but let's stay with the star schema due to its greater simplicity.

Populating DML Objects from the Data Warehouse

You need to make a correspondence between the objects in the world of the data warehouse and objects in the AW, so that data can be moved from one to the other. These correspondences are designated by drawing lines connecting the related objects. Let's do that now and then perform the data load.

Loading the Dimension Table Data

I will illustrate the procedure using the product dimension; the other dimensions are loaded similarly. Go into Product, and expand the product icon. Click on the mappings icon at the bottom. This will cause the right-hand portion of AWM to create a display area where you can bring the visual representation of an AW object (the product dimension) next to a visual representation of the data warehouse object (the product dimension lookup table).

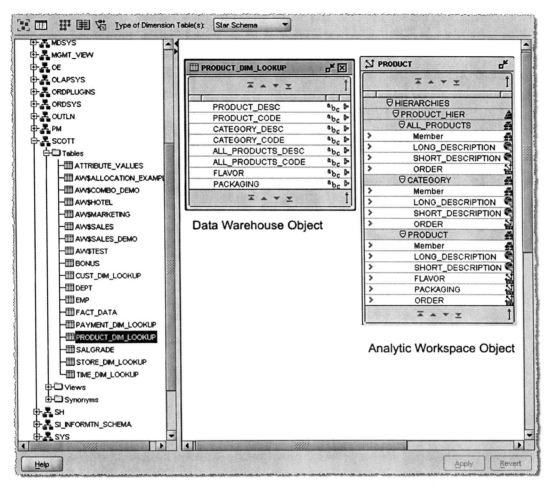

Figure 16.5. Mapping Data Warehouse Objects to AW Objects

Take a look at the Product description panel in Figure 16.5. Because the flavor and packaging attributes only apply to the very lowest level, they are only shown at that level. The order attribute applies at all levels and appears at all levels.

Now you're going to map the DML data elements onto the columns of your source tables using graphical interactions with the display. Expand and look at the tables under the SCOTT schema: that's where you'll find the product dimension look-up table. If you click that, it will appear in the window inside the other tab. Now draw the links between the corresponding elements of these two to arrive at a display like this:

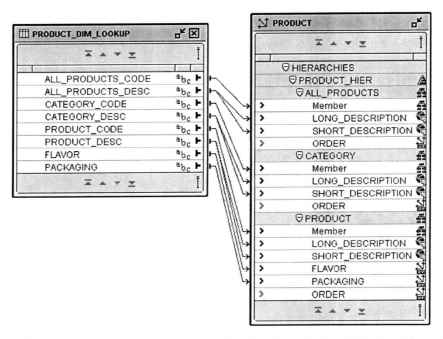

Figure 16.6. Mappings are Made by Connecting the Associated Objects with an Arrow

(In this example, data for the order attribute is not in the product dimension table; we'll enter it manually to illustrate the process of populating the data from the OLAP Worksheet.) Once you've completed all the mappings, click the apply button to commit those mappings. With the mappings established, you're ready to load the dimension members and their descriptive information from the table.

Chapter 16
The Star Schema and Beyond

To do this, right-click the dimension and select MAINTAIN DIMENSION as shown below:

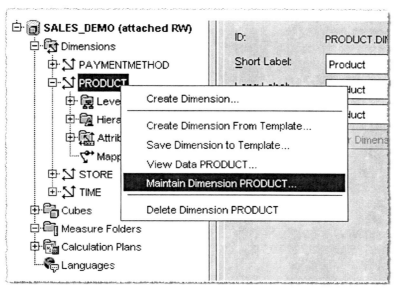

Figure 16.7. Bringing Up the Maintenance Wizard to Populate the Product Dimension

This brings up the Maintenance Wizard. You can simply click "Finish" and the data will be loaded into the dimension.

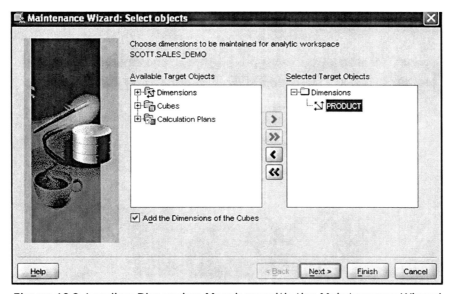

Figure 16.8. Loading Dimension Members with the Maintenance Wizard

Now let's go back to populate the order attribute. We'll enter the data manually through the OLAP Worksheet:

```
PRODUCT_ORDER(PRODUCT 'ALL_PROD') = 1
PRODUCT_ORDER(PRODUCT 'CTP') = 2
PRODUCT_ORDER(PRODUCT 'CMW') = 7
PRODUCT_ORDER(PRODUCT 'CDC') = 15
PRODUCT_ORDER(PRODUCT 'CBF') = 11
PRODUCT_ORDER(PRODUCT 'MW001') = 8
PRODUCT_ORDER(PRODUCT 'MW003') = 10
PRODUCT_ORDER(PRODUCT 'DC002') = 17
PRODUCT_ORDER(PRODUCT 'BF001') = 12
PRODUCT_ORDER(PRODUCT 'TP001') = 3
PRODUCT_ORDER(PRODUCT 'TP002') = 4
PRODUCT_ORDER(PRODUCT 'MW002') = 9
PRODUCT_ORDER(PRODUCT 'TP003') = 5
PRODUCT_ORDER(PRODUCT 'BF003') = 14
PRODUCT_ORDER(PRODUCT 'TP004') = 6
PRODUCT_ORDER(PRODUCT 'DC001') = 16
PRODUCT_ORDER(PRODUCT 'BF002') = 13
```

The above statements specify that you want the member ALL_PROD to be first in the display, CTP second, TP001 third, and so on. Since this is a hierarchical dimension, only certain assignments make sense. You wouldn't, for instance, put TP001 second, because then it would immediately follow the ALL_PROD value and in the hierarchy there is a parent value between them.

We now have all the information for the product dimension entered and you can right-click on the dimension, choose View Data PRODUCT, and look at that dimension.

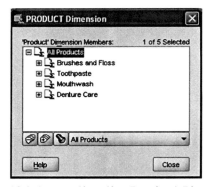

Figure 16.9. Inspecting the Product Dimension

A similar process is followed to load the other dimensions: store, payment method, and time. Once that's done, you're ready to load the data from the table.

Loading the Fact Table Data

Loading the fact data is a similar process to loading the dimensional data: map the DML data elements onto the columns of the table and do the maintain step. Click the Mappings icon under APPL_DAT, double-click on the FACT_DATA table under the SCOTT schema, and link the corresponding elements by drawing a line between as shown below.

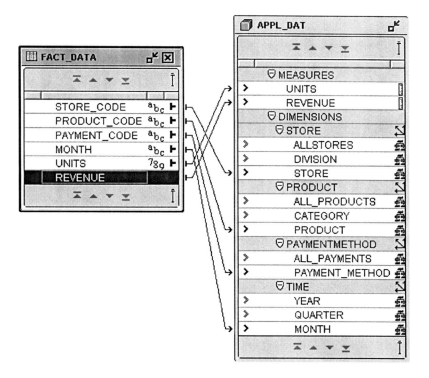

Figure 16.10. Mapping Fact Table Columns to AW Objects

Once you've established the mappings, right-click the cube and choose "Maintain Cube." This will not only load in the leaf-level data, it will also perform the aggregations.

Now you can inspect the data. Right-click the measure and choose View Data UNITS. You'll get the window where the screens from the Chapter 3 Demo Application were created. When it first comes up, it looks like Figure 16.11.

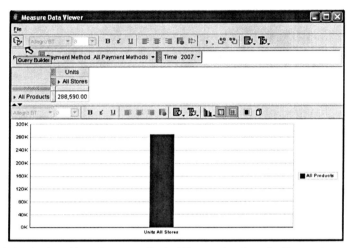

Figure 16.11. Using the Measure Data Viewer to Create Reports and Charts

In Figure 16.11, the top half of the display is for data reporting, while the bottom half is for charts. I've placed the mouse pointer over the Query Builder icon in the top left corner of the screen to cause the pop-up tip to display. In the next chapter, you'll actually click that button to cause the Query Builder (Query Wizard) to be displayed. Clicking the down arrow under "All Products" expands the report portion of the window. Expanding the store and product hierarchies one level gives us Figure 16.12.

	Units		
	All Stores	Convenience Store	Supermarket
All Products	288,590.00	118,666.00	169,924.00
Brushes and Floss	60,481.00	24,320.00	36,161.00
Denture Care	47,615.00	19,450.00	28,165.00
Mouthwash	66,412.00	28,015.00	38,397.00
Toothpaste	114,082.00	46,881.00	67,201.00

Figure 16.12. Basic Report of the Four Dimensional Units Measure

Dragging the handle on the store tile and moving it over the products area causes it to turn colors, like that shown in Figure 16.13.

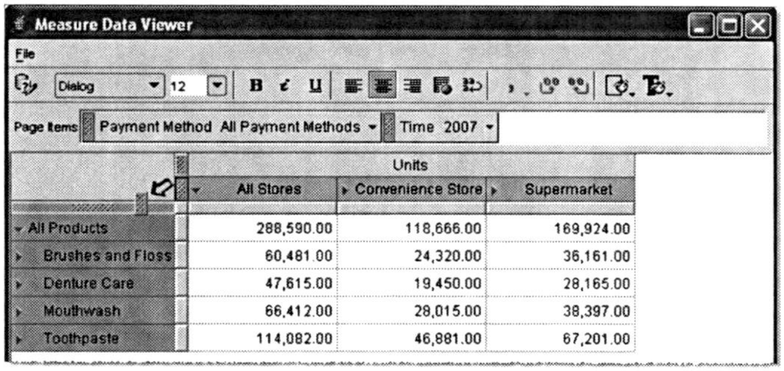

Figure 16.13. Swapping the Store and Products Dimensions

Dropping the tile gives the new report with stores going down and products across as shown in Figure 16.14.

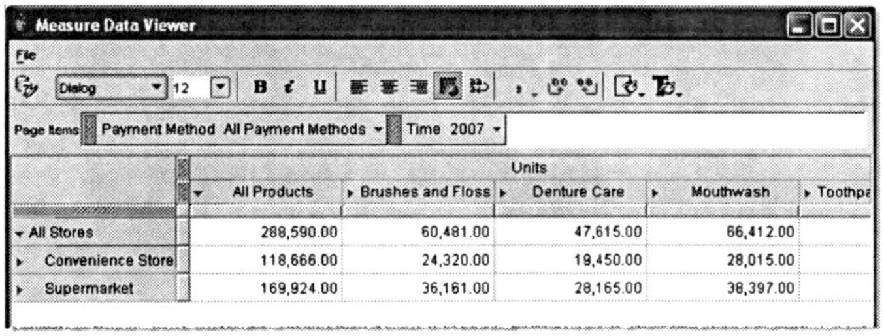

Figure 16.14. Report of Units with Store on Rows and Product on Columns

Playing with this report you can explore the many possible orientations such as the ones shown in Chapter 3: *What is the Oracle OLAP DML?*

The bottom half of the Measure Data Viewer can be used to produce graphical presentations of the data. There are numerous graph types available and many configuration options. Figure 16.15 and Figure 16.16 show two examples.

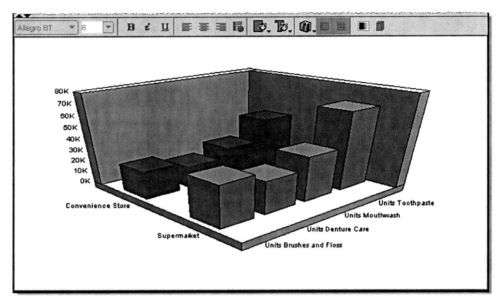

Figure 16.15. 3D Bar Graph

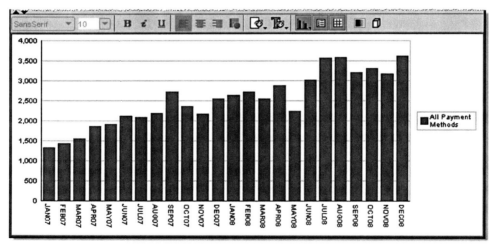

Figure 16.16. Trend Display

The Classic Business Intelligence Application

The basic strategies for hosting data within a relational data warehouse environment have names attached to them. We've seen star schema, snowflake schema, and constellation schema. What about the designs within a multidimensional environment?

Although designs in the AW aren't usually named, I'd like to give a name to the design we have just worked with. The Demo Application we just created is an example of what I will call the Classic Business Intelligence Application (CBIA).

CBIA refers to an OLAP application with the following characteristics:

- One or more multidimensional measures are included.

- Each measure is loaded at the leaf level from a data source, normally a relational data warehouse. The values of the leaf level represent the intensity of some process. For example, the values may be the number of units of product sold or the dollars of revenue collected.

- For any dimension that has hierarchies defined, aggregate values are computed either as part of a build process or at display time.

- There are attributes defined (optionally) for any of the dimensions.

- Formulas can be used to render the data; they may perform on-the-fly aggregations or other calculations such as percents, ratios, or indexed values.

CBIA is what the graphical interface we just used builds for you. I think it's useful to name this process, because it makes it easier to talk about designs that are not CBIA—and that's where things get interesting.

Analytic Workspace as Information Foundry

One of the greatest value-adds of the OLAP calculation engine is that it can be used to create derived measures. A derived measure is a new measure created by manipulating more basic data. In simple cases, you can create a new measure by applying a simple transformation of an existing measure via a formula. A number of examples of this were shown in Chapter 11: *Calculating Data On-the-Fly.*

More involved derived measures warrant precalculation or may be complex enough that they require a program to compute them. In this section, we'll take a look at a few processes for creating derived measures that will be familiar from your prior work. In Chapter 21: *Design Principles for Creating Multidimensional Information* and Chapter 22: *Migrations: Tracking Changes in Customer Choices,* I will show some more sophisticated examples.

Breaking Out Data by Related Dimensions

In the Demo Application, the units measure was populated with data broken out by product, store, payment method, and time. Such a measure satisfies many analysis requirements. But now suppose you need to investigate how sales vary as a function of product flavor and geography (and for good measure, let's say you don't care about payment method). How do you do that?

You create a measure based on data broken out by flavor, geography, and time. You will populate this variable using the information contained in the units variable and the attributes that map products to their flavor and stores to their location (zip code, for example).

Defining a variable to hold this data is straightforward:
```
DEFINE UNITS2 VARIABLE DECIMAL <FLAVOR GEOGRAPHY TIME>
```

The trick is how to populate this variable with data. This is just the "aggregating by attribute" process described in Chapter 14: *Aggregation.*

Note that you're creating one data element entirely on the basis of another one within the AW; you didn't access the data warehouse to do it.

Behavior-Based Attributes

Let's suppose a manufacturer has an incentive program for stores based on sales performance for selected products over time. There are multiple qualification levels. Membership into those qualification levels is defined by a set of rules provided to the stores. The manufacturer wants to track numbers of stores qualifying at the various levels as a function of time and geography.

Assume that the manufacturer can determine satisfaction of the incentive program criteria on the basis of the information contained in the UNITS measure. How would you create a measure that provides such information? You'd create a variable dimensioned by a qualification level dimension, geography, and time. Next a DML program is written that applies the business rules to the units data and determines the standing of each store for each month (i.e., it populates a two-dimensional attribute mapping store and time to qualification level). An aggregation program is then used to populate the data variable created.

DIMENSION PROFILER

You want a display that shows a count of products in the system, broken out by flavor and packaging type. From the dimensional information that was loaded, this profile information can be calculated using the approach like the one illustrated in Chapter 7: *Categorizing Dimension Members with Attributes.*

These measures clearly fall outside of the CBIA framework. They are calculated within the AW from existing data found there. They are not loaded from an external data source and there is no explicit representation of them within the data warehouse. They often have a different dimensionality from the data from which they were calculated. They may employ dimensions that no "CBIA measure" uses.

OLAP by Bill Blass

The examples above illustrate the information foundry concept. The idea is this: business fundamentals are loaded into the system and then additional information is obtained from them. Tailored from innovative combinations of the source information, the new metrics address specific business concerns in direct and compelling ways. These are likely to be more complicated transformations than can be performed by appending a formula to the end of one of the base measures. Think of them as "designer measures" created to address unique aspects of the application area.

OLAPistas Attend the Multidimensional Data Modeling Show

Making Data Visible in the GUI

One final step: you usually need to make the derived measures visible to the GUI (though if it's part of a "one-off" study being conducted in the back end, it may not be desired). To accomplish this, first determine if any of its dimensions are not already represented in the metadata. (For example, you may need to represent the FLAVOR dimension.) For any such dimension, create a dimension lookup table in the format described above and load it in to the system using the process illustrated. Next, create a cube that has the desired dimensionality. Now create a measure to represent your derived measure.

As we saw in the last chapter, this results in a default definition. For example:
```
DEFINE DERIVED1_UNITS2 FORMULA NUMBER <FLAVOR GEOGRAPHY -
TIME>
EQ this_aw!DERIVED1_PRT_TOPFRML(this_aw!DERIVED1_PRT_ -
MEASDIM 'UNITS2')
```

Finally, replace the EQ of the formula so that it displays your derived data.
```
CONSIDER DERIVED1_UNITS2
EQ UNITS_2
```

17 | Selectors

A selector is the graphical user interface that is used to select the dimension members that define the rows, columns, and pages of a report. The applications that are capable of creating reports from Oracle OLAP data—OracleBI Discoverer Plus for OLAP, OracleBI Spreadsheet Add-In, and Oracle BI Beans all use the interface that we will explore in this chapter.

For Oracle OLAP, a selector is the translation of the LIMIT command into GUI elements. In this chapter, we are going to explore the Query Wizard that comes with Oracle OLAP. The Query Wizard takes care of all the steps needed to define a report: selecting measures, assigning breakout dimensions to display edges, as well as selecting and ordering dimension members. I am using the term "selector" in an informal sense to refer to the portion of the Query Wizard that is responsible for doing dimension member selections.

You won't see its every nuance, but you will see the basics of how to use the Query Wizard. You will see how the LIMIT command's options you are familiar with translate into graphical elements, and your knowledge of the LIMIT command will undoubtedly make the Query Wizard easier to understand!

Now, bring up the Query Wizard. Right-click a measure from the "Measures" folder. Choose view data to get a multidimensional report of the data. In the upper left hand corner of that report you will find the icon for the Query Builder. Click on it and the Query Wizard will appear as shown in Figure 17.1.

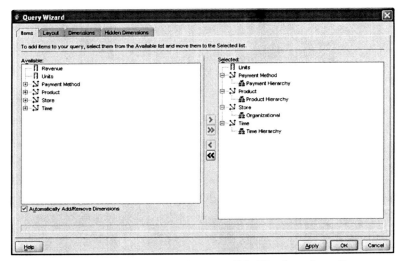

Figure 17.1. Query Wizard: Items Tab Displayed on Open

In Figure 17.1 you see four tabs: Items, Layout, Dimensions, and Hidden Dimensions. These tabs are generally worked in just this order. Click on Units (which highlights it) then click the button with the right-hand arrow to move it over to the right-hand pane. In the right-hand pane, you see an icon representing the Units measure—its four breakout dimensions are beneath it. Units is the only measure that will be shown in the report. You are ready for the next step.

Click on the Layout tab (see Figure 17.2). This tab is where you specify how the dimensions will be oriented in the report that will be generated: which dimensions will be along the row edge, which along the column edge, and which will be in the page edge. The display shows the data breakout dimensions, as well as the Measure dimension that is created automatically when the metadata is built.

Each dimension is represented by a pane. The panes are dragged and dropped to get the desired orientation for the report. In Figure 17.2, Payment Method and Time have been positioned as page items, Product defines the rows, and Measure and Store define the columns.

Chapter 17 | **231**
Selectors

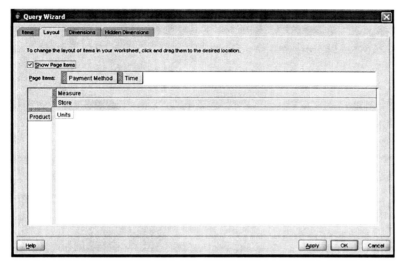

Figure 17.2. Query Wizard: Layout Tab (Layout Manager)

This sets the orientation of the report. Now, click the "Dimensions" tab. This is where you will access the dimension member selector, shown in Figure 17.3 (to expedite the discussion, I have labeled several of the elements in the figure).

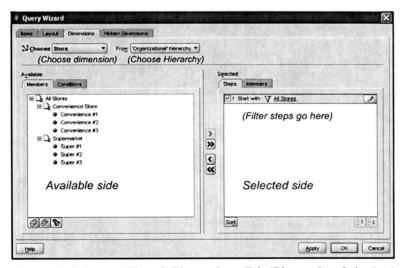

Figure 17.3. Query Wizard: Dimensions Tab (Dimension Selector)

Notice that this panel is a little more complex than the others. It is divided into two halves: an "Available" side and a "Selected" side. Each of these sides has its own tabs: the "Available" side has "Members" and "Conditions"; the "Selected" side has "Steps" and "Members."

There are two listboxes near the top: one for selecting a dimension and one for choosing a hierarchy for the selected dimension.

You can specify as many filter steps as you choose; each step creates a line in the "Selected" side to document the list of filtering steps. Figure 17.3 shows one step, documented with the line "Start with All Stores." You can click the Members tab if you want to run the filter steps and see what the results are.

There are two basic ways of making selections. Either select from the hierarchical display (being shown in the "Available" side of Figure 17.3) or use one of the filtering tools that are accessed by clicking the "Conditions" tab. You will explore some of the filtering tools later.

Let's explore the two listboxes near the top of the panel. Click on the listbox following the word "Choose" to get a list of dimensions.

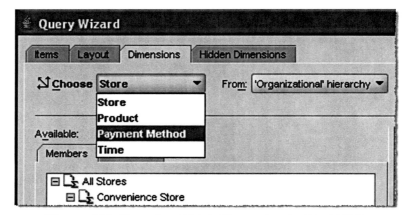

Figure 17.4. Choosing Which Dimension to Work With

Clicking on a dimension selects it. Payment Method is highlighted in Figure 17.4, but let's stay with the Store dimension.

The listbox on the right will be populated with the hierarchies that go with the selected dimension. Click on it to see the hierarchies.

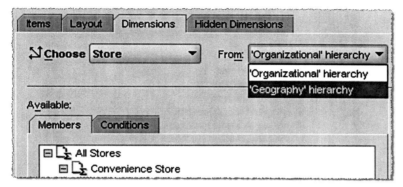

Figure 17.5. Choosing Which Hierarchy to Work With

The available side of Figure 17.3 has been displaying the Organizational hierarchy. You could switch over to the Geography hierarchy by selecting it. You would, in effect, be doing this:

```
LIMIT STORE_HIERLIST TO 'GEO_HIER'
```

Now, click the "Conditions" tab to gain access to the filtering tools as shown in Figure 17.6. The tools are grouped into functional groupings. The first two tool groupings: Exception and Top/Bottom, both provide data value-based filtering tools. Each specific tool is presented as series of templates initialized with sample values that can be changed to match your requirements.

Let's take a look at a few.

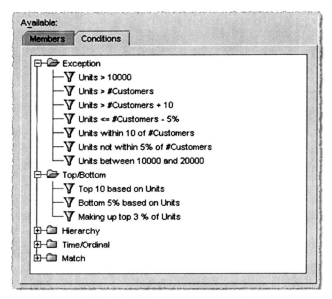

Figure 17.6. Filtering Tools

You will recognize the first template, Units>10000, as the LIMIT command:
```
LIMIT STORE TO UNITS GT 10000
```

Recall from Chapter 10: *Storing Data in Analytic Workspaces* that if you want to do a value filter on a four-dimensional variable, you will need to limit three dimensions to a single value; the other dimension is the one that will be searched. Then the single limit statement for the store dimension is not really a complete specification. The complete specification would look like this:

```
LIMIT PRODUCT TO 'ALL_PRODUCTS'
LIMIT PAYMENT_METHOD TO 'ALL_METHODS'
LIMIT TIME TO '2007'
LIMIT STORE TO UNITS GT 10000
```

Where are these first three limit statements represented? How would you change their values?

When you click on a filtering choice, the "Edit Step" dialog box appears as shown in Figure 17.7.

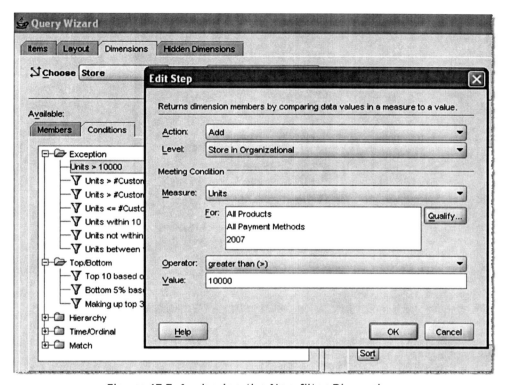

Figure 17.7. Anchoring the Non-filter Dimensions

The selected values for the other three dimensions are displayed in the "Measure"/"For" box. They can be changed by clicking "Qualify." You select the limit type (ADD, KEEP, REMOVE) from the "Action" listbox. You can also change the operator and threshold value.

Now move to the next tool group. Beneath the "Exception" and "Top/Bottom" group of tools, are the "Hierarchy" tools where selections based on the parent and level relations are made. Expanding the "Hierarchy" icon you see Figure 17.8.

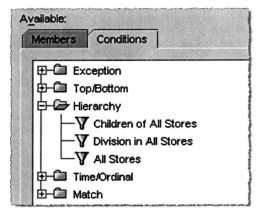

Figure 17.8. Hierarchy Selection Tools

You recognize "Children of All Stores" as being:
```
LIMIT STORE TO 'ALL'
LIMIT STORE TO CHILDREN USING STORE_PARENTREL
```

And "Division in All Stores" as:
```
LIMIT STORE TO STORE_LEVELREL 'DIVISION'
```

By clicking on the templates you get choices related to hierarchical selection as shown in Figure 17.9:

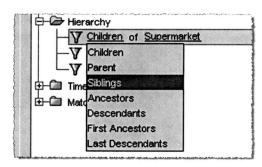

Figure 17.9. Setting Parameters for Hierarchical Selections

At the bottom you see the "Match" tools. If you open them up you see a display like the one shown in Figure 17.10.

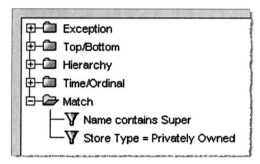

Figure 17.10. Selecting Based on Attributes and Descriptions

The criterion, "Name contains Super," is equivalent to the DML limit:
```
LIMIT STORE TO FINDCHARS(STORE_LONG_DESCRIPTION 'Super') -
GT 0
```

And "Store Type = Privately Owned" is equivalent to:
```
LIMIT STORE TO STORE_TYPE 'Privately Owned'
```

The Match tool takes care of selections based on both labels and attributes.

Click on the underscored items to get choices. For instance, if you click on "Store Type = Privately Owned" you will see Figure 17.11.

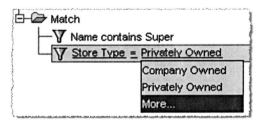

Figure 17.11. Setting Parameters for Attribute Selection

This has been a whirlwind introduction to using the selection capabilities of the Query Wizard. You can experiment with the Query Wizard or refer to the documentation to explore all of the choices.

Part V:
OLAP DML Programming

18 | Writing DML Programs

You have already seen so many of the OLAP DML elements that you are just a few short steps away from being able to write powerful programs. Let me start by making a few general observations about the language.

The DML includes all the standard control flow elements familiar to anyone with experience in a structured programming language. Elements such as FOR loops, WHILE statements, procedural blocks, GOTO statements, and so on are all there. Although you can define properties for most objects, the DML is not an object-oriented language.

All of the commands and functions you have seen—the LIMIT and MAINTAIN commands, the OBJ and STATLEN functions, REPORT and SHOW, DEFINE and DELETE—are all part of the programming language. The variables and other objects you have created have global scope. In this chapter, you will see how to create variables of local scope.

Finally, like most programming languages, programs can return a value or not. Recursive programs and formulas are permitted.

The Reasons for Writing Programs

Before you write your first program, I'd like to point out the most common reasons for writing programs to support business intelligence applications: loading data, building data, exporting data, diagnostics and testing, and measure "getter" programs.

- **LOADING DATA**—The process of bringing data from one repository into another. This usually means taking data from a flat file or relational table and bringing it into the AW.

- **BUILDING DATA**—This refers to the process of calculating data. It includes performing aggregations and populating derived quantities.

- **EXPORTING DATA**—Sometimes it is necessary to have a flat file of data exported. There are occasions where the customer wants large data files with many thousands of lines or volumes of data that are not practical to be displayed through a GUI window. Also, you may want to export the contents of the AW as a backup.

- **DIAGNOSTICS AND TESTING**—There may be a need to write diagnostic programs to help verify the correctness of a procedure. You may need a program to generate and evaluate a large number of test cases or collect performance measurements of load or build times.

- **MEASURE "GETTER" PROGRAMS**—When a user accesses data through a GUI front end, they are accessing data through a formula. The formula may have an "EQ" that is one of the default definitions generated by the system, such as the ones shown in Chapter 16: *The Star Schema and Beyond* or some other expression, like the ones from Chapter 11: *Calculating Data On-the-Fly*. For complex calculations, you can set the EQ property of a formula to a program. When the formula is evaluated, the program will be run. This makes it possible to respond at any level of complexity.

Creating a DML Program

To learn the process of writing programs, we'll use a series of examples.

PROGRAM 1: A SIMPLE AGGREGATION PROGRAM

Let's write a program to aggregate a variable over its various dimensions. The first step in writing a program is to create the program object itself.

```
DEFINE AGGREGATE_CUST_REV PROGRAM
```

This gives us an empty program shell. To enter statements into it, type:
```
EDIT AGGREGATE_CUST_REV
```

Chapter 18
Writing DML Programs

Now a window pops up into which you can enter program statements. Once the program has been entered, choose FILE | SAVE from the program window to save the statements entered.

In this example, we will enter a simple program that aggregates the CUST_REV variable and updates the AW. It prints a message at the end giving the number of seconds the program took to run. The program is shown in Figure 18.1.

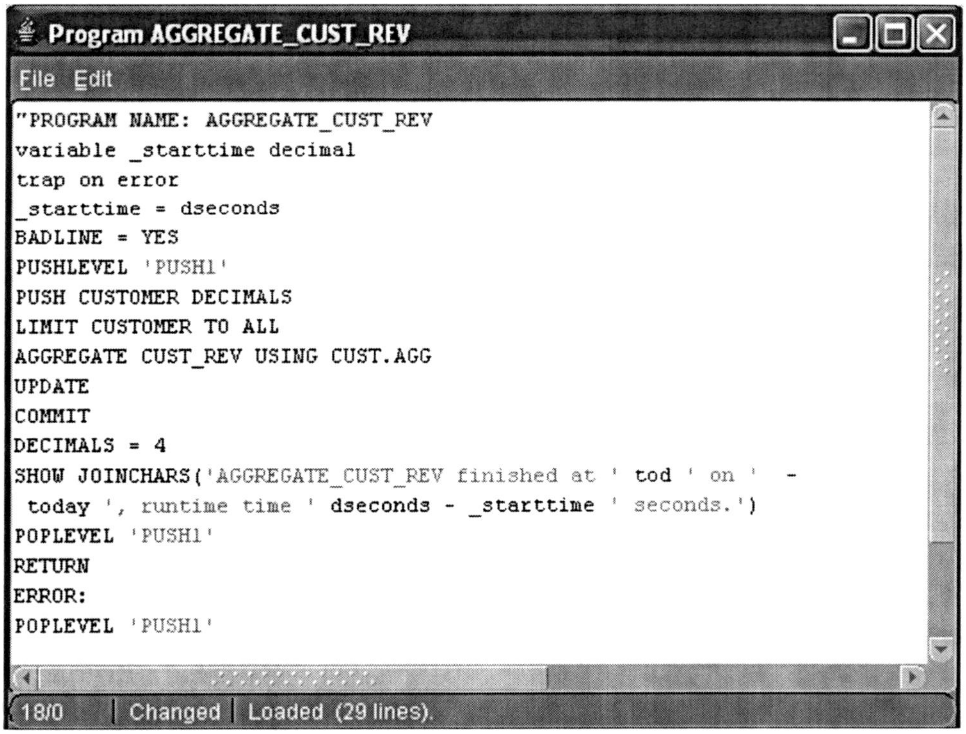

```
"PROGRAM NAME: AGGREGATE_CUST_REV
variable _starttime decimal
trap on error
_starttime = dseconds
BADLINE = YES
PUSHLEVEL 'PUSH1'
PUSH CUSTOMER DECIMALS
LIMIT CUSTOMER TO ALL
AGGREGATE CUST_REV USING CUST.AGG
UPDATE
COMMIT
DECIMALS = 4
SHOW JOINCHARS('AGGREGATE_CUST_REV finished at ' tod ' on ' -
 today ', runtime time ' dseconds - _starttime ' seconds.')
POPLEVEL 'PUSH1'
RETURN
ERROR:
POPLEVEL 'PUSH1'
```

Figure 18.1. Edit Window

I'll explain each statement in order, starting at the top.

The first line starts with a quotation marks; this means the line is a comment and will not be executed.

The variable statement creates a scalar, decimal-valued variable. This is a local variable that will be known inside the program only and will exist only while it is running. Before going on to the next program statement, let me make a few comments about local variables.

First, note the difference in syntax between defining a local variable and a global DML variable. A local variable is defined like this:

VARIABLE _STARTTIME DECIMAL

A global DML variable is defined like this:
DEFINE STARTTIME VARIABLE DECIMAL

Second, local variables may be at most 16 characters in length, whereas global variables may be up to 64 characters in length. Also, local variables can start with an underscore, but global variables cannot. Some programmers always start the name of local variables with an underscore to make it easy to identify local versus global variables. Local variables are always scalars; they cannot be dimensioned!

Third, the VARIABLE statement can only be used inside a program, whereas DEFINE can be used inside or outside a program. On to the next program statement.

In the next statement, the value of DSECONDS is copied into the local variable, _starttime. The DSECONDS option returns the number of seconds since Oracle Corporation was founded. Near the end of the program, the program accesses the value of DSECONDS a second time and subtracts it from _STARTTIME. This gives the elapsed time for the program run.

The PUSHLEVEL statement is used to name a series of push statements. In this program, we push the CUSTOMER dimension and the DECIMALS option because we are going to change their status, then restore it at the end of the program. It is normally good programming practice to restore the status of any dimension changed to its original value (unless the purpose of the program is to set status).

Now the customer dimension is limited to ALL and the aggregation is performed. The results are committed with the UPDATE and COMMIT commands and are ready to be displayed.

A SHOW command is used to print a message; then the program returns. If the program encounters a run-time error, it will go to the line labeled "ERROR:". You can see the use of the hyphen as a continuation character in the SHOW command.

Run the program by typing its name in the OLAP Worksheet and pressing enter:
```
->AGGREGATE_CUST_REV
AGGREGATE_CUST_REV finished at 14:02:58 on 05AUG08, runtime
time 0.1250 seconds.
```

Program 2: Meta-business Intelligence

In a production environment where large data loads and build sequences are conducted on a regular schedule under demanding circumstances (huge amounts of data!), it is important to be able to see, monitor, and understand the factors that influence run times.

Load or build processes are typically run on a periodic basis (every week, every month, etc.). They are run with varying amounts of data or under varying load conditions. In this next example, we will enhance Program 1 to store timing information in DML objects. This way, the run-time information of the aggregation program can be analyzed using the DML's analytical capabilities.

Thus, in this example we will be "taking our own medicine" so to speak, by embedding what could be called a "meta-business intelligence application" that uses the analytical capabilities of the DML to analyze its own operations.

I won't go into great depth with the meta-application, but I will lay the groundwork, showing how basic run-time metrics can be captured and set up for analysis. With your knowledge of dimensional analysis, you should be able to envision how a more comprehensive application for analyzing run times could be created.

To begin with, you need to define the objects that will store the timing information.

Create a dimension to identify each run of the program:
```
DEFINE RUN_ID DIMENSION INTEGER
```

Create a time dimension that will be used to specify the date it was run:
```
DEFINE D.RUN_DATE DATE
```

Create a relation that maps each run ID to its run date:
```
DEFINE R.RUN_DATE RELATION D.RUN_DATE <RUN_ID>
```

Create other variables that will be used to record other information about the run:
```
DEFINE TIME_OF_RUN VARIABLE TEXT <RUN_ID>
DEFINE RUN_DSECONDS VARIABLE DECIMAL <RUN_ID>
DEFINE EXECUTE_TIME VARIABLE DECIMAL <RUN_ID>
```

Now let's enhance Program 1 to capture this new information. The enhanced program will capture that information in these DML objects so that it can be analyzed more systematically.

Take a look at the following program; the discussion will be in the coding comments.

```
"PROGRAM NAME: AGGREGATE_CUST_REV2
variable _starttime decimal
trap on error
_starttime = dseconds
PUSH CUSTOMER
MAINTAIN D.RUN_DATE MERGE TODAY

"Find the first RUN_ID value with no data:
LIMIT RUN_ID TO R.RUN_DATE EQ NA
LIMIT RUN_ID KEEP FIRST 1

"Populate the data for this run:
R.RUN_DATE = TODAY
TIME_OF_RUN = TOD
RUN_DSECONDS = DSECONDS

"Perform the aggregation:
LIMIT CUSTOMER TO ALL
AGGREGATE CUST_REV USING CUST.AGG

"Save the results:
UPDATE
COMMIT

"Compute and store the elapsed time for running the program:
EXECUTE_TIME = dseconds - _starttime
POPLEVEL CUSTOMER
RETURN
ERROR:
POPLEVEL CUSTOMER
SHOW 'RUN NOT SUCCESSFUL'
RETURN
DECIMALS = 4
LIMIT RUN_ID TO R.RUN_DATE NE NA
RPR R.RUN_DATE TIME_OF_RUN W 12 RUN_DSECONDS W 12 -
EXECUTE_TIME
```

Here are some performance metrics:

```
RUN_ID     R.RUN_DATE  TIME_OF_RUN  RUN_DSECONDS  EXECUTE_TIME
---------- ----------- ------------ ------------- ------------
         1    30JUL08     13:46:45  145,830.7030        0.1090
         2    30JUL08     13:46:48  145,834.2180        0.0780
         3    30JUL08     13:46:51  145,836.8280        0.0780
         4    30JUL08     13:47:41  145,886.9530        0.0930
         5    30JUL08     13:48:24  145,930.2340        0.0940
         6    30JUL08     13:48:37  145,942.9530        0.0940
```

You know how to use data like this to compute simple metrics. For example, suppose this program is run several times a day, on a daily basis. A time trend showing average run times could be generated with commands like:

```
LIMIT RUN_ID TO RUN_DATE '30JUL08'
REPORT AVERAGE(EXECUTION_TIME, RUN_DATE)
```

There are many ways to extend the analysis. If you were dealing with a complex load/build process that encompassed many DML programs, you could create a "program dimension" and break out total run times by program. You could look at execution times as a function of both program and date of the run. You might want to organize such a program dimension into a hierarchy. The top "ALL" level would be used to represent all programs of the load/build process. A category level could be created having the values LOAD and BUILD. Leaf-level values would represent an individual program.

I have seen development groups struggling to get user acceptance of a new OLAP tool with the users not wanting to work outside of Excel. In a back room, the same development group can be seen using Excel to analyze their production statistics. Using OLAP to analyze production performance not only gives a more powerful platform, it helps to develop a better understanding of the end-user's mindset and challenges.

PROGRAM 3: THE ACCUMULATION PROGRAM

At the end of Chapter 14: *Aggregation* we discussed the idea of accumulations. This operation is used in situations where the application data consists of dimension members (rather than numbers). In such applications, the data associated with the non-leaf-level nodes are computed by set unions rather than aggregations.

Accumulations were illustrated in Chapter 14 using a hierarchical promotion dimension. In that illustration, the base application data was comprised of the customers who were members of the given loyalty program or who received a given sales offer. These customers constitute the information associated with leaf-level nodes of the promotion dimension.

In this example, I will show a program that determines which customers belong to the aggregate nodes of the promotion hierarchy. The data will be stored in a valueset that is dimensioned by promotion. The program will climb up the promotion hierarchy, starting at the level above leaf. It populates the data for each node by taking the union (i.e., LIMIT ADD) of its children.

In Chapter 14, the following objects were created:
```
DEFINE PROMOTION DIMENSION TEXT
DEFINE PROMOTION_PARENTREL RELATION PROMOTION <PROMOTION>
DEFINE PROMO_CUSTS VALUESET CUSTOMER <PROMOTION>
```

The valueset PROMO_CUSTS was populated manually at the end of Chapter 14. The program below populates this valueset for the non-leaf-level values of PROMOTION by doing set unions.

The program comments explain the logic.
```
"PROGRAM NAME: PROMO_CUSTS.AGGPROG
"How it works: This program will populate PROMO_CUSTS
"one level at a time. Leaf level is assumed populated. This
"program will start with the first level above leaf level.
"We will need a local variable that will be used to hold the
"value of the promotion being worked on.
VARIABLE _CURRENT_PROMO TEXT

"Here, set the levels that will be processed.
LIMIT PROMOTION_LEVELLIST TO 2 1

"For each of those levels, find the nodes represented and
"ADD (= set union) the sets of children to the valueset.
FOR PROMOTION_LEVELLIST
```

```
DO
  LIMIT PROMOTION TO PROMOTION_LEVELLIST
  FOR PROMOTION
  DO
    _CURRENT_PROMO = PROMOTION
    TEMPSTAT PROMOTION
    DO
      LIMIT PROMOTION TO CHILDREN
      FOR PROMOTION
      LIMIT PROMO_CUSTS(PROMOTION _CURRENT_PROMO) ADD -
      PROMO_CUSTS
    DOEND
  DOEND
DOEND
RETURN
```

Run the program to do the accumulations:
```
PROMO_CUSTS.AGGPROG
```

The program produces no output. You can do report statements to see the results. The following report, for example, shows how many customers are associated with each member of the PROMOTION dimension.

```
->RPR HEADING '#CUSTOMERS' STATLEN(PROMO_CUSTS)

PROMOTION         #CUSTOMERS
--------------    ----------
ALL_PROMOS              14
LOYALTY_PRG              7
OFFERS                  11
LP_A                     5
LP_B                     4
OF_A                     4
OF_B                     5
OF_C                     6
```

To identify the customers themselves, limit CUSTOMER to the contents of the valueset. For instance, to set the status of CUSTOMER to the customers that received any offer, you would do this:

```
LIMIT PROMOTION TO 'OFFERS'
LIMIT CUSTOMER TO PROMO_CUSTS
```

PROGRAM 4: POPULATING THE RELATIVE TIME VARIABLE

In Chapter 11: *Calculating Data On-the-Fly*, I gave an example of a formula enabling the use of "relative time." Relative time selections are values like "Current Month" or "Two Months Ago." Exactly which months are being referred to depends on when (i.e., the date) the formula is evaluated. As you saw, the formula used a variable that maps relative times into absolute times. At the beginning of each month, as part of the system administration, the mappings must be re-established since "Current Month" now points to something different.

In this example, I show a program that populates the mappings from relative to absolute time.

Here's the formula from Chapter 11:
```
DEFINE F1.REVENUE FORMULA DECIMAL <CUSTOMER PRODUCT TIME>
EQ REVENUE(TIME ABSOLUTE_TIME)
```

The EQ translates the relative time into an absolute time using a variable called ABSOLUTE_TIME. This variable is defined as:

```
DEFINE ABSOLUTE_TIME VARIABLE TEXT <TIME>
```

Now let's say you have 13 months of relative time values:
```
MAINTAIN TIME ADD 'CURR_MONTH' 'CURR_MINUS_01' -
'CURR_ MINUS_02' 'CURR_MINUS_03' 'CURR_MINUS_04' -
'CURR_MINUS_05' 'CURR_MINUS_06' 'CURR_MINUS_07' -
'CURR_MINUS_08' 'CURR_MINUS_09' 'CURR_MINUS_10' -
'CURR_MINUS_11' 'CURR_MINUS_12'
```

Create an order attribute that tells the system what order these values belong in:
```
DEFINE REL_TIME_ORDER VARIABLE INTEGER <TIME>
```

Populate the order attribute with statements like this:
```
REL_TIME_ORDER(TIME 'CURR_MONTH')    = 1
REL_TIME_ORDER(TIME 'CURR_MINUS_01') = 2
REL_TIME_ORDER(TIME 'CURR_MINUS_02') = 3
REL_TIME_ORDER(TIME 'CURR_MINUS_03') = 4
```

The following program populates the ABSOLUTE_TIME variable. It uses the ADD_MONTHS function, which returns the date that is N months after the specified date.

```
"PROGRAM NAME: RELATIVE_TIME.POP
"Populate for relative time values
LIMIT TIME TO 'CURR_MONTH' TO 'CURR_MINUS_12'
FOR TIME
ABSOLUTE_TIME = JOINCHARS(EXTCHARS(ADD_MONTHS(TODAY, -
REL_TIME_ORDER + 1), 4 3) EXTCHARS(ADD_MONTHS(TODAY, -
REL_TIME_ORDER + 1), 8 2))

"Populate for absolute time values
LIMIT TIME COMPLEMENT
ABSOLUTE_TIME = TIME
RETURN
```

After running the program, the absolute time values are mapped to themselves and the relative time values are mapped to the appropriate values.

```
->LIMIT TIME TO 'CURR_MONTH' TO 'CURR_MINUS_12'
->REPORT HEADING 'ABSOLUTE' ABSOLUTE_TIME
TIME              ABSOLUTE
--------------    ----------
CURR_MONTH        NOV08
CURR_MINUS_01     OCT08
CURR_MINUS_02     SEP08
CURR_MINUS_03     AUG08
CURR_MINUS_04     JUL08
CURR_MINUS_05     JUN08
CURR_MINUS_06     MAY08
CURR_MINUS_07     APR08
CURR_MINUS_08     MAR08
CURR_MINUS_09     FEB08
CURR_MINUS_10     JAN08
CURR_MINUS_11     DEC07
CURR_MINUS_12     NOV07
```

PROGRAM 5: CREATING RANDOM SAMPLES

A random sample is a subset of dimension members in which every member has an equal chance of being selected. Random samples can be useful both for software testing and for testing a business process. In the case of software testing, random samples can be used to generate a set of test cases that can be run, then compared with hand calculations to verify correctness. In business processes, they can be used to create treatment and control groups.

It is easy to generate random selections of dimension members using the DML. Suppose, for example, you want to generate a random sample of customers from a CUSTOMER dimension. The basic process is this:

- Create a decimal variable dimensioned by CUSTOMER.
- Populate the variable with random numbers using the RANDOM function.
- Choose the top N based on the value of the variable (bottom N would work as well).

Below you will see a program that creates a random sample of customers and stores them in a valueset. Define the objects you need per the process outlined above:

```
DEFINE RAND_SAMPLE_CUSTS VALUESET CUSTOMER
DEFINE RAND_NUMS VARIABLE DECIMAL <CUSTOMER>
```

Since CUSTOMER is a hierarchical dimension, you will want to select from leaf-level values to get a random sample of CUSTOMER dimension values that represents actual customers.

Let's describe a program that generates a random sample of five customers and populates RAND_SAMPLE_CUSTS with them.

```
DEFINE PROGRAM RAND_SAMPLE_CUSTS.POP
"PROGRAM NAME: RAND_SAMPLE_CUSTS.POP
LIMIT CUSTOMER TO CUSTOMER_LEVELREL 1
RAND_NUMS = RANDOM(0,1)
LIMIT CUSTOMER KEEP TOP 5 BASEDON RAND_NUMS
LIMIT RAND_SAMPLE_CUSTS TO CUSTOMER
RETURN
```

Now, let's inspect the random sample of customers.
```
->RPR RAND_SAMPLE_CUSTS
```

```
RAND_SAMPLE_CUSTS
----------
CU012
CU006
CU009
CU016
CU007
```

PROGRAM 6: CREATING RANDOM COMBINATIONS

In some applications, you may need a random set of dimension member combinations. The program below selects a random selection of store/product/payment method/months and stores them in a valueset called VS.RANDCOMBOS.

Assume you have created these supporting objects:
```
DEFINE RANDCOMBOS COMPOSITE -
<STORE PRODUCT PAYMENTMETHOD TIME>
DEFINE RANDCOMBODATA VARIABLE DECIMAL -
<RANDCOMBOS<STORE PRODUCT PAYMENTMETHOD TIME>>
DEFINE VS.RANDCOMBOS VALUESET RANDCOMBOS
```

This program uses the CHGDFN command that you saw at the end of Chapter 12: *Filtering, Relationships, and Combinations*.

```
"PROGRAM NAME: RANDCOMBOS.POP
IF EXISTS('VS.RANDCOMBOS')
THEN DELETE VS.RANDCOMBOS
IF OBJ(TYPE 'RANDCOMBOS') EQ 'DIMENSION'
THEN CHGDFN RANDCOMBOS COMPOSITE
LIMIT PAYMENTMETHOD TO PAYMENTMETHOD_LEVELREL 1
LIMIT PRODUCT TO PRODUCT_LEVELREL 1
LIMIT STORE TO STORE_LEVELREL 1
LIMIT TIME TO TIME_LEVELREL 1
RANDCOMBODATA = RANDOM(0,1)
CHGDFN RANDCOMBOS DIMENSION
LIMIT RANDCOMBOS TO TOP 10 BASEDON RANDCOMBODATA
IF NOT EXISTS('VS.RANDCOMBOS')
THEN DEFINE VS.RANDCOMBOS VALUESET RANDCOMBOS
LIMIT VS.RANDCOMBOS TO RANDCOMBOS
RETURN
```

Now, let's run the program and inspect the output.
```
->RANDCOMBOS.POP
->RPR W 28 VS.RANDCOMBOS

VS.RANDCOMBOS
----------------------------
<FEB08, CH, BF001, SUP03>
<JUL07, CR, TP001, CNV03>
<AUG07, CH, MW002, SUP02>
<AUG08, CA, MW001, SUP01>
<JUL08, CR, TP003, SUP02>
<JUN08, DC, DC002, SUP03>
<JUL07, DC, MW003, SUP02>
<JUL07, DC, TP003, SUP03>
<OCT08, CH, TP003, CNV03>
<JUN08, CA, BF001, CNV02>
```

What Determines Program Output?

In this section, I am going to cover a number of "gotchas" that I have noticed tend to cause problems for developers who are new to the DML.

What is a program, but a set of instructions? It is a set of DML commands like the ones we have been entering into the OLAP Worksheet grouped together into a container and executed by a single instruction. The program is designed to do something and starts with something. So we could think of this as a simple input-output process represented like this:

Figure 18.2. Simple Input-Output Process

But what exactly is the input? If the purpose of a program is to compute some new data based on existing data, the input might be a variable containing that data. Or it could be a numerical value passed as an argument to the program, or even a combination of these two.

But consider the following program:
```
DEFINE DEMO_PROG PROGRAM
ARG _FRACTION DECIMAL
ARG _OFFSET DECIMAL
RETURN(_FRACTION*TOTAL(CUST_REV) + _OFFSET)
->SHOW DEMO_PROG(.9, 10)
4,471.02
```

Now observe this:
```
->LIMIT CUSTOMER TO CUSTOMER_LEVELREL 'CUST_LEV'
->SHOW DEMO_PROG(.9, 10)
753.50
```

You run the same program with the same arguments and get a different result! The reason is that output from this program depends on something outside the program: the status setting of the CUSTOMER dimension.

Here's another anomalous situation. Limit the CUSTOMER dimension to all values. Now, leave off the second argument. The value of _offset will be NA and the program returns a value that is 10 less than the original run.

```
->SHOW DEMO_PROG(.9)
4,461.02
```

Now set the value of the NASKIP2 option to No and re-run the program.
```
->NASKIP2 = NO
->SHOW DEMO_PROG(.9)
NA
```

This program also depends on the setting of the NASKIP2 option!

These examples underscore how care must be taken to control all the factors that determine the program's output. In addition to the situations just illustrated, there are situations where the attachment order of multiple AWs can affect the outcome.

Thus, a more realistic model of system behavior would be as shown in Figure 18.3.

Figure 18.3. Realistic Input-Output Process

To ensure you get the results you expect, make sure you properly manage all relevant status settings, option settings, and AW attachment order.

19 | Getting Data In and Out of Analytic Workspaces

In this chapter, you will learn how to write programs that will load in dimension members, populate variables, relations, and valuesets, and even to read in program elements that don't store data, such as formulas and aggmaps.

In Chapter 15: *Exploring Metadata,* we loaded data using AWM's GUI. Using the information entered in the various templates and setting the mappings, AWM is able to create load programs that are run when the Maintenance Wizard is run.

There are occasions when you will want to write your own programs for loading data in order to get additional flexibility. Suppose, for example, you need to load a small subset of the data to replace some bad values, or you want to load data into an object that is not user visible (and thus won't display in the AWM GUI so it can't be loaded that way), or is of an object type not handled by the graphical interface, such as valuesets and relations.

This chapter will be based on three DML commands: FILEREAD, SQL, and INFILE. In a nutshell, the FILEREAD command is used for reading from a flat file, the SQL command is used to access data stored in relational tables, and INFILE is used to read in object definitions. The product documentation covers the many options available to these programming statements; our mission here is to illustrate loading techniques.

Writing Programs to Read Data from an External Source

Using DML programs, data from any flat file or table can be loaded; they don't have to be part of a star schema or any other specific data warehouse design.

Data is normally loaded in two passes. In the first pass, dimensions are populated (effecting a MAINTAIN operation). In the second pass, objects that depend on those dimensions, such as variables, are populated (effecting assignment statements).

PROGRAM 7: MAINTAINING A DIMENSION FROM A TEXT FILE USING FILEREAD

Before reading in data from a text file, a directory alias needs to be set up so that the AW will know where to find the file. This setup must be done using SQL statements. They can be entered from a standard interface such as SQL+ or directly from the OLAP Worksheet by switching into SQL mode. Let's do the latter.

Under Options check SQL Mode:

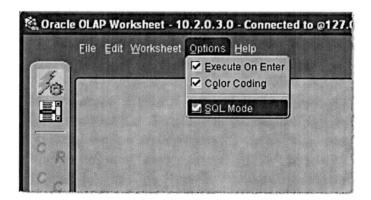

Now enter commands like these:
```
create directory OLAP_DATA as 'C:\OLAP_DATA'
grant read on directory OLAP_DATA to public
grant write on directory OLAP_DATA to public
```

That completes the set up. Switch back to DML mode by going back to Options and unchecking SQL Mode.

In this example, we are going to work with a text file named PRODUCT_DIMDATA.txt that contains the data displayed below:

```
TP001     CTP       ALL_PRODCATA
TP002     CTP       ALL_PRODCATB
TP003     CTP       ALL_PRODCATB
TP004     CTP       ALL_PRODCATC
MW001     CMW       ALL_PRODCATA
MW002     CMW       ALL_PRODCATA
MW003     CMW       ALL_PRODCATC
DC001     CDC       ALL_PRODCATC
DC002     CDC       ALL_PRODCATB
BF001     CBF       ALL_PRODCATA
BF002     CBF       ALL_PRODCATB
BF003     CBF       ALL_PRODCATC
```

This file is in a fixed field width format, three eight-character fields followed by one four-character field. The first field contains leaf-level values for PRODUCT, the second field contains its parent, the third contains its parent, and at the end is the category code for the product. This is the same data that would be contained in a dimension lookup table except the labels are missing.

Assume this file is in the c:\OLAP_DATA directory. Issue the command:
```
->CDA OLAP_DATA
The current directory is OLAP_DATA
```

You can now run the following program to read the data:
```
"PROGRAM NAME: MAINTAIN_DIM_WITH_FILEREAD
vrb FI integer
VRB _NUM_LINES INTEGER
_NUM_LINES = 0
CDA OLAP_DATA
TRAP ON ERROR
FI=FILEOPEN('PRODUCT_DIMDATA.txt', READ)
FILEREAD FI -
COL 1 WIDTH  8 APPEND PRODUCT = BLANKSTRIP(VALUE, -
TRAILING) -
COL 9 WIDTH 8 APPEND PRODUCT = BLANKSTRIP(VALUE, -
TRAILING) -
```

```
     COL 17 WIDTH 8 APPEND PRODUCT = BLANKSTRIP(VALUE, -
     TRAILING)
     _NUM_LINES = _NUM_LINES + 1
     SHOW JOINCHARS(_NUM_LINES ' lines of data read at ' tod)
     FILECLOSE FI
     RETURN
     ERROR:
     FILECLOSE FI
     RETURN
```

The first step is to open the file so that the data can be read. The FILEOPEN statement assigns a number to the file by which it will be referred to by the FILEREAD statement. The FILEREAD statement reads the data. Although logically on a single line, it usually runs over many physical lines as it does here. Thus you will note the use of continuation characters. The FILEREAD statement loops over all the lines in the file until it hits the end of the file.

It is possible to do some modifications to the input data as it is read. In this program the BLANKSTRIP function is used to remove trailing blanks. The term VALUE is a special term used to refer to what is being read.

Finally, it is possible to perform simple arithmetic operations as part of that looping process. In this program, the NUM_LINES counter is being incremented. At the end it is used to display how many lines were read.

Program 8: Populating Relations from Data in a Flat File

The last program populates PRODUCT with its dimension members. In this program, you will populate the parent-child relations and the values for the category attribute. This program loads only two objects to keep things simple; in actual application, you would probably load in the values for the labels as well in this step.

```
"PROGRAM NAME: POPULATING_RELATIONS_WITH_FLAT_FILE
vrb FI integer
VRB _NUM_LINES INTEGER
_NUM_LINES = 0
CDA OLAP_DATA
badline = yes
TRAP ON ERROR
FI=FILEOPEN('PRODUCT_DIMDATA.txt', READ)
FILEREAD FI STOPAFTER 100 -
     COL 1 WIDTH 8 PRODUCT = BLANKSTRIP(VALUE, TRAILING) -
```

```
COL 9 WIDTH 8 PRODUCT_PARENTREL = -
BLANKSTRIP(VALUE, TRAILING) -
COL 17 WIDTH 8 APPEND -
PRODUCT_PARENTREL(PRODUCT PRODUCT_PARENTREL) = -
BLANKSTRIP(VALUE, TRAILING) -
COL 25 WIDTH 4 R.PRODUCT.CATEGORY -
_NUM_LINES = _NUM_LINES + 1
SHOW JOINCHARS(_NUM_LINES ' lines of data read at ' tod)
FILECLOSE FI
RETURN
ERROR:
FILECLOSE FI
RETURN
```

From the FILEREAD statement you can see that the program first reads in a product value, then the value of its parent, then its parent's parent. Finally, it reads in the value of the product category.

Program 8 is similar to Program 7, with a few differences that are worth pointing out. For one, in Program 8 the keyword, APPEND, is absent before PRODUCT. That means it will not load dimension values, which were loaded in Program 7. Also take a look at the line populating the category relation. Since no modification of the input data is performed (for example, no BLANKSTRIP), there is no right-hand expression.

Sometimes when I'm developing a program I will include a line that says BADLINE = YES. This will cause the system to tell you which line had the problem in the event of an error.

PROGRAM 9: READING IN COMBINATIONS

In this next program you will populate a conjoint dimension. Now assume the data file is called "COMBOS.txt" and the first few lines look like this:

```
SUP02|BF003|CR|SEP08|
CNV03|TP004|CR|SEP08|
SUP03|TP004|CR|SEP08|
CNV01|TP004|CR|SEP08|
CNV02|TP004|CR|SEP08|
```

You will populate a conjoint dimension—TESTCOMBOS—based on the dimensions from the SALES_DEMO application. The definition of the dimension that will be populated is:

```
DEFINE TESTCOMBOS DIMENSION <STORE PRODUCT PAYMENTMETHOD -
TIME>
```

The following program is designed to populate TESTCOMBOS with the dimension combinations from the first 10 data lines only (note the use of the STOPAFTER keyword).

```
"PROGRAM NAME: READ_COMBINATIONS
"IN AW: SALES_DEMO
vrb FI integer
VRB _NUM_LINES INTEGER
_NUM_LINES = 0
CDA OLAP_DATA
TRAP ON ERROR
FI=FILEOPEN('COMBOS.txt', READ)
FILEREAD FI STOPAFTER 10 -
COL 1 WIDTH 5 STORE = BLANKSTRIP(VALUE, TRAILING) -
COL 7 WIDTH 5 PRODUCT = BLANKSTRIP(VALUE, TRAILING) -
COL 13 WIDTH 2 PAYMENTMETHOD = BLANKSTRIP(VALUE, TRAILING) -
COL 16 WIDTH 5 TIME = BLANKSTRIP(VALUE, TRAILING) -
APPEND TESTCOMBOS = <STORE PRODUCT PAYMENTMETHOD TIME> -
_NUM_LINES = _NUM_LINES + 1
SHOW JOINCHARS(_NUM_LINES ' lines of data read at ' tod)
FILECLOSE FI
RETURN
ERROR:
FILECLOSE FI
RETURN
```

This program requires the base dimensions—STORE, PRODUCT, PAYMENTMETHOD, and TIME—to have been populated. The only dimensional maintenance that occurs in the program is for the TESTCOMBOS dimension. That's why it is the only dimension with the word APPEND preceding it.

Program 10: Loading in Programs, Aggmaps, and TheKitchenSink

DML objects of any kind can be read in from a text file, not just dimensions and other data items. The process is simple. Create a text file with the definitions of the objects you want to load in, and then use the INFILE statement to bring in the definitions. For instance, you could create a text file called EVERYTHING.TXT containing the following lines:

Chapter 19
Getting Data In and Out of Analytic Workspaces

```
DEFINE SAMPLE_PROG PROGRAM
PROGRAM
SHOW 'HELLO WORLD'
RETURN
END
DEFINE PRODUCT.AGG AGGMAP <PRODUCT>
AGGMAP 'RELATION PRODUCT_PARENTREL'
DEFINE TheKitchenSink FORMULA TEXT
EQ TODAY
```

Once created and placed in the OLAP_DATA subdirectory, these definitions can be imported into the AW using the INFILE command:

```
INFILE 'EVERYTHING.TXT'
```

PROGRAM 11: EXPORTING DATA TO A TEXT FILE

Delivering data through a GUI as a multidimensional report is not the only way of providing data. Sometimes, large flat files of data are requested. These "reports" might have many thousands or even millions of lines of data. The next program uses the ROW command to output the data. To cause the output to go to a flat file instead of the OLAP Worksheet, use the OUTFILE command.

```
DEFINE RP PROGRAM
ARG OUTFILE_NAME TEXT
PUSH COMMAS
COMMAS = NO
"Directs the output to an external file
OUTFILE OUTFILE_NAME
FOR PRODUCT PAYMENTMETHOD TIME
ROW ACROSS STORE: APPL_DAT_UNITS
POP COMMAS
"Redirects the output to the screen
OUTFILE EOF
RETURN
```

You call the program supplying an argument that tells it the name of the file where the output should be stored:

```
CALL RP('OUTFILE.TXT')
```

PROGRAM 12: LOADING DATA FROM A RELATIONAL TABLE USING EMBEDDED SQL

Now let's see how to read data from a relational data table. To do this, you will use the embedded SQL facility. As the program below shows, the statements are completely different from the ones used to read a flat file with FILEREAD.

```
DEFINE DATALOAD PROGRAM
PROGRAM
"PROGRAM NAME: DATALOAD
"IN AW SALES_DEMO
BADLINE = YES
TRAP ON ERROR
SQL DECLARE C2 CURSOR FOR SELECT STORE_CODE, PRODUCT_CODE,-
PAYMENT_CODE, MONTH, UNITS, REVENUE FROM FACT_DATA
SQL OPEN C2
"RPR SQLERRM
SQL FETCH C2 LOOP INTO -
:STORE -
:PRODUCT -
:PAYMENTMETHOD -
:TIME -
:APPL_DAT_PRT_TOPVAR(APPL_DAT_PRT_MEASDIM 'UNITS') -
:APPL_DAT_PRT_TOPVAR(APPL_DAT_PRT_MEASDIM 'REVENUE')
SQL CLOSE C2
SQL CLEANUP
RETURN
ERROR:
SHOW 'THERE WAS AN ERROR'
RPR SQLCODE SQLERRM
RETURN
END
```

PROGRAM 13: A PROGRAM THAT WRITES A PROGRAM

This example demonstrates a powerful capability of the DML: the ability to write a program that writes a program. Programs that do this are called *code generators*. Along with ampersand substitution, code generators are a key technique for getting very flexible, dynamic behavior. That flexibility is used here to get the ability to pass in the data table name as an argument. The program, WRITESPROGRAM, below, composes the lines of another program, TEMP_PROG. The program lines are composed using the character manipulation functions JOINLINES and JOINCHARS. They are stored in a local text variable called PROGLINES

Chapter 19
Getting Data In and Out of Analytic Workspaces

that is used to set the program property of TEMP_PROG. Once that has occurred, TEMP_PROG is ready to be run. The data is read in by TEMP_PROG, not WRITESPROGRAM. So now take a look at WRITESPROGRAM:

```
"PROGRAM NAME: WRITESPROGRAM
"THIS PROGRAM CREATES THE PROGRAM LINES FOR A PROGRAM
"CALLED TEMP_PROG. THE LINES OF THIS PROGRAM ARE STORED
"IN A TEXT VARIABLE CALLED PROGLINES
ARG _DATA_SOURCE TEXT
VRB _PROG_LINES TEXT
_DATA_SOURCE = NAFILL(_DATA_SOURCE, 'FACT_DATA')
BADLINE = YES
TRAP ON ERROR
_PROG_LINES = JOINLINES('"PROGRAM NAME: TEMP_PROG' -
JOINCHARS('SQL DECLARE C2 CURSOR FOR SELECT STORE_CODE, -
PRODUCT_CODE, PAYMENT_CODE, MONTH, UNITS, REVENUE FROM '-
_DATA_SOURCE) -
'SQL OPEN C2' -
' ' -
'SQL FETCH C2 LOOP INTO -' -
':STORE -' -
':PRODUCT -' -
':PAYMENTMETHOD -' -
':TIME -' -
':APPL_DAT_PRT_TOPVAR(APPL_DAT_PRT_MEASDIM \'UNITS\') -' -
':APPL_DAT_PRT_TOPVAR(APPL_DAT_PRT_MEASDIM \'REVENUE\') ' -
'SQL CLOSE C2' -
'SQL CLEANUP' -
'RETURN')
"_PROG_LINES HAS NOW BEEN POPULATED
IF NOT EXISTS('TEMP_PROG')
THEN DEFINE TEMP_PROG PROGRAM
"HERE WE TAKE THE TEXT IN PROGLINES AND MAKE IT THE LINES
"OF TEMP_PROG
CNS TEMP_PROG
PROGRAM _PROG_LINES
DSC TEMP_PROG
CMP TEMP_PROG
"TEMP_PROG
"IF EXISTS('TEMP_PROG')
"THEN DELETE TEMP_PROG
RETURN
ERROR:
RETURN
```

You can call WRITESPROGAM with an argument or leave it off to get the default value of "FACT_DATA" for the source data table name. Once WRITESPROGRAM has been run, you can describe TEMP_PROG to see the program that was written:

```
DEFINE TEMP_PROG PROGRAM
PROGRAM
"PROGRAM NAME: TEMP_PROG
SQL DECLARE C2 CURSOR FOR SELECT STORE_CODE, PRODUCT_CODE, -
PAYMENT_CODE, MONTH, UNITS, REVENUE FROM FACT_DATA
SQL OPEN C2
SQL FETCH C2 LOOP INTO -
:STORE -
:PRODUCT -
:PAYMENTMETHOD -
:TIME -
:APPL_DAT_PRT_TOPVAR(APPL_DAT_PRT_MEASDIM 'UNITS') -
:APPL_DAT_PRT_TOPVAR(APPL_DAT_PRT_MEASDIM 'REVENUE')
SQL CLOSE C2
SQL CLEANUP
RETURN
END
```

Run WRITESPROGRAM to load the data into the variable: APPL_DAT_PRT_TOPVAR.

Program 14: Loading Valuesets

There are occasions when you may need to populate a valueset from an external source. You may have a set of dimension members of special interest that have been identified through a manual process or say you created a set of special test cases. You want to load them into the AW so you can use them in an analysis. Suppose you loaded a set of dimension members into a relational table.

How do you read a set of dimension members contained in an external data source into a valueset? While relations are essentially loaded just like variables, there's a programming trick required with valuesets because *there is no direct way of loading a valueset using either SQL or FILEREAD.*

The program shown in this section illustrates one way of accomplishing this. There are three basic steps:

- Create a "throwaway" dimension that is populated with the values from the data source.

- Limit the valueset to all the dimension members in the throwaway dimension using the VALUES function.

- Optionally, the throwaway dimension can be deleted.

Let's see this approach in action. Assume you have a set of product dimension members you wish to use to populate a valueset. You will store them in VS.SPECIAL_PRODS:

```
DEFINE VS.SPECIAL_PRODS VALUESET PRODUCT
```

The following program populates VS.SPECIAL_PRODS from the values in a table called SPECIAL_PRODS.

```
"PROGRAM NAME: VALUESETLOAD
TRAP ON ERROR
IF NOT EXISTS(THROWAWAY)
THEN DEFINE THROWAWAY DIMENSION TEXT

"Delete all values of THROWAWAY
MAINTAIN THROWAWAY DELETE ALL

"Now populate THROWAWAY with the values in the table
SQL DECLARE C2 CURSOR FOR SELECT PRODUCT_CODE FROM -
SPECIAL_PRODS
SQL OPEN C2

"RPR SQLERRM
SQL FETCH C2 LOOP INTO :APPEND THROWAWAY
SQL CLOSE C2
SQL CLEANUP

"You want to limit SPECIAL_PRODS to all the values
"in THROWAWAY, but SPECIAL_PRODS holds PRODUCT values
"and THROWAWAY is a distinct, unrelated dimension.
"Use the VALUES function to convert the status list of
"THROWAWAY into a multiline text list.
"This solves the problem.
LIMIT VS.SPECIAL_PRODS TO VALUES(THROWAWAY)
IF EXISTS(SPECIAL_PRODS)
THEN DELETE SPECIAL_PRODS DIMENSION TEXT
RETURN
ERROR:
SHOW 'THERE WAS AN ERROR'
RPR SQLCODE SQLERRM
RETURN
```

20 | Tune-Up: Working with Analytic Workspaces

This chapter is, in a way, a continuation of Chapter 4: *Pit Stop: Analytic Workspace Manager Administration Basics.* In that chapter, you learned the basic operations with AWs. Here you will add to your capabilities for working with AWs by learning:

- How to make a backup of an AW.
- How to use export-import cycles to defragment an AW.
- How to save AW information with AWXML.
- How to determine space usage.
- How to work with multiple AWs attached simultaneously.
- How to create a program that executes automatically when the AW is attached (i.e., an event-driven program).

Backing Up an Analytic Workspace

As I mentioned in Chapter 3: *What is the Oracle OLAP DML?*, Oracle's implementation of native multidimensional capabilities can be thought of as a world-within-a-world. An analytic workspace has multidimensional storage structures and a language for retrieving the data. That system is contained in a LOB. The LOB is stored in rows of tables in a relational database.

The backup procedures that apply to any Oracle database can be used to back up one that contains an AW. But suppose you want to back up only the AW component. The EXPORT command can be used to create such a backup. It creates a compact binary file that it places in the directory on the server that you set via the CDA command. The file created is called an Express Interchange File (EIF).

The following statement can be used to make a backup of the SALES_DEMO AW.
```
EXPORT ALL TO EIF FILE 'SALES_DEMO.EIF'
```

Now for a few caveats.

- When multiple AWs are attached, only the first AW in the attachment list is exported, so you need to make sure the AW you want to export is placed first in the attachment order.

- The export command is sensitive to status—the ALL keyword in the above statement actually means *all that are in status*. If your intention is to make a complete backup of the AW, you should set all statuses to ALL.

- Recall that ALLSTAT sets the status of all dimensions to "ALL" *except the special NAME dimension,* which it does not affect. So the status of the NAME dimension needs to be set separately.

To take care of all these details, the complete set of statements to do a full backup would be:
```
CDA OLAP_FILES
AW ATTACH SALES_DEMO FIRST
LIMIT NAME TO ALL
ALLSTAT
EXPORT ALL TO EIF FILE 'SALES_DEMO.EIF'
```

You may find it convenient to put a set of instructions like this into a program so that they can be executed by a single command.

If you only want to back up some of the objects or some of the dimension values, limit the NAME dimension to the objects you wish to back up, and set the individual dimension statuses to the values you need.

Alternatively, instead of using the ALL keyword, you can get a partial backup by listing the objects you want in the export command itself:

```
EXPORT UNITS REVENUE TO EIF FILE 'SALES_DEMO2.EIF'
```

And by the way, the export command *knows* what UNITS and REVENUE are dimensioned by and will automatically include those dimensions in the export along with the two variables specified in the export file.

To bring content into an AW from an EIF file, the IMPORT command is used. It looks like this:

```
IMPORT ALL FROM EIF FILE 'SALES_DEMO.EIF'
```

You will probably want to do an UPDATE, COMMIT after the import.

Take a look at the product documentation for the many options available with the EXPORT and IMPORT commands.

Using Export-Import Cycles to Defragment an AW

In Chapter 5: *Creating Dimensions,* I mentioned that dimensional maintenance can result in inefficient storage usage. In some applications, the dimensional maintenance occurs at the initial load time; thereafter, little is required. That is the desirable situation.

In some applications; however, ongoing dimensional maintenance is needed. Especially if dimension member deletions or permanent re-orderings using MAINTAIN MOVE are being performed with frequency, you will start to use storage inefficiently and/or suffer performance degradations.

The inefficiencies introduced by such dimensional maintenance can be eliminated through a defragmentation process we'll call an export-import cycle. The new AW will be "clean," without the holes created by dimension value deletions or pointers created from MAINTAIN MOVE. The basic steps are:

- STEP 1: Export the entire AW to an EIF file, creating a backup.
- STEP 2: Delete the AW.
- STEP 3: Create a fresh AW under the same name as the deleted AW.
- STEP 4: Import the EIF backup file.
- STEP 5: Update and commit after the import completes.

Saving AW Information with AWXML

There is also a way to save (what I have been calling) the metadata layer of an AW into an external text file that uses XML-based information encoding. This kind of export can be initiated via the Java API or using the GUI interface. To do it from the GUI perform the following steps (see Figure 20.1):

- STEP 1: Right-click the AW you want to save.
- STEP 2: Choose "Save Analytic Workspace to Template."
- STEP 3: Give the location for the file.

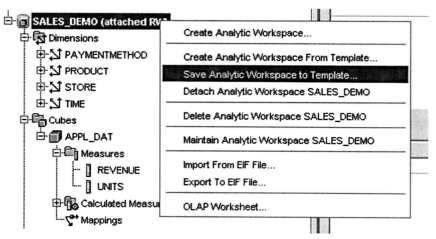

Figure 20.1. Saving Metadata to an XML File

Whereas the EXPORT command does its work on the server, the work performed by this operation will occur on the client machine (normally your PC). The XML file will be stored on the client as well. Only descriptions of the objects that were created using the Java API will be exported. The export will not, for example, contain any programs or the actual data stored in the data variables.

Estimating Storage Usage

Due to the complexities of how the database releases space and other factors, determining the actual amount of storage used by an AW is not a straightforward matter. The issue of space usage has been commented about on the Oracle forums and various blogs. It is beyond the scope of this book to get into those issues, but I do want to share a useful program that shows you where the storage is being consumed as a function of the object.

Below is a program that will produce a formatted report telling, by object, how much storage is required. The list reported is sorted by size; there is an input parameter that lets you limit the number of items reported. A grand total of storage usage is given at the end.

```
DEFINE ANALYZE_SIZE PROGRAM
PROGRAM
"PROGRAM NAME: ANALYZE_SIZE
ARG _NUM_LINES INTEGER
VRB _TOTAL_SIZE DECIMAL
VRB _COUNTER INTEGER
VRB _DISKSIZE DECIMAL
VRB _PAGESIZE DECIMAL
_TOTAL_SIZE = 0
_COUNTER = 1
_PAGESIZE = aw(pagesize)
_NUM_LINES = NAFILL(_NUM_LINES, 10)
LIMIT NAME TO ALL
LIMIT NAME KEEP OBJ(DISKSIZE NAME) GT 0
SORT NAME D OBJ(DISKSIZE NAME)
PUSH DECIMALS
DECIMALS = 0
push commas
commas = yes
show joinchars('Report Produced at ' tod ' on ' today)
blank
FOR NAME
DO
   _DISKSIZE = OBJ(DISKSIZE NAME)
   IF _COUNTER LE _NUM_LINES
   THEN SHOW JOINCHARS(extchars(joinchars('00000' -
   _COUNTER), numchars(joinchars('00000' _COUNTER)) -
   4, numchars(joinchars('0000' _COUNTER)) ) ': The ' -
   OBJ(TYPE NAME) ' ' NAME ' used ' _DISKSIZE*_PAGESIZE ' -
   Bytes')
```

```
    "THEN SHOW JOINCHARS(OBJ(TYPE NAME) ','  NAME ',' -
    _DISKSIZE*_PAGESIZE )
    _TOTAL_SIZE = _TOTAL_SIZE + _DISKSIZE
    _COUNTER = _COUNTER + 1
DOEND
BLANK
SHOW JOINCHARS('TOTAL SPACE USED IS '_TOTAL_SIZE*_PAGESIZE)
POP DECIMALS
pop commas
RETURN
SHOW OBJ(DISKSIZE NAME)*aw(pagesize)
END
```

Run the program without supplying the argument. This will give information for the first 10 largest objects. The output looks like this:

```
Report Produced at 15:12:20 on 09SEP08
00001: The VARIABLE APPL_DAT_PRT_TOPVAR used 1,942,592 Bytes
00002: The COMPOSITE APPL_DAT_COMPOSITE used 568,960 Bytes
00003: The DIMENSION RANDCOMBOS used 438,912 Bytes
00004: The DIMENSION TESTCOMBO used 130,048 Bytes
00005: The DIMENSION GEN_OBJ_ROLES used 65,024 Bytes
00006: The DIMENSION DIM_OBJ_LIST used 65,024 Bytes
00007: The DIMENSION ALL_LEVELS used 65,024 Bytes
00008: The DIMENSION GID_DIMENSION used 65,024 Bytes
00009: The DIMENSION MAPGROUP_DIM used 65,024 Bytes
00010: The DIMENSION MEASURE_PROP used 65,024 Bytes
TOTAL SPACE USED IS 8,249,920
```

Working with Multiple Analytic Workspaces

All of the examples in this book have been based on a single user-created AW. There are reasons for creating more than one AW for your application.

One is to have a separate code AW that is dedicated to holding the DML programs. This makes it possible to attach to the code AW read/write, but attach to the data AWs in read-only mode. In this way you can do program development or testing without danger of permanently altering the stored data.

Another occurs when there are very large amounts of data. In such situations it is sometimes desirable to spread that data over more than one AW. For example, you can partition the data based on time frames, with different AWs storing the data for different time slices. This makes parallel loads possible since each data AW can be attached read/write and loaded concurrently, or even have them running on different machines.

Sometimes partitioning can be used to control composite growth, making it possible to lower the total number of composite values in any given AW, making it substantially below what it would be if all data were in a single AW.

Fully Qualified Names

When you have multiple user AWs attached simultaneously, it becomes important to refer to objects with their fully qualified names. The format of the fully qualified name is:
Schema_name.aw_name!object_name

We have been writing statements like this:
```
SHOW PRODUCT
```

Here is how it would look using fully qualified names:
```
SHOW SCOTT.SALES_DEMO!PRODUCT
```

If you have multiple AWs, it is usually best to have each in its own schema.

Event-Driven Programs

Finally, I will mention there is some capability for creating event-driven programs. Notably, it is possible to create a program that will automatically run when the AW that contains it is attached. Such programs are frequently used to do initializations, set statuses, or attach other required AWs.

To create such a program, simply give it the special name ONATTACH.

Part VI:
Analytical Alchemy

21 | Design Principles for Creating Multidimensional Information

Oracle OLAP includes both native multidimensional data storage technology and a computational engine with a feature-rich programming language. As a data storage technology, it stands as a peer to other data storage technologies, most notably relational data storage. As a data storage technology, specialized for hosting and marshalling multidimensional data, its advantages are largely performance related. Through the use of specialized data structures, preaggregated data, indexed dimensions and relations, and the absence of table joins, Oracle OLAP is usually able to deliver substantial boosts in query performance for dimensional applications over what can be obtained with a purely relational solution.

As a computational engine, OLAP stands as a peer to other analysis software including statistical packages and data mining software or computationally oriented languages such as S or Mathematica. As a programming language specialized for representing and manipulating multidimensional information, its advantages rest in its computational power and richness, as well as the uniqueness of its capabilities. You have already had more than a taste of these unique capabilities:

- Feature-rich programming language that supports both 3GL and 4GL operations.

- Specialized data structures that denominate information in functional categories—not rows and columns; not integer subscripts.

- Debundling selection and reporting functions via the "setting status" facility.

- Multidimensional storage of not only numbers or text, but ordered sets of dimension members as well.

- Fast, implicitly specified calculations for multidimensional arrays of data.

Getting maximum leverage out of this computational engine is much more than knowing the DML programming language—you have to be an analytical alchemist! You have to know how to use the language to create meaningful, actionable measures. You should be able to work with the information analysis process itself; understanding the business processes and how information is used in them.

Andrew attempts analytical alchemy when all of a sudden there is a combinatorial explosion

There will always be low-hanging fruit. There will be the basic metrics that should clearly be made available. These will become the foundations of your OLAP application. Then there will be the measures, less obvious, the derived measures, perhaps denominated in derived dimensions. These have a special potential to give you a unique competitive advantage.

In this chapter, I want to present some concepts that define and give power to the OLAP analysis platform. These are practical principles to guide your work, principles that will serve as a springboard for innovation. The design principles presented will stand on their own two feet, independent of any implementation language. To make sure you see how to apply them; however, in the later half of this chapter I will show you how to put them to work with the DML showing concrete examples.

This chapter will be a way of revisiting some of the analysis techniques you have learned, giving a conceptual framework in which to place them.

The OLAP Advantage: Dimensionalizing an Analysis

What is the fundamental element that distinguishes OLAP analysis? The essence of what OLAP contributes is captured in a process I call *dimensionalizing an analysis.*

To explain this, I need to use the term "analysis" in a particular way. For the purposes of this discussion, I will define an analysis as being the process of transforming one set of data into a new set that more directly addresses a business issue or question.

Aggregation is the simplest case of an analysis. In the case of aggregation, the new dataset consists of a single value that summarizes or represents the original set. Aggregates address the question, What happened with this group?

Moving averages are a slightly more complicated example. This is a transformation that modifies a time series to produce a similar, but smoother version. Moving averages address the question, What is the trend in these data?

I am defining dimensionalizing an analysis to be the process of taking an analysis, then repeating it for the numerous scenarios that are defined by combinations of breakout dimension values. With this understanding in mind, we can say that OLAP is a facility for dimensionalizing an analysis. It has the computational wherewithal to compute the data, organize it in a multidimensional format, and present it through specialized interfaces designed to showcase its dimensional structure.

Let's explore the concept of dimensionalizing an analysis using the above two examples.

Suppose you have sales figures for a group of customers. You want to assess performance, asking for instance, what is the average sales level per customer? Rather than compute a single average value for all the data, you first segregate the data into compartments on the basis of the store where the customer shopped and the week that the purchases were made. Then you compute averages for each of the subsets created. By doing this, you are able to look at performance movements over time or to compare the results from different stores. This simple example has store and week as breakout factors or dimensions.

A time series is a sequence of measurements taken at successive points in time. To calculate a moving average, the values of neighboring data points are averaged together. But in the OLAP environment, you don't just have "a time series," you have a multidimensional array of time series. The moving-average example of Chapter 11: *Calculating Data On-the-Fly* was based on a three-dimensional revenue variable. The formula illustrated provides a separate moving average time series for each combination of customer and product dimension members.

The Presentation of OLAP Data

It's not just enough to produce the information; there must be an interface that can manage the display of it, taking advantage of the structural characteristics that distinguish OLAP data. It is with data organized in such a fashion that an OLAP-aware interface delivers its core value: the ability to easily, quickly, conveniently, and logically switch from one scenario to the next, showing the results of the organization's efforts from any desired perspective. This is the process commonly called *slicing and dicing the data*.

The elements of such an interface were illustrated in Chapter 15: *Exploring Metadata*. They are the ability to:

- Choose which measures to show.
- Determine which dimensions provide headings for the row, column, and page edges.
- Select dimension members to be shown using a rich set of filtering tools.
- Sort the selected dimension members into a desired order.
- Create reports or graphical charts of the data.

CHAPTER 21 | 283
Design Principles for Creating Multidimensional Information

Think of this business intelligence function as providing *seeing eye numbers* without which an organization would be operating blindly.

Not wanting to operate blindly, management uses numbers for guidance

The Genesis of OLAP Data: Dimensions

OLAP data begins with dimensions. Are dimensions any old attribute column found in the database? Are there principles that can assist in choosing meaningful dimensions?

Whatever the activity of interest in your application, there are innumerable descriptions of it that could be made—*at least in principle*. Someone buys shoes in a store. There will be a *reason* they are buying the shoes. The person will be of a certain *age* and *income*. There may be a particular *purpose* for the shoes. The shoes are a certain *model* and *size*. You could go on and on describing a given transaction with more and more detail. A process will have quantitative data associated with it as well, for example, the price of the shoes.

Some of the descriptions you could come up with may not have relevance to your objectives; some of them may be impractical or impossible to record. But in the end, there are data collected along with descriptions of them. These data must be crafted into useful measures that will power the business intelligence system. With so many possibilities, how do you identify the dimensions that should be selected?

What is needed are principles that yield the basics *and an extendable information architecture,* one that is responsive to not only today's known issues, but is adaptable so it can be made responsive to questions unforeseen. The starting point for creating such an architecture is the identification of the dimensions that describe the data in the most fundamental sense. These dimensions will be used to create a set of *baseline data*. The baseline data supplies the information foundation upon which extensions can be built.

So how do you identify the "fundamental" (i.e., base) dimensions? After years of working with many different applications and data modeling scenarios, I have observed that the fundamental descriptions of data are the ones that correlate with interrogatory pronouns; they are the answers to the questions that journalists seek to address in writing a story about a newsworthy event. In the business intelligence world, the event is the transaction that generates the data.

Table 21.1 shows the interrogatory pronouns and examples of typical corresponding dimensions.

Table 21.1. Identifying Base Dimensions

Interrogatory Pronouns	Typical Corresponding Dimensions
Who	Customer, store, patient, student, advertiser, account
What	Product, treatment, course, line item
When	Time, month, quarter, year
Where	Geography, place of business, school
How	Channel, payment method, rate plan, distributor

For example, you could have product sales broken out by store, product, and month, telling who, what, and when. Or you could have student graduation data broken out by student and year, telling who and when. The baseline data is the quantitative data broken out by these dimensions.

Table 21.1 serves as a guideline for thinking about dimensional data. Nothing is black and white. Store could be a *who* in one context (they are carrying the product or not) or a *where* in another (it is where the purchase was made). There could be two *whos:* in a distribution process, for example, a shipper and a receiver, and so on.

(By the way, you may have noticed I left out *why*. It's a great question to answer, but it is usually not observable in the information processing sequence.)

Data created in such a format—a measurement and the dimension values that describe it—are very intuitive, because they are formulated in terms that we naturally think in. *This is the breakthrough of the multidimensional data concept.*

From the fundamentals, the next logical step is deriving information that is denominated in terms that possess additional explanatory value or insight. For instance, you may want to see sales figures broken out not by product, but by style or size. You may want to see graduation rates broken out by student demographics, or school attended, or by private versus public schools.

In other words, breaking data out by attributes of the fundamental dimensions can help explain what is going on. Table 21.2 shows some sample attributes that typically accompany the base dimensions.

Table 21.2. Identifying Attributes for Base Dimensions

Interrogatory Pronouns	Typical Corresponding Attributes
Who	Demographics, behavioral attributes
What	Color, packaging, size, method
When	Weekend, holiday, weekday, season
Where	Weather, language, population density
How	Preferred versus not preferred payment method, brick and mortar versus online

This data transformation could be described like this: take a dimension of the baseline data, substitute for it one or more related dimensions to create a new measure. The new measure provides new information.

Designing Measures

We looked at the dimensions; now let's look at the measures. In creating dimensioned data I gave a name to the simplest scenario: The Classic Business Intelligence Application. In that scenario, the measures start with leaf-level data that measures the intensity of some process. With dimensions organized into hierarchies and the aid of an aggregation method, you create a measure capable of displaying the information at varying degrees of granularity.

I have shown other mechanisms by which measures can be generated:

- Derived data created by breaking out on related dimensions (discussed in the above section and exemplified in REVCAT from Chapter 14: *Aggregation*).

- Dimensioned profiles by breaking out a count of dimension members on the basis of one or more attributes (see dimension profiler example with PRODUCT dimension in Chapter 7: *Categorizing Dimension Members with Attributes*).

- Non-numerical data where the data consists of sets of dimension members (see RFM_CUSTOMERS in Chapter 13: *Working with Sets*).

In this chapter and the next, I will show two other powerful measure-generating paradigms. Each will be based on first defining a basic analysis, then dimensionalizing it to create multidimensional data.

Filters-to-Measure

When I discussed value-based filtering in Chapter 10: *Storing Data in Analytic Workspaces,* I pointed out that there is normally one dimension whose members are searched (the "filtering dimension") while the members of all other dimensions are fixed to a single specified value. By applying the "dimensionalizing" principle to the non-filtering dimensions, filters can be used to generate *counting measures*. Counting measures provide very specific, actionable information, based on business rules that define concrete objectives or requirements.

Let's take a look at an example. As you know, filters are used to identify dimension members that satisfy a criterion. In actual application, sometimes the requirement is to identify the members satisfying the criteria, but other times only the number of members is needed.

For example, suppose you are a manufacturer running an incentive program that grants special benefits to stores that sell some minimum number of a specially designated item. You want to know how many stores are qualifying, and you would like to see a trend of that over time. Maybe you are actively promoting the incentive program and you want to see if your promotion is working or not.

The number of units sold is stored in a variable:
```
DEFINE UNITS VARIABLE INTEGER <STORE PRODUCT TIME>
```

Let's use an integer dimension to set the minimum number of items that must be sold to qualify for the incentive program. You might think of that number as something that should be stored in a variable, but I am making it a dimension to get some reporting flexibility, which you will see later on in the discussion.

```
DEFINE N DIMENSION INTEGER
```

Now let's write a program that determines the number of qualifying stores:
```
DEFINE COUNT_QUALIFYING PROGRAM
ARG _N INTEGER
ARG _TIME TIME
ARG _PRODUCT TEXT
VRB _NUMQUAL INTEGER
"If the arguments are not supplied in the calling
"statement, grab the values from what is in status
_N = NAFILL(_N,N)
_TIME = NAFILL(_TIME,TIME)
_PRODUCT = NAFILL(_PRODUCT,PRODUCT)
TEMPSTAT STORE
DO
   LIMIT STORE TO STORE_LEVELREL 'STORE'
   LIMIT STORE(PRODUCT _PRODUCT TIME _TIME) KEEP UNITS GT _N
   _NUMQUAL = STATLEN(STORE)
DOEND
RETURN(_NUMQUAL)
```

You could use the program to see how many stores sold at least five units of TP003 during JUL09 like this:

```
SHOW COUNT_QUALIFYING(5 TP003 JUL09)
```

But you wanted to create a trend report, not a single value. How would you do that? Create a formula as an interface to this program and use the formula to iterate over the time values you want.

```
DEFINE F.COUNT_QUALIFYING FORMULA <N PRODUCT TIME>
EQ COUNT_QUALIFYING
```

Now you can generate your trend report like this:
```
LIMIT N TO 5
LIMIT PRODUCT TO 'TP003'
LIMIT TIME TO 'JUL09' TO 'JUL10'
REPORT F.COUNT_QUALIFYING
```

This formula does a lot more than give the trend report! It has "what-if" functionality. It lets you see what would have happened if the qualifying number were different, or how things would have worked out with other choices of the "special product." In fact there are many ways of extending this analysis. You could add the store dimension to it and, with some modifications of the program, give the ability to break out the information by aggregate values of store to give a count of qualifying stores broken out by geography as well as time.

This example demonstrates how by understanding OLAP on a non-superficial level, you can more realize its full value. OLAP is a powerful tool that can help you do a lot more than provide *access enterprise information to help make decisions*. You can actually *create* enterprise information with it.

22 | Migrations: Tracking Changes in Customer Choices

In this chapter, I am going to explore an analytical model that provides a powerful tool for understanding the dynamics of a business process. Based on *state-transition analysis,* this is a model that can be applied in situations where it is possible to track the actions or choices of a customer over time. The model will yield multidimensional reports like those with which you are already familiar—reports that show you what happened—*but it also yields a new type of report that offers new and powerful ways to see how the results were achieved.*

You will see from the presentation of this methodology how seeing conventional summary reports can be like getting the final score of a football game—they give you the results but don't show the plays that produced the score. *The methodology here shows the plays.* To be an effective coach—to make the right business choices—knowing the dynamics of how the results were produced is of unquestionable relevance and that is what the analysis you will see in this chapter provides.

The methodology applies to situations where there is an interest in understanding buying patterns and how they are changing over time. The problem of understanding how customers change their purchase decisions is sometimes called *migration analysis.* These are sales situations with a *recurrence characteristic*—the customer has, over time, multiple opportunities to engage in a purchase decision with the same vendor, regarding the same sets of products or addressing the same need.

You may have the ability to track customer actions because they are your ongoing customer or because they are in a loyalty program. You may be working with individuals who are part of a panel of people who have been recruited to participate in market research studies on an ongoing basis. These are the situations where this analysis can be applied.

The discussion will be built around a hypothetical sales situation involving automobile purchases. You are going to see how to develop a powerful OLAP analysis system for tracking and understanding choice flows, movements from one choice of product to another.

I developed an application based on transition analysis like this for a Fortune 100 company for studying changes in advertising purchases; I think you will easily see how the method could be used for analyzing the way customers switch their telephone service provider, healthcare provider, or how they make a myriad of other ongoing purchase decisions. At the end of the chapter I will show how to set up this analysis methodology for a variety of applications.

The State-Transition Analysis Framework

The conceptual elements for state-transition analysis consists of a collection of discrete states; one or more agents capable of movement among those states; and movements between the states, which will be called transitions. The states represent the choices that can be made; the agents make the choices; and the transitions represent the progression of choices. The agents may be customers; the states may be buying decisions.

In a sales process, here are examples of the kinds of situations the transitions could represent:

- Buying product A, then product B instead.
- Choosing rate plan A, then switching to rate plan B.
- Choosing no special feature, then purchasing special feature A.
- Purchasing a product in category A, then switching to a product in category B.
- Choosing vendor A, then choosing vendor B.

A graphical representation makes this model easy to understand, so we'll make one now using a simple example.

Table 22.1 shows three states. The states are product choices. The information in the table includes a short symbolic representation of the state (the "Code") and a description of what the state refers to.

Table 22.1. The States Associated with the Sales Process

Code	Description
A	Customer Selected Product A
B	Customer Selected Product B
C	Customer Selected Product C

In this example, we have a customer who makes purchases on a periodic basis choosing from among three products. The customer has a *current* product. They need a refill and get a *next* product. A transition is the representation of that change from the current product to the next product. Figure 22.1 depicts a customer who starts in state "A" then goes to state "B." As shown, the states are represented by circles and the transitions by links originating at the current state and terminating with an arrowhead at the next state.

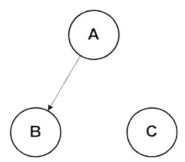

Figure 22.1. State-Transition Diagram Representing a Change from A to B

Now suppose we had purchase information like this for many customers. The collection of data could be depicted by drawing an arc for every occurring transition and annotating each arc to show the number of customers that made the given transition as shown in Figure 22.2.

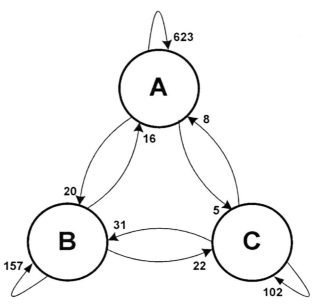

Figure 22.2. State-Transition Diagram Showing Transitions for Many Customers at Once

You would read this diagram: 623 customers chose product A both the first and the second time (i.e., no change of buying decision); 5 customers chose A the first time, then C; 31 customers chose C the first time, then B; and so on.

With this basic understanding, let's introduce the sample sales application.

A Sales Application

Suppose that a study has been commissioned in which the purchase choices of 12,000 automobile buyers have been collected. In this study, each buyer is replacing an existing vehicle. You record the manufacturer of their original car and of the replacement car as well as other information about the customer.

To keep things simple, let's assume there is a choice of four manufacturers: Chrysler, General Motors, Ford, and Other. Table 22.2 shows that customer CUST001 started with a Chrysler and replaced it with another Chrysler; customer CUST002 started with a Chrysler and replaced it with a GM; and so on.

Table 22.2. Basic Fact Data for a Sales Application

CUST_ID	Current	Next
CUST001	CHRY	CHRY
CUST002	CHRY	GM
CUST003	FORD	GM
CUST004	GM	FORD

For the study population of 12,000 customers, how did the various manufacturers fare? You could address this question by tallying the number of times each manufacturer is represented in the "Current" column and then for the "Next" column and compare the figures to see if there was a net gain or loss. I have done this in Table 22.3 for a hypothetical dataset. I am going to refer to the report shown in Table 22.3 a number of times, so I'll give a name to it. I'll call the report shown in Table 22.3 the "Basic Report."

Table 22.3. Conventional Summary Report ("Basic Report")

Manufacturer	Current	Next	Net Change	Percent Change
Chrysler	1,694	2,054	360	21.25%
Ford	2,721	2,831	110	4.04%
General Motors	3,985	3,590	(-395)	(-9.91%)
Other	3,600	3,525	(-75)	(-2.08%)

In Table 22.3, you can see that of the 12,000 people in the study, 1,694 customers came in with a Chrysler and 2,054 left with a Chrysler, for a net gain of 360 Chrysler customers.

The data in Table 22.3 is what is referred to in the last chapter as an analysis of data. The data from Table 22.2 is too grainy—it is difficult to see any patterns of activity from it. You perform the analysis to transform the data of Table 22.2 to that of Table 22.3. You need only glance at the data in Table 22.3 to glean useful information.

How do we translate this analysis into our world of OLAP? For starters, anything categorical is a dimension. So we have a customer dimension. Next, there are manufacturers (our states) giving another dimension. There are two customer choices represented in the data:

the manufacturer of their current car (current state) and the manufacturer of their next car (next state). You may recognize the two customer choices to be behavioral attributes.

To translate these statements into DML, proceed as follows.

Create the dimensions:
```
DEFINE CUSTOMER DIMENSION TEXT
DEFINE STATE DIMENSION TEXT
```

Model the two behavioral attributes:
```
DEFINE R.CURRENT_STATE.CUSTOMER RELATION STATE <CUSTOMER>
DEFINE R.NEXT_STATE.CUSTOMER RELATION STATE <CUSTOMER>
```

Using the techniques of Chapter 19: *Getting Data In and Out of Analytic Workspaces* you can load in dimension values for customer and manufacturer, then populate the two relations. Assuming that has been done, you can use the COUNT function to get the Current and Next figures.

```
->REPORT HEADING 'Current' -
COUNT(CUSTOMER EQ CUSTOMER, R.CURRENT_STATE.CUSTOMER) -
HEADING 'Next' -
COUNT(CUSTOMER EQ CUSTOMER, R.NEXT_STATE.CUSTOMER)
STATE              Current     Next
--------------    ----------  ----------
CHRY                 1694        2054
FORD                 2721        2831
GM                   3985        3590
OTHER                3600        3525
```

Here lies an opportunity employ your skill in using formulas to restructure the presentation of information. How would you create a formula that can produce the Basic Report shown in Table 22.3?

Define a measure dimension with four values to represent the four columns—Current, Next, Net Change, and Percent Change— of the Basic Report. Then create a formula dimensioned by this measure dimension and the STATE dimension. Now set the EQ of the formula to generate the desired data. Can you see what it should be? The first two measure expressions are given above, the other two are simple arithmetic expressions.

Observe, the Basic Report is really one-dimensional data. There is a STATE dimension that gives the manufacturer; there are four measures based on it. To enjoy *the OLAP advantage* you break out the data by more dimensions—*you "dimensionalize" the analysis.*

Getting the OLAP Advantage

Let's suppose, for example, the gender of each customer was recorded as part of the study. Then a gender attribute can be modeled using a relation to map each customer to their gender.

Now you can break out the data by manufacturer *and* gender; you can get a Basic Report for male customers and one for female customers.

With a simple hierarchy, defined on gender and an aggregation process, you would be able to create the Basic Report as well as male-customer-only and female-customer-only versions. This makes it possible to compare the changes for male versus female customers.

Of course you could break out by more than one attribute-based dimension. You could break out the data by numerous demographic factors (marital status, age category, etc.) generating true multidimensional data. You might even conduct the study on an ongoing basis, introducing a time dimension. *These are all ways of dimensionalizing the analysis.*

Using State-Transition Analysis

Now consider the following questions:

- Where do new customers come from who switch to Chrysler?

- Where do customers go who choose to switch from Chrysler to a competitor?

- Has customer loyalty been increasing or decreasing?

It is not difficult to see that the Basic Report provides no information that addresses these questions. To do that we will create a new report based on state-transition analysis.

We will use a state-transition model to represent the purchase choices recorded in our hypothetical database of 12,000 car buyers graphically. We cycle through the database records and count the number of occurrences of each type of transition. Using a diagram with each manufacturer represented as a circle, we annotate the arcs that represent the transitions with the number of customers making that transition. The result for the hypothetical database is show in Figure 22.3.

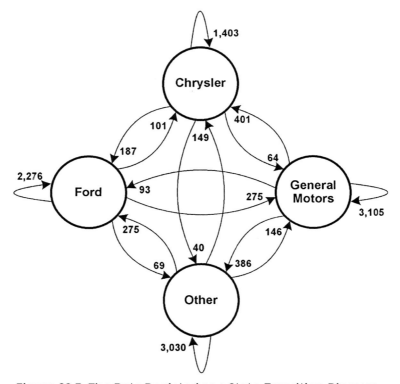

Figure 22.3. The Data Depicted as a State-Transition Diagram

From the information contained in Figure 22.3, you can address the new questions. You can see, for example, that 1,403 Chrysler owners stayed with Chrysler. You see that Chrysler lost 187 customers to Ford, 64 to GM and 40 to Other—for a total loss of 291. On the other hand, Chrysler brought 401 General Motors owners into the fold, along with 101 Ford owners and 149 from Other for a total gain of 651. The net gain is:

Net Gain for Chrysler = (401 + 101 + 149) − (187 + 64 + 40) = 651 − 291 = 360

This is the number shown in the Basic Report in the Chrysler row under the Net Change column.

It should be easy to convince yourself that the state-transition diagram has practical and revealing information that the Basic Report does not. *Notably, this data display shows the flow of choices that produced the results.*

Displaying the State-Transition Information in Tabular Format

The information seen on the transition diagram can also be displayed in a tabular format. This presentation will be called a *state-transition table* or a *state-transition report*. The graphic gives an intuitive, easy-to-interpret depiction of what's going on, but the table format can be printed using conventional reporting and works better for large numbers of states.

The state transition report has one row corresponding to each starting or current state and a column corresponding to each terminating or next state. It will be convenient to refer to these as the "From" and "To" states. The data value will be a count of the number of customers making the transition.

For our sample sales application, the state-transition report has four rows and four columns of numbers (plus the headings). The information from Figure 22.3 is represented in the report as seen in Table 22.4.

Table 22.4. State-Transition Diagram Data in Tabular Format

From State (Current)	To State (Next)			
	Chrysler	Ford	General Motors	Other
Chrysler	1,403	187	64	40
Ford	101	2,276	275	69
General Motors	401	93	3,105	386
Other	149	275	146	3,030

It is easy to see that Table 22.4 displays exactly the same data as the state-transition diagram of Figure 22.3. The downward diagonal cells have a special significance: they represent customers that repeated their original decision (i.e., loyal customers). All other cells represent customers that switched.

Creating the State-Transition Report with DML

You have seen how to create the Basic Report using DML, now let's create the state-transition report with DML. One of the unique features of this report is that it seems to use the state dimension twice, as both rows and columns. But it is actually not possible to use a dimension twice in an object definition. You will have to use two different dimensions that have the same dimension members. When there is more than one dimension that mirrors each other like this, the dimension is called a *shadow dimension.*

So whereas the Basic Report was done with a single state dimension, the state-transition report will use two. Let's name the Current state FROM_STATE and the Next state TO_STATE:

```
DEFINE FROM_STATE DIMENSION TEXT
DEFINE TO_STATE DIMENSION TEXT
```

Now we can add values to these two dimensions:
```
MAINTAIN FROM_STATE ADD 'CHRY' 'FORD' 'GM' 'OTHER'
MAINTAIN TO_STATE ADD 'CHRY' 'FORD' 'GM' 'OTHER'
```

Note that in this sample sales application, any one of our states could be a Current state and any one of our states could be a Next state. In some applications; however, this is not the case. In some applications there may be a Current state that could not be a Next state, and vice versa, and in those cases these two dimensions would not have the same members.

Next, we need a dimension to represent the transitions themselves; these are what we will count and show in the report. A transition is a combination of a FROM_STATE and a TO_STATE. As you have seen, combinations of dimension values are modeled using conjoint dimensions and that's what you'll do here:

```
DEFINE TRANSITION DIMENSION <FROM_STATE TO_STATE>
```

We created the customer dimension in the previous section. Now we need a way to map each customer to the transition representing their choices. This is done with a relation:

```
DEFINE R.TRANSITION.CUSTOMER RELATION TRANSITION -
<CUSTOMER>
```

Chapter 22
Migrations: Tracking Changes in Customer Choices

Now, suppose we have populated this relation (using the data in Table 22.4). Create a formula to count the number of customers represented by each transition like this:

```
DEFINE TRANS_COUNT_T FORMULA INTEGER <TRANSITION>
EQ COUNT(CUSTOMER EQ CUSTOMER, R.TRANSITION.CUSTOMER)
```

Let's use this formula to get a sorted list of the transitions:
```
->SORT TRANSITION D TRANS_COUNT_T
->REPORT TRANS_COUNT_T
```

-----TRANSITION------		TRANS_COUN
FROM_STATE	TO_STATE	T_T
----------	----------	----------
GM	GM	3105
OTHER	OTHER	3030
FORD	FORD	2276
CHRY	CHRY	1403
GM	CHRY	401
GM	OTHER	386
FORD	GM	275
OTHER	FORD	275
CHRY	FORD	187
OTHER	CHRY	149
OTHER	GM	146
FORD	CHRY	101
GM	FORD	93
FORD	OTHER	69
CHRY	GM	64
CHRY	OTHER	40

As you can see, of the 12,000 customers the most frequently occurring transition is for a GM customer to remain a GM customer.

Now create a transition report by using a formula to break the transition dimension into its endpoints.

```
DEFINE TRANS_COUNT FORMULA INTEGER <TO_STATE FROM_STATE>
EQ TRANS_COUNT_T
```

Report on this formula to get the transition table:
```
->REPORT TRANS_COUNT

                    ----------------TRANS_COUNT----------------
                    ----------------TO_STATE------------------
FROM_STATE          CHRY          FORD          GM          OTHER
----------          ----          ----          --          -----
CHRY                1403           187          64            40
FORD                 101          2276         275            69
GM                   401            93        3105           386
OTHER                149           275         146          3030
```

Extending the Transition Analysis

The transition report tells us how many of each possible transition was taken. I will now show some simple extensions to get even more focused information. *This new information will allow you to see two important aspects of the sales dynamics: customer loyalty and changes in customer composition.* Customer loyalty is concerned with the propensity for a vendor to get repeat customers. Change in customer composition is concerned with seeing what proportion of the customer base came from former non-customers.

Customer Loyalty

Let's add the row totals to the numbers from Table 22.4. This is shown in Table 22.5.

Table 22.5. Adding the Row Totals to the State-Transition Diagram Data

From State (Current)	To State (Next)				Total From
	Chrysler	Ford	General Motors	Other	
Chrysler	1,403	187	64	40	1,694
Ford	101	2,276	275	69	2,721
General Motors	401	93	3,105	386	3,985
Other	149	275	146	3,030	3,600

If we divide each number in Table 22.5 by its corresponding row total and multiply by 100 we get *the percentage of customers who went to state Y from state X*. In Table 22.6 this calculation has been performed.

Table 22.6. The "To" Percentages

From State (Current)	To State (Next)				Total
	Chrysler	Ford	General Motors	Other	
Chrysler	82.82%	11.04%	3.78%	2.36%	100%
Ford	3.71%	83.65%	10.11%	2.54%	100%
General Motors	10.06%	2.33%	77.92%	9.69%	100%
Other	4.14%	7.64%	4.06%	84.17%	100%

Table 22.6 is packed with information; the diagonals give a measure of customer loyalty; the off-diagonal elements show where the customers who switched went.

You might think of collecting the diagonal elements together and putting them into one measure to arrive at a customer loyalty figure broken out by manufacturer as shown in Table 22.7.

Table 22.7. Customer Loyalty Broken Out by Manufacturer

Manufacturer	Percent Loyal
Chrysler	82.82%
Ford	83.65%
General Motors	77.92%
Other	84.17%

DML Code for the Extension

Performing this extension is an application of the programming techniques you have learned. You can get the row totals with a formula:

```
->DEFINE ROW_TOTALS FORMULA INTEGER <FROM_STATE>
->EQ TOTAL(TRANS_COUNT, FROM_STATE)
->RPR ROW_TOTALS
```

FROM_STATE	ROW_TOTALS
CHRY	1694
FORD	2721
GM	3985
OTHER	3600

You will recognize these numbers as the Current column of the Basic Report of Table 22.3. Using them you calculate the "To" percentages of Table 22.6 with this formula:

```
->DEFINE PCT_TO FORMULA DECIMAL <FROM_STATE TO_STATE>
->EQ 100*TRANS_COUNT/ROW_TOTALS
->RPR DOWN FROM_STATE PCT_TO
```

	PCT_TO			
	TO_STATE			
FROM_STATE	CHRY	FORD	GM	OTHER
CHRY	82.82	11.04	3.78	2.36
FORD	3.71	83.65	10.11	2.54
GM	10.06	2.33	77.92	9.69
OTHER	4.14	7.64	4.06	84.17

Next, suppose you want to pick out the diagonal elements to produce a measure of customer loyalty as in Table 22.7. You can do this with a simple formula dimensioned by STATE:

```
->DEFINE LOYALTY FORMULA DECIMAL <STATE>
->EQ PCT_TO(FROM_STATE STATE TO_STATE STATE)
->REPORT LOYALTY
```

STATE	LOYALTY
CHRY	82.82
FORD	83.65
GM	77.92
OTHER	84.17

Measuring Changes in Customer Composition

As the percent of row total tells where your customers went to, the percent of column total tells where your customers came *from*. Table 22.8 shows the column totals. Where the row totals gave the numbers in the Current column of the Basic Report, *the column totals give the Next column of the Basic Report.*

Table 22.8. Adding the Column Totals to the State-Transition Diagram Data

From State (Current)	To State (Next)			
	Chrysler	Ford	General Motors	Other
Chrysler	1,403	187	64	40
Ford	101	2,276	275	69
General Motors	401	93	3,105	386
Other	149	275	146	3,030
Total To	2,054	2,831	3,590	3,525

The Basic Report tells you that 2,054 customers ended up with a Chrysler; Table 22.8 tells you whose customer they were before they purchased that Chrysler.

Dividing each number in Table 22.8 by the corresponding column total and multiplying by 100 gives a percent expression shown in Table 22.9.

Table 22.9. The "From" Percentages

From State (Current)	To State (Next)			
	Chrysler	Ford	General Motors	Other
Chrysler	68.31%	6.61%	1.78%	1.13%
Ford	4.92%	80.40%	7.66%	1.96%
General Motors	19.52%	3.29%	86.49%	10.95%
Other	7.25%	9.71%	4.07%	85.96%
Total	100%	100%	100%	100%

In Table 22.9, the diagonal elements tell what percentage of a manufacturer's customer base is composed of former customers.

If you subtract each of the diagonal element figures in Table 22.9 from 100%, you get the percent of current customers who were not customers last time—*the new blood*. This calculation is done in Table 22.10.

Table 22.10. Percent of Customer Base Who Bought from Some Other Manufacturer Last Time

Manufacturer	Percent from Outside
Chrysler	31.69%
Ford	19.60%
General Motors	13.51%
Other	14.04%

Whereas you would probably want to see the diagonals of the "To" picture as large as possible (i.e., loyal customers), a low value would be favored for the "From" diagonals. In fact, it is not too difficult to reason that if the "To" percentage is greater than the "From" percentage, there has been a net growth in the customer base.

The DML for the "From" picture is similar to that for the "To" picture. I won't show the code, but you might want to try to work it out for yourself.

Different Plays Leading to the Same End Score

Before closing our illustration of state-transition analysis, I would like to demonstrate, in a rather dramatic way, how significant the value of the information it provides can be. This will be accomplished by comparing the analysis of two sets of data: one is the example we have been working with and the other is a second hypothetical dataset with a curious relationship to it. Please take a look at the data in Table 22.11.

Table 22.11. State-Transition Report for a Contrasting Report

From State (Current)	To State (Next)				Total From
	Chrysler	Ford	General Motors	Other	
Chrysler	335	187	646	526	1,694
Ford	101	440	2,111	69	2,721
General Motors	193	828	687	2,277	3,985
Other	1,425	1,376	146	653	3,600
Total To	2,054	2,831	3,590	3,525	12,000

Note that the row and column totals in Table 22.11 match those of the original state-transition report of Table 22.4—*but that's where the similarities end.* The data of Table 22.4 exhibits customers mainly making the same choice in the Current and Next time frames; whereas in Table 22.11, most of the customers are making a switch.

Let's calculate the "To" percentages to get the loyalty and other information as shown in the format of Table 22.6; however, if you inspect the percentages in Table 22.12 you see a much lower degree of loyalty than is evidenced in Table 22.6.

Table 22.12. The "To" Percentages for the Contrasting Report

From State (Current)	To State (Next)				Total
	Chrysler	Ford	General Motors	Other	
Chrysler	19.78%	11.04%	38.13%	31.05%	100%
Ford	3.71%	16.17%	77.58%	2.54%	100%
General Motors	4.84%	20.78%	17.24%	57.14%	100%
Other	39.58%	38.22%	4.06%	18.14%	100%

Comparing the extended state-transition analysis figures for the two datasets side-by-side in Table 22.13 reveals how different the customer choice dynamics were for these two cases.

Table 22.13. Comparison of the Extended State-Transition Data for the Two Datasets

Manufacturer	Loyalty Measure		Customers from Outside	
	Dataset 1	Dataset 2	Dataset 1	Dataset 2
Chrysler	82.82%	19.78%	31.69%	83.69%
Ford	83.65%	16.17%	19.60%	84.46%
General Motors	77.92%	17.24%	13.51%	80.86%
Other	84.17%	18.14%	14.04%	81.48%

Here you see two very different sets of numbers, even though the summary figures from the Basic Report are exact matches. Imagine yourself as the manager responsible for setting marketing strategy. If you only had the Basic Report and you represented Chrysler, you would probably be happy with the results, maybe looking for ways to create more "conversions" (non-customers becoming customers). But if the situation were really represented by the second dataset *and* you saw the state-transition-analysis results, you would undoubtedly be happy with the conversion rate and be more concerned with building the loyalty of your customer base.

Dimensionalizing the State-Transition Analysis

We have defined the various elements of the state-transition analysis. We have the Basic Report, we have the "To" and "From" percentages, we have the loyalty and changes in customer-composition measures. Armed with these analytical components you are ready for the next step, dimensionalizing the data: you break the data out by demographic attributes of the customers or by characteristics of the automobiles; you do a "longitudinal study" to produce data displays broken out by time. These are the workings of the analytical alchemist, the practice of multidimensional acrobatics!

With this example under our belt, I would like to make a remark about the strategy for developing analytical models and business intelligence systems in general. More than in conventional systems design, business intelligence systems should make use of the iterative design process with numerous prototyping cycles.

As one begins a development effort, there may be a dizzying array of choices for structuring and organizing information. Sometimes the best way to achieve mental clarity or to uncover the design issues, is to dig in and create and explore some simple models. Do this, keeping your eyes open and mind alert as you grapple with the questions that will arise as you deal with a concrete model. You will unquestionably see opportunities for extensions whose merits and applicability you can access.

The design process can be made more manageable by starting with simplified scenarios. Even if you know that you are going to want to look at an analysis broken out by customer demographics, you should consider developing the initial model without those breakout factors so that you can work with a simplified situation to define the basic analysis. *Dimensionalizing a given result is generally a straightforward extension; the real crux is to get the analysis right in the first place.*

The state-transition analysis makes a good display of the power and flexibility of DML as a language for programming and data modeling. If your background is in statistics or data mining, you are familiar with specialized languages for creating and employing analytical models, and you will see the OLAP DML as yet another. On the other hand, if your experience is from a relational database or other computer technology background, you might find that the DML not being part of an industry-sanctioned standard disconcerting. In any case, I think that the future of OLAP as an analytic platform, hinges, in part, on the continuing practice of designing and creating specialized analytics that address business problems in very specific ways. The Oracle OLAP DML is surely a powerful platform for doing that.

Other Applications of State-Transition Analysis

Seeing ways of creating new metrics is a part of the craft of business intelligence; so is the ability to see new applications. Before leaving this chapter, let's take a look at some different scenarios in which the state-transition models of this chapter could be applied.

University Graduation Rate Analysis

A university administration is interested in studying the graduation rate of its students. It performs a study to track students' progress toward graduation. The status of the student is looked at once a year. They define a study using states like the ones in Table 22.14.

Table 22.14. The Path of Students

Code	Description
FS	Freshman
SO	Sophomore
JR	Junior
SR	Senior
TR	Transfer to another school
NS	No longer in school
GR	Graduate

The "customers" are students; the transitions are things like moving from freshman to sophomore. We are not interested in loyalty, but in promotion.

As you can see, the agents don't have to be customers; they could be students, trainees, prizewinners, parolees—any designation of people. In fact, the agents don't have to be people, they could be any choice-making entity, for example business entities such as advertisers or stores.

Drug Treatment Program Assessment

A drug treatment facility wishes to evaluate the efficacy of a drug treatment program. It defines patient cohorts as groups of people who are in the same stage of treatment, based on time in the program. Patients begin treatment. There is a follow up every three months and the status of each patient is determined. A state-transition analysis is performed using a set of states such as those in Table 22.15.

Table 22.15. The Path of Patients

Code	Description
PS	Program start
AB	Abstinence
QI	Quality of life improvement
OP	Out of program
CC	Charged with major crime

STORE INCENTIVE PROGRAM ANALYSIS

Suppose a manufacturer has an incentive program for outlets that sell its products. It will look at performance on a quarterly basis for each store and determine if the store has met the requirements to receive the rewards of the incentive program or not. A state-transition analysis based on states such as the ones shown in Table 22.16 is performed.

Table 22.16. The Path of Stores

State Code	State Description
NO	Met requirements for no incentive program
YESA	Met requirements of incentive program at Level A
YESB	Met requirements of incentive program at Level B

RFM ANALYSIS

In the RFM analysis, customers are classified into "cells" on the basis of three behavioral attributes. Assuming the "treatments" (advertising and promotional actions) take effect, you would expect to see customers being moved into the desired cells. To study such movements, use those cells to define the states in a transition analysis.

23 | The Relationship Between OLAP, Statistics, and Data Mining

I hope you enjoyed the multidimensional acrobatics! In this volume, you have been introduced to a substantial set of data modeling concepts and programming techniques for creating and working with multidimensional data. It is through an appreciation of the full capabilities of OLAP as an analysis platform that the greatest intelligence can be built into business intelligence systems.

Multidimensional Acrobatics

To round out your concept of the capabilities of the OLAP analysis platform, I want to examine where it stands in relation to other analysis approaches. In this chapter, I will make a comparison among OLAP dimensional analysis, the field of statistics, and data mining.

Any one of these three can be described, at a high level, as using data to enhance the understanding of a process. They do, however, differ in the core set of problems they address, their approaches, their breadth, and complexity. But are there points where they overlap? What are the synergies among them?

It is beyond the scope of this book to try to define statistical techniques or explain the methods used in data mining. But if you already have familiarity in these fields and want to see a comparison between them and OLAP, these next two sections are for you.

MOLAP is from Mars, Statistics is from Venus

There are many ways in which the field of statistics and OLAP analysis are different. Whereas statistics is a mathematical science that is, in a sense, an expression of the scientific method, OLAP is fairly un-mathematical and is concerned with showing the user what happened. More than a science, OLAP is an expression of accounting. Statistics is about quantifying relationships and reproducibility, estimating model parameters, and hypothesis testing; OLAP structures information into a multidimensional format to display what happened.

Different as these seem, there are points at which the two touch. For example, the aggregates ubiquitous in multidimensional analysis are usually one of the common "descriptive statistics" used in the field of statistics. Within the purview of statistical methodology, there exist techniques from categorical data analysis that work with data displays (for example, contingency tables and crosstabs) in the formatting you have seen for multidimensional data variables. The technique of stratified sampling very much resembles the OLAP process of breaking out data by dimensions.

Exploratory data analysis (EDA) is an approach to data analysis based in maximizing insight into a data set and uncovering its underlying structure by allowing the data itself to reveal that structure. EDA makes heavy use of graphics and other data displays. This is similar to the goals of OLAP reporting (even if the types of data displays employed in these two disciplines are rather different).

There are some statistical functions in the DML. There are built-in functions for computing means, medians, and standard deviations. You have seen how to use the DML's random number generator to create simulated data and generate random samples. There is a REGRESS function that calculates the coefficients of a linear regression. The REGRESS.REPORT command will display those coefficients along with the standard regression diagnostics one would expect from a statistical package.

Table 23.1 summarizes some of the similarities and differences between OLAP and statistics:

Table 23.1. Multidimensional Analysis (OLAP) vs. Statistics

	Multidimensional Analysis (OLAP)	Statistics
Similarities	Mission concerns enhancing understanding of data.	Mission concerns enhancing understanding of data.
	Largely based on making aggregate data values available; aggregates are usually some form of descriptive statistic.	Use of descriptive statistics is a basic technique of statistical analysis.
	Produces displays of dimensional data.	Crosstabs and contingency tables.
	Breaks out a universe of values into dimensionalized data.	Similar to the idea of a stratified sample.
Differences	Like accounting: What happened?	Like science: Is it reproducible?
	Only marginal use of mathematics.	Often employs sophisticated mathematics.
	Calls it a dimension.	Calls it a discrete independent variable.
	Calls it a measure or variable.	Calls it a dependent variable.
	Core value is in offering dimensional views of data; time is a "required" dimension.	Usually not "dimensionalized"; frequently based on a snapshot in time.
	What the mathematician would call a discrete-valued variable is called a dimension.	Most often works with continuous valued variables, categorical analysis is a specialty.
	Dimensions are most often subdivisions of the universe based on its characteristics (not treatments, interventions, or outcomes).	Discrete variables are most often treatments, interventions, or outcomes.
	Obvious, intuitive representation. For example, you will naturally think in terms of time, product, and geography.	Not obvious representation. Business thinking is not usually framed in terms of confidence intervals, p-values, chi-squared values, etc.
	We're slicing and dicing data and showing it in a report or chart.	We're doing a significance test, or estimating a parameter value, or designing an experiment.

Data Mining is from Pluto

Data mining is concerned with *discovering knowledge*. It is about uncovering relationships or patterns hidden in data that can be used to predict behaviors, outcomes, or provide some other useful function.

The discoveries of data mining are typically cast into one of the following frameworks:

- CLASSIFICATION—We have a customer, are they a high credit risk or low risk?

- CLUSTERING—We have a large universe of customers, can we define a small set of customer types that does a good job, in some sense, of describing the entire universe?

- ASSOCIATIONS—When this happens, that tends to happen.

- SCORING—What is the probability that this customer will cancel their service? What is the likelihood that this is a fraudulent transaction?

In part, data mining is an application of the techniques of statistics. However, it frequently goes outside of that field, employing methods of artificial intelligence or other mathematical approaches to arrive at solutions that are more robust for working with messy, real-world data.

The end product is usually an operational model. The model may be a decision tree, neural network, or some other procedure defined by an algorithm. The model performs the task for which it was created: to classify an item, determine meaningful clusters, display associations, or score an item.

What about OLAP? Can OLAP be used to do these kinds of analyses? In Chapter 7: *Categorizing Dimension Members with Attributes* and Chapter 13: *Working with Sets* you saw an example of data-mining-like analysis—classification—with the RFM model. In RFM, a DML program populates three behavioral attributes for a set of customers based on the data in a multidimensional variable. Each customer is then classified into an RFM cell on the basis of those attribute values.

There is one respect in which this is different from most data-mining classifiers. The attributes recency, frequency, and monetary were given to us as the basis for classifying the customers. These factors have been identified, through marketing experience, to be highly correlated with response rates in direct marketing campaigns.

Usually, in data mining, determining the factors that correlate most powerfully with the outcome of interest is part of the project. In such cases, data mining replaces human expertise with knowledge implicit in the data, knowledge it will extract in its analysis process. It employs optimization algorithms to select the factors from a broad set of candidates or perhaps even construct them from other data elements.

OLAP applications that are similar to data mining applications are complex. For that reason, it was not feasible to detail them in this book. But I will briefly describe a customer loyalty application I developed, using the OLAP framework you now know, that is even more like a data-mining project than an RFM model. This will give you an even better idea of what could be done using the OLAP computational engine that comes with Oracle OLAP.

The principle output of the loyalty application was a probability figure, telling the likelihood that a customer would cancel their service within a prescribed period of time. In addition to probability figures, the output included *lift figures*—diagnostic information giving a measure of the effectiveness of the model for predicting cancellations.

The input data consisted of customer demographics, billing and payment history, as well as product usage data. The DML's statistical and other built-in functions were used, with some assistance from a statistical package, to evaluate the input data and select the segmentation factors. Similar to the RFM model, a multidimensional segmentation of the customer base was generated, but with more than three dimensions.

I used a "supervised learning" approach to score each cell of the multidimensional segmentation with a probability of service cancellation. The scoring process used historical data stored in multidimensional variables. Lift figures were computed by a DML program. Random samples were used to define control and test groups used in evaluating the accuracies of the model.

The resulting solution enjoyed *the OLAP advantage:* a dimensional model formulated in an intuitive, understandable format. The predictive model was a hypercube of probabilities that could be perused as a report. Thus, the model not only scored the customers, it generated understandable reports showing the patterns of vulnerability as a function of the breakout dimensions.

Table 23.2 summarizes some of the similarities and differences between OLAP and data mining.

Table 23.2. Multidimensional Analysis (OLAP) vs. Data Mining

	Multidimensional Analysis (OLAP)	**Data Mining**
Similarities	A tool for making discoveries: shows you what's happening so you can make them.	A tool for making discoveries: makes them autonomously.
	Makes heavy use of hierarchies.	Makes heavy use of decision trees.
Differences	White box—model is transparent.	Black box—many types of data mining algorithms not intuitively understandable.
	Rigid, structured.	Flexible, unstructured.
	Displays data.	Scores or classifies data.
	Intuitive, easy to understand.	Complex and often difficult to understand.
	Optimized for understandability.	Optimized for accuracy.
	Main purpose is displaying information.	Main purpose is modeling information.

Synergy Between OLAP and the Other Analysis Platforms

OLAP provides a vehicle for exploring data. With it, you will get a feel for the numbers; you will see the interactions among the dimensional factors. As desirable as it is to have systems make valuable discoveries autonomously, in practice, the ability to push things in a given direction on the basis of prior knowledge can be invaluable. The familiarity with the data you will gain from *navigating through the multidimensional superhighway* can provide critical insight that will help to maximize the effectiveness of your statistics or data-mining project.

Chapter 23
The Relationship Between OLAP, Statistics, and Data Mining

Cruising down the Multidimensional Superhighway

Bon Voyage!

Index

Symbols
-> (arrow), precedes user-entered commands when system output is also shown, 32
- (hyphen), continuation character for command lines, 32
& (ampersand), ampersand substitution, 130
" (quotation mark), precedes comment lines in programs, 243

Numerics
30,000-foot view, 21–26
10g Release 2 database, Oracle, 5
3GL and 4GL operations, supported by DML, 279

A
abbreviations, creating for commands, 38
accumulations, 182–185
 program for, 248–249
ACROSS keyword, REPORT command, 121
advantages of OLAP, 19–20
AGGMAP command, 170
aggmaps, 170, 172
 models and, similarities and differences, 178
AGGREGATE command, 169–170
 implicit looping, 172
aggregating a variable over its dimensions, program for, 242–245
aggregating by attributes, 178–182, 226
 multi-attribute breakouts and pivot tables, 180–181
 percent of category formula, 179–180
 unnatural hierarchies, 181–182
aggregating over all hierarchies, 168–173
aggregating over selected hierarchies, 173–174
aggregating selected values only, 175
AGGREGATION function, 177
aggregations, 281
 calculation operators, specifying, 176
 core principles, 166
 definition, 165
 group specification methods, 167–168
 skip-level, 169
 values stored with leaf-level values in same object, 171–172
ALLSTAT command and NAME dimension, 270
ampersand substitution, 130, 264
Analytic Workspace Java API, 20
Analytic Workspace Manager. *See* AWM
analytic workspaces. *See* AWs
Analytic Workspaces Node, Object View vs. Model View, 192–193
analytical alchemy, 279–281
ancestors, hierarchically based filtering, 92
application data, 22, 109
approach, book's, 5–6, 6–7, 13
arrow (->), precedes user-entered commands when system output is also shown, 32
Art of War, 15
attachment order of multiple AWs, affect on output, 255–256
attributes, 65, 66–67
 aggregating by, 178–182, 226
 aggregation, group specification method, 167
 as application data, 75
 for base dimensions, how to identify, 285–286
 behavior-based, 226–227
 default order, creating (AWM Model View), 199–200
 dimension profilers, 69–73
 indexed, creating (AWM Model View), 198
 non-indexed, creating (AWM Model View), 197–198
 performance attributes, 73–74
 treatment attributes, 74–75
 unnatural hierarchies, 98–99, 101
audience, book's, 4–5

AVERAGE function, 151
AW ATTACH, 34
AW CREATE, 32
AW DELETE, 35
AW DETACH, 34
AW LIST, 31
AW objects, mapping data warehouse objects to (AWM Model View), 216–219
AWM
    Maintenance Wizard, 219
    Measure Data Viewer, 23–26, 222–224
    Object View vs. Model View, 191–193
    OLAP Worksheet
        starting, 31
        using as a calculator, 31
    Oracle OLAP option, 21
    Query Wizard, 229–237
AWs, 13, 15
    access modes, 33
        after reordering, 36
        changing, 34
    attached vs. detached, 33
    attaching other required AWs with event-driven programs, 275
    backup, creating, 269–271
    case sensitivity of names, 37, 38
    creating
        from the command-line, 32–33
        graphically, 28–32
        for program development or testing, 274
    defragmenting, 271
    deleting, 35
    exporting and attachment order, 270
    fully qualified name, 32
    getting information about, 36–37
    as information foundry, 225–227
    listing the objects in, 35
    metadata, saving information to an XML file (AWXML), 272
    multiple
        attachment order, affect on output, 255–256
        reasons for creating, 274–275
    object types vs. relational database object types, 18–19
    Object View vs. Model View, 28–29
    Oracle OLAP option, 20
    ordering multiple, 35–36
    page size, show, 112
    parallel loads, 274–275
    partitioning to control composite growth, 274–275
    saving changes permanently, 34

AWs (*continued*)
    standard-form, 189
        vs. non-standard-form, 27–28
    standard set of objects created in Model View, 208–210
    storage usage, estimating, 273–274
    tablespace, 30
AWXML, saving metadata information to an XML file, 272

B

backup, creating for AWs, 269–271
BADLINE option, 261
base dimensions, 65
    how to identify attributes for, 285–286
    how to identify them, 284–285
base dimensions vs. related dimensions, 65–66
basic report, state-transition analysis, 293
behavior-based attributes, 226–227
BI, 3
    Cindi Howson's description, 14
    military intelligence and, 15–16
    OLAP and, 14
    as seeing eye numbers, 283
    Wikipedia definition, 14
BI applications
    how sets are used in, 158
    reasons for writing programs supporting them, 241–242
BLANKSTRIP function, 260
book's approach, 5–6, 6–7, 13
book's audience, 4–5
book's conventions, 32, 243
book's software requirement, 21
breaking out data by related dimensions, 226
breakout dimensions, 22
BTREE, indexing and conjoint dimensions, 147
building data, 242
business intelligence. *See* BI

C

calc this, not that, 125–126
calculating data on-the-fly, 125–126
calculation operation, core principle of aggregation, 166
calculation operators, specifying, 176
calculation timing, core principle of aggregation, 166
capstoning, 134
cardinality, low, 198
cascading formula architecture, troubleshooting, 133

case sensitivity
    AW names, 37, 38
    commands and functions, 38
    dimension members, 45
categorical entities and dimensions, 22
categorical vs. quantitative information, 22
CBIA (Classic Business Intelligence Application), 225, 286
CDA command, 270
character manipulation functions, 59, 60, 93, 264–265
charts and reports, using Measure Data Viewer to create (AWM Model View), 222–224
CHGDFN command, 153–154, 253
child nodes, 78, 89
children, hierarchically based filtering, 89
Classic Business Intelligence Application (CBIA), 225, 286
Codd, Dr. E.F., 12
code generators, 264
combinations
    conjoint dimensions and, 143–144, 145–146
    counting and selecting with
        Example 1: Find the distinct items in a given order, 146–147
        Example 2: Find the distinct items contained in any (of more than one) specified orders, 148
        Example 3: Find which orders contain at least one of the specified items, 148–149
        Example 4: A formula that tells if an item is in an order, 149
        Example 5: Calculate the number of distinct items per order, 149
        Example 6: Trend report on the number of distinct items ordered, 150
        Example 7: Trend report on the average number of items per order, 151
    factless fact table, 144
combinatorial explosion, 122
commands
    abbreviations, creating, 38
    case sensitivity, 38
    vs. functions, 36
    more than one on a line, 38
    shortcuts, 38
    See also individual command names
COMMIT command, 34
Common Warehouse Metadata, version 2 (CWM2), 190
comparison of objects created in Object View Worksheet vs. Model View GUI, 204–207
comparison operators, 58

compliance, metadata, 190
composite growth, controlling via AW partitioning, 274–275
composites, 123–124
compressed composites, 124
conjoint dimensions, 143
    examples, 143–144, 145–146
    indexing, 147
    populating, 261–262
CONSIDER command, 62
constellation schema, 214
conventions, book's, 32, 243
core principles of aggregation, 166
COUNT function, 69–70
counting measures, 286–287
cubes, 112. *See also* variables: dimensionality
cubes and measures, creating (AWM Model View), 200–203
custom groupings, aggregation, group specification method, 167, 176–178
customer profiling, 72–73
CWM2 (Common Warehouse Metadata), 190

D

data food chain, OLAP's position in, 14–15
data manipulation language. *See* DML
data mining vs. OLAP, 314–316
data storage, order, 113–115
data type, show, 111
data visibility, GUI and, 228
data warehouse, populating DML objects from (AWM Model View), 216–224
data warehouse objects, mapping to AW objects (AWM Model View), 216–219
decision support field, 3
default order attributes, creating (AWM Model View), 199–200
DEFINE command, 42
    shared dimensions, ordering for optimal performance, 111
defragmenting, AWs (export-import cycle), 271
Demo Application, 21–26
Demo Application, creating (AWM Model View), 191–203
denormalized and normalized tables, 215–216
depth of a node, 78, 83, 103, 104
derived measures, 225–226
descendants, hierarchically based filtering, 90
DESCRIBE command, 111
designer measures, 227

designing measures, 286
destination sets and source sets, 141–143
developer friendly code, 43–44, 85
development or testing, creating AWs for, 274
diagnostics and testing, 242
dimension profilers, 69–73, 227
    vs. RFM analysis, 74
dimension selector, Query Wizard (AWM Model View), 231–232
dimension table data, loading (AWM Model View), 216–221
dimensional maintenance, 271
dimensionality, determining, 110
dimensionality, show, 111
dimensionalizing an analysis, OLAP advantage, 281–282
dimensionalizing the state-transition analysis, 306–307
dimensions
    base dimensions, 65
        vs. related dimensions, 65–66
    breaking out data by related dimensions, 226
    breakout, 22
    cardinality, low, 223
    categorical entities, 22
    combinations, counting and selecting with
        Example 1: Find the distinct items in a given order, 146–147
        Example 2: Find the distinct items contained in any (of more than one) specified orders, 148
        Example 3: Find which orders contain at least one of the specified items, 148–149
        Example 4: A formula that tells if an item is in an order, 149
        Example 5: Calculate the number of distinct items per order, 149
        Example 6: Trend report on the number of distinct items ordered, 150
        Example 7: Trend report on the average number of items per order, 151
    combinations, factless fact table, 144
    conjoint, 143
        examples, 143–144, 145–146
        indexing, 147
        populating, 261–262
    creating, 42
    data types, 42
    defining and maintaining, 42–43

dimensions (*continued*)
    dimension members
        case sensitivity of, 45
        choosing codes for, 43–44
        creating/adding from the command line, 42
        creating labels in more than one language, 60–61
        creating numerical descriptions, 62
        deleting, 111
        filtering, 48–49
        getting information about, 45
        ordering, 46–47
        sorting
            permanently, 64
            temporarily, 63–64
        uniqueness, 43
    dimension values (*See* dimension members)
    dimensional maintenance, 47
    display dimensions, 120–21
    fastest- and slowest-varying, 114–115
    getting information about, 45
    how to identify base dimensions, 284–285
    measure dimensions, 118–119
    object type, 41
    performance strategies, 117–118
    properties, using to describe the dimension itself, 62–63
    related dimensions, 66
    rotation, 25
    setting status based on labels, 58–60
    shadow, 298
    shared
        consequences of, 110–111
        DEFINE command ordering for optimal performance, 111
    status, 47
    status list, push-down stack, 163–164
    swapping to exchange display role, 24
dimensions (AWM Model View)
    creating, 193–194
    lookup tables, 215–216
Dimensions tab, Query Wizard (AWM Model View), 231–232
directory alias, setting up, 258
display dimensions, 120–21
DML, 4, 17–18
    advantages, 19–20
    general observations, 241
    object types vs. relational database object types, 18–19
    Oracle OLAP option, 20
    properties, 62

DML (*continued*)
  vs. SQL, 17–18
  supports 3GL and 4GL operations, 279
DML objects, populating from the data warehouse (AWM Model View), 216–224
DOWN keyword, REPORT command, 120
drilling down into a hierarchy, 25
drug treatment program assessment, state-transition analysis, 308–309
DSECONDS option, 244

E

EDA (exploratory data analysis), 312
EIFs (express interchange files), 270, 271
embedded SQL, use to load data from relational table, 264
engineering tradeoffs in developing BI applications, 7–8
EQ (equal to, comparison operator), 58
EQ, changing a formula's, 127
EQ command, 127
equal to, comparison operator (EQ), 58
Equation 1: Moving average with three data values, 135–136
Equation 2: FIR filter with N weights, 136–137
error handling in programs, 244
error trapping, BADLINE option, 261
event-driven programs, 275
Example 1: Find the distinct items in a given order, 146–147
Example 2: Find the distinct items contained in any (of more than one) specified orders, 148
Example 3: Find which orders contain at least one of the specified items, 148–149
Example 4: A formula that tells if an item is in an order, 149
Example 5: Calculate the number of distinct items per order, 149
Example 6: Trend report on the number of distinct items ordered, 150
Example 7: Trend report on the average number of items per order, 151
Excel, 247
exploratory data analysis (EDA), 312
explosion, combinatorial, 122
EXPORT command
  AWXML and, 272
  EIF and, 270
  status and, 270
export-import cycles (defragmenting AWs), 271
exporting data, 242

exporting data to a text file with OUTFILE command, 263
express interchange files (EIFs), 270, 271
EXTCHARS function, 93
extendable information architecture, 284

F

fact table data, loading (AWM Model View), 221
fact tables
  constellation schema, 214
  star schema, 213–214
  vs. variables, 213–214
factless fact table, 144
FASMI, 12
fast analysis of shared multidimensional information (FASMI), 12
fastest-varying dimensions, 114
FILEREAD command, 257, 258–260, 261, 262
  STOPAFTER keyword, 262
filtering. *See* LIMIT command
filtering dimension, 115
filtering tools, Query Wizard (AWM Model View), 233–235
filters
  saving the results into a named set, 159
  storing a series of results using a one-dimensional valueset, 160
filters-to-measure, 286–288
FINDCHARS function, 59
finite impulse response. *See* FIR
FIR digital filters, formula, 136–137
FIR filter with N weights, equation, 136–137
food chain, data, OLAP's position in, 14–15
FOR loop
  implicit, 56
  explicit, 248
Formula 1: Revenue index, 128
Formula 2: Percent of revenue (customer), 128
Formula 3: Percent of revenue (product), 128
Formula 4: Percent of revenue (category), 128–129
Formula 5: Ampersand substitution, 130
Formula 6: Substituting a forecast value for a missing actual, 130–131
Formula 7: Relative time, 131–132
Formula 8: Revenue a year ago, 132
Formula 9: Revenue delta, 133
Formula 10: Hiding a dimension from a measure, 134
Formula 11: Stitching variables together, 134
Formula 12: Smoothing a time series with moving averages, 135–136

Formula 13: Implementing finite impulse response digital filters, 136–137
formulas, 125
    changing the EQ, 127
    for common calculations, 128–137
    defining, 126–127
    dynamically assigning variables, ampersand substitution, 130
    how GUIs display information, 201
    using to restructure data or output, 134
FULLDSC command, 63
fully qualified names, 275
functions
    case sensitivity, 38
    character manipulation, 59, 60, 93, 264–265
    vs. commands, 36
    See also individual function names
fundamental dimensions. *See* base dimensions

G

GE (greater than or equal to), 58
global scope vs. local scope of variables, 241, 243–244
greater than (GT), 58
greater than or equal to (GE), 58
group specification, core principle of aggregation, 166
group specification methods of aggregation, 167–168
GT (greater than), 58
GUIs
    displaying information through formulas, 201
    how to make data visible in, 228
    LIMIT command and, 229

H

HASH, indexing and conjoint dimensions, 147
headings, reports
    changing default display, 120–121
    default display, 114
healthcare example, many-to-many relationships with valuesets, 162–163
hiding a dimension from a measure, formula, 134
hierarchaeologists, 97, 106
hierarchies
    aggregation, group specification method, 167, 168–175
    balanced, 103
    balanced but not regular, 103
    balanced vs. any, data file formats compared, 105
    balanced vs. ragged, 103–104
    codes and labels, 82–83, 85, 102
    customer, developing a, 79–80

hierarchies (*continued*)
    definition, 78–79
    design considerations, 79–80
    diagram format, 78
    DML representation, creating, 79, 84–85
    drilling down into, 25
    filtering
        hierarchically based, 88–92
        level based, 94
    geographical, 85–87
    GUI format, 80
    levels, 78, 92–93, 94, 100–101
    multiple, 85–87, 105–106
    natural, 97–98
    natural vs. unnatural, 97–99
        qualitative differences, 99–101
    nodes, 78, 82, 83
    organizational chart format, 77
    ragged, 104–105
    regular balanced, 103
    reports, generating, 94–95
    self relations, 79
    star schema, 105–106
    tabular format, 81–84, 105
    unnatural, 98
        aggregating by attributes, 181–182
        alternative, attributes as breakout dimensions, 101
        attributes, 98–99, 101
        creating, 102
hierarchies, creating (AWM Model View), 194–196
hierarchy tools, Query Wizard (AWM Model View), 236
HOLAP, 12–13, 27
Howson, Cindi, 14
hybrid online analytical processing. *See* HOLAP
hypercubes, 112. *See also* variables: dimensionality
hyphen (-), continuation character for command lines, 32

I

implicit calculations, 172
implicit looping, 56–57
IMPORT command and EIF, 271
indexed attributes, creating (AWM Model View), 198
indexing, conjoint dimensions, 147
INFILE command, 257, 262–263
information architecture, extendable, 284
information foundry, AW as, 225–227
initializations with event-driven programs, 275
input data, modify with BLANKSTRIP function, 260
INSTAT function, 50

interrogatory pronouns
  attributes for base dimensions and, 285–286
  base dimensions and, 284–285
INTPART function, 88
ISVALUE function, 45
Items tab, Query Wizard (AWM Model View), 230

J
JOINCHARS function, 264–265
JOINLINES function, 264–265

K
Kimball, Ralph, 12

L
labels in more than one language, 60–61
large object binary (LOB), 27, 269
layout manager, Query Wizard (AWM Model View), 230–231
Layout tab, Query Wizard (AWM Model View), 230–231
LE (less than or equal to), 58
leaf nodes, hierarchies, 78, 82
less than (LT), 58
less than or equal to (LE), 58
levels, hierarchies, 100–101
levels, working with, 92–94
lift figures, 315
LIKE operator, 58
LIMIT ADD, 248, 249
  Venn diagram, 140
LIMIT command, 48–49
  GUI and (AWM Model View), 229
  Query Wizard and (AWM Model View), 229
  selectors and (AWM Model View), 229
  vs. SQL SELECT command, 51
  unexpected or inconsistent results, 116
limit types, 139–141
LISTNAMES command, 35
  standard-form AW objects created in Object View vs. Model View, 208–210
loading data, 242
loading data from relational table using embedded SQL facility, 264
loading dimension table data (AWM Model View), 216–221
loading fact table data (AWM Model View), 221
loading valuesets from an external source, 266–267
LOB (large object binary), 27, 269
local scope vs. global scope of variables, 241, 243–244

lookup tables, dimensions (AWM Model View), 215–216
looping, implicit, 56–57
low cardinality, 198
LT (less than), 58

M
MAINTAIN ADD, 42
MAINTAIN ADD vs. MAINTAIN MERGE, 43
MAINTAIN command and status, 50
MAINTAIN DELETE, 111
MAINTAIN MERGE, 43
MAINTAIN MOVE, 46–47
  dimensional maintenance and, 271
  sorting (permanently), dimension members, 64
maintenance, dimensional, 271
Maintenance Wizard, using to load dimension members (AWM Model View), 219
many-to-many relationships, 142–143
  example, 145–146
  valuesets, healthcare example, 162–163
mapping data warehouse objects to AW objects (AWM Model View), 216–219
match tools, Query Wizard (AWM Model View), 237
Mathematica, 279
Measure Data Viewer, using to create reports and charts (AWM Model View), 222–224
measure dimensions, 118–119
measure getter programs, 242
measures
  counting, 286–287
  cubes and, creating (AWM Model View), 200–203
  derived, 225–226
  designer, 227
  designing, 286
  quantitative information, 22
mentoring, 8
metadata
  of AWs, saving information to an XML file (AWXML), 272
  definition, 190
  structures (AWM Model View), 208–210
Microsoft Analysis Services, 13
Microsoft SQL Server, 13
migration analysis, 289
military intelligence
  BI and, 15–16
  nationmaster.com definition, 15
Minitab, 5
model, object type, 177–178

Model View GUI vs. Object View Worksheet,
    comparison of objects created, 204–207
Model View vs. Object View in AWM, 191–193
models and aggmaps, similarities and differences, 178
MOLAP, 12–13
    vs. data mining, 279, 314–316
    vs. statistics, 279, 312–314
    synergy with other analysis platforms, 316
MOLAP vs. ROLAP, 13
moving average with three data values, equation, 135–136
moving averages, 281, 282
    formula, 135–136
MOVINGAVERAGE function, 135–136
multi (MULTI), access mode, 33
multi-attribute breakouts and pivot tables, aggregating by attributes, 180–181
multicube approach, 112. *See also* variables: dimensionality
multidimensional online analytical processing. *See* MOLAP
multidimensional vs. relational, switching between data presentations, 151–155
multistep filtering, 139–141
MySQL, 13

N
NAFILL function, 130–131
named composites, 123–124
named sets, saving the results of a filter into, 159
nationmaster.com, military intelligence definition, 15
NE (not equal to), 58
NOHASH, indexing and conjoint dimensions, 147
non-indexed attributes, creating (AWM Model View), 197–198
normalized and denormalized tables, 215–216
not equal to (NE), 58
numerical descriptions, creating for dimension members, 62

O
OBIEE (Oracle Business Intelligence Enterprise Edition), 5
OBJ function, 45
    data type, show, 111
    dimensionality, show, 111
    storing, show total memory pages required, 112
object attributes, 66–67
object types
    aggmaps, 170
    AWs vs. relational databases, 18–19
    dimensions, 41
    formulas, 125
    model, 177–178
    programs, 241
    relation, 65, 67–69
    valuesets, 157–158
    variables, 54
Object View vs. Model View in AWM, 191–193
Object View Worksheet vs. Model View GUI,
    comparison of objects created, 204–207
objects
    comparison of those created in Object View Worksheet vs. Model View GUI, 204–207
    data type, show, 111
    dimensionality, show, 111
    fully qualified names, 275
    populating from the data warehouse (AWM Model View), 216–224
    standard set created for standard-form AW in Model View, 208–210
    storing, show total number of memory pages required, 112
OFA (Oracle Financial Analyzer), 5
OKNULLSTATUS option, 49
OLAP, 3, 11
    acronym, shortcomings of, 12
    advantages, 19–20
    BI and, 14
    data food chain, position in, 14–15
    vs. data mining, 279, 314–316
    FASMI and, 12
    Oracle OLAP option, 20–21
    vs. other analysis software and languages, 279–281
    vs. relational solutions, 279–281
    vs. statistics, 279, 312–314
    synergy with other analysis platforms, 316
OLAP advantage
    dimensionalizing an analysis, 281–282
    state-transition analysis, 295
OLAP analytic engine, 20
OLAP API, 20
OLAP DML. *See* DML
OLAP Worksheet
    Oracle OLAP option, 21
    SQL mode, 258
    starting from AWM, 31
    using as a calculator, 37

Olapistas, 228
OLTP, 12, 15
on-the-fly, calculating data, 125–126
ONATTACH program, 275
one-to-many relationships, 142
one-to-one relationships, 142
online analytical processing. *See* OLAP
online transaction processing. *See* OLTP
option settings, affect on program output, 255–256
Oracle BI Beans, 20
   creating reports with, 229
Oracle Business Intelligence Enterprise Edition (OBIEE), 5
Oracle Discoverer PLUS OLAP, 5
Oracle Essbase, 13
Oracle Express, 5
Oracle Financial Analyzer (OFA), 5
Oracle 11g OLAP, 5
Oracle 10g Release 2 database, 5
Oracle 9i OLAP, 5
Oracle OLAP. *See* OLAP
Oracle OLAP Application Developer's Guide, 10g Release 2, 20
Oracle OLAP DML. *See* DML
Oracle OLAP option, 20–21
Oracle RDBMS, 13
Oracle Sales Analyzer (OSA), 5
OracleBI Discoverer Plus OLAP, creating reports with, 229
OracleBI Spreadsheet Add-In, creating reports with, 229
OSA (Oracle Sales Analyzer), 5
OUTFILE command, 263
output data to a text file with OUTFILE command, 263

P

page size, show for AWs, 112
parallel loads and AWs, 274–275
parent-child relationship, hierarchies, 78
parent nodes, hierarchies, 78, 84–85
parents, hierarchically based filtering, 91
partitioning AWs to control composite growth, 274–275
Pendse, Nigel, 12
percent of category formula, aggregating by attributes, 179–180
percent of revenue (category), formula, 128–129
percent of revenue (customer), formula, 128
percent of revenue (product), formula, 128
performance
   aggregating selected values only, 175
   data (variable) storage order considerations, 114–115

performance (*continued*)
   dimensional maintenance, 47, 271
   fastest- and slowest-varying dimensions, 114–115
   implicit calculations, 172
   implicit looping, 56–57
   indexed attributes, 198
   indexing and conjoint dimensions, BTREE, 147
   maximize through dimension ordering, 117–118
   OLAP advantages, 19
   relations vs. variables, 68
   shared dimensions, DEFINE command ordering, 111
   sparsity, 122–124
performance attributes, 73–74
pivot tables and multi-attribute breakouts, aggregating by attributes, 180–181
PL/SQL vs. DML, 18
populating conjoint dimensions, 261–262
populating DML objects from the data warehouse (AWM Model View), 216–224
populating valuesets from an external source, 266–267
presentation of OLAP data, 282–283
profilers, dimension, 227
profiling, customer, 72–73
Program 1: A simple aggregation program, 242–245
Program 2: Meta-business intelligence, 245–247
Program 3: The accumulation program, 248–249
Program 4: Populating the relative time variable, 250–251
Program 5: Creating random samples, 252–253
Program 6: Creating random combinations, 253–254
Program 7: Maintaining a dimension from a text file using FILEREAD, 258–260
Program 8: Populating relations from data in a flat file, 260–261
Program 9: Reading in combinations, 261–262
Program 10: Loading in programs, aggmaps, and thekitchensink, 262–263
Program 11: Exporting data to a text file, 263
Program 12: Loading data from a relational table using embedded SQL, 264
Program 13: A program that writes a program, 264–266
Program 14: Loading valuesets, 266–267
program development or testing, creating AWs for, 274
programs, 241
   controlling all factors that affect output, 254–256
   event-driven, 275
   reasons for writing programs supporting BI applications, 241–242
properties, using to describe the dimension itself, 62–63
push-down stack, 163–164

Q

QDRs, 57, 61
qualified data references. *See* QDRs
qualitative differences, natural vs. unnatural hierarchies, 99–101
quantitative information and measures, 22
quantitative vs. categorical information, 22
Query Builder (AWM Model View), 229
Query Wizard (AWM Model View), 229–237
  LIMIT command and, 229
quotation mark ("), precedes comment lines in programs, 243

R

random combinations, program for creating, 253–254
RANDOM function, 88
random number generator, create test data, 115
random samples, program for creating, 252–253
random samples, uses of, 252
read-only (RO), access mode, 33
read/write (R/W), access mode, 33
read/write exclusive (RWX), access mode, 33
reasons for writing programs supporting BI applications, 241–242
recency, 73
recursive programs and formulas, 241
REGRESS function, 312
REGRESS.REPORT command, 312
related dimensions, 66
relational databases object types vs. AW object types, 18–19
relational online analytical processing. *See* ROLAP
relational solutions vs. OLAP, 279–281
relational vs. multidimensional, switching between data presentations, 151–155
relations, 67
  attributes as application data, 75
  multidimensional, 75–76
  naming conventions, 67
  performance, 68
  performance attributes, 73–74
  treatment attributes, 74–75
  versatility of, 76
relationships
  many-to-many, healthcare example, 162–163
  types of, 141–143
relative time, formula, 131–132
relative time variable, program for populating, 250–251

REPORT command, 36
  ACROSS keyword, 121
  default width, 54
  DOWN keyword, 120–121
  headings
    changing default display, 120–121
    default display, 114
  hierarchies and, 95
reports
  creating with
    Oracle BI Beans, 229
    OracleBI Discoverer Plus OLAP, 229
    OracleBI Spreadsheet Add-In, 229
    Query Wizard (AWM Model View), 229–237
  display dimensions, 120–121
  hierarchies, 94–95
  hierarchies, drilling down into, 25
  multidimensional vs. relational, 71–72
  state-transition reports, creating with DML, 298–300
  trend reports, creating, 287–288
reports and charts, using Measure Data Viewer to create (AWM Model View), 222–224
revenue a year ago, formula, 132
revenue delta, formula, 133
revenue index, formula, 128
RFM analysis, 74
  example, 152–155
  state-transition analysis, 309
RO (read-only), access mode, 33
rock, paper, scissors, 88
ROLAP, 12–13
ROLAP vs. MOLAP, 13
root nodes, hierarchies, 78, 82, 85
rotation, dimensions, 25
ROW command, 263
run-time metrics, program for capturing them, 245–247
RW (read/write), access mode, 33
RWX (read/write exclusive), access mode, 33

S

S (mathematical programming language), 279
sales application example, state-transition analysis, 292–295
SAS, 5
saved selection, 159
scope of variables, global vs. local, 241, 243–244
seeing eye numbers, 283
selectors, 229

self relations
  hierarchies, 79
  non-hierarchies, 88
set unions, 248
sets
  how they are used in BI applications, 158
  named, saving the results of a filter into, 159
  source and destination, 141–143
shadow dimensions, 298
sharing dimensions, 110–111
SHOW command, 36–37
skip-level aggregations, 169
slicing and dicing data, 23–24, 282
slowest-varying dimensions, 114
smoothing a time series
  digital filters, formula, 136–137
  moving averages, formula, 135–136
snowflake schema, 216
software required for book, 21
SORT command, 63
sorting dimension members
  permanently, 64
  temporarily, 63–64
source sets and destination sets, 141–143
space usage, estimating for AWs, 273–274
spaghetti calcs, troubleshooting, 133
SPARSE keyword, 123
sparsity, 122–124
SPSS, 5
SQL, use embedded facility to load data from relational table, 264
SQL command, 257
SQL interface to OLAP, 20
SQL mode, OLAP Worksheet, 258
SQL SELECT command vs. LIMIT command, 51
SQL vs. DML, 17–18
standard-form AWs, 189
  standard set of objects created in Model View, 208–210
  vs. non-standard-form, 27–28
star schema
  definition, 211–213
  fact table, 213–214
  hierarchies, 105–106
state-transition analysis
  basic report, 293
  contrasting report with same end score, 304–306
  definition, 290
  dimensionalizing, 306–307
  displaying in tabular format, 297

state-transition analysis (*continued*)
  extending with changes in customer composition, 303–304
  extending with customer loyalty, 300–302
  framework, 290–292
  OLAP advantage, 295
  RFM analysis, 309
  sales application example, 292–295
  store incentive program analysis, 309
  university graduation rate analysis, 308
  using, 295–297
state-transition reports, creating with DML, 298–300
statistics vs. OLAP, 312–314
STATLEN function, 50
status, 47
  EXPORT command, 270
  finding out about, 50
  null, 49
  setting with event-driven programs, 275
  settings, affect on program output, 255–256
  valuesets and, 159, 161
STATUS command, 50
status lists
  aggregation, group specification method, 167
  push-down stack, 163–164
stitching variables together, formula, 134
STOPAFTER keyword, 262
storage usage, estimating for AWs, 273–274
store incentive program analysis, state-transition analysis, 309
structures, metadata (AWM Model View), 208–210
substituting a forecast value for a missing actual, formula, 130–131
Successful Business Intelligence: Secrets to Making BI a Killer App, 14
swapping dimensions to exchange display role, 24

T
tablespace, AWs, 30
test data, create with RANDOM function, 115
testing or program development, creating AWs for, 274
throwaway dimension, 266–267
time, absolute vs. relative, formula, 131–132
time lag, formula, 132
time series
  moving averages, 281, 282
  smoothing with digital filters, formula, 136–137
  smoothing with moving averages, formula, 135–136
treatment attributes, 74–75
trend reports, creating, 287–288

troubleshooting
  AW created under Object View has disappeared, 28–29
  commands, more than one on a line and one fails, 38
  DML program output, 254–256
  formulas calling other formulas, 133
  LIMIT command, unexpected or inconsistent results, 116
Tzu, Sun, 15

U

university graduation rate analysis, state-transition analysis, 308
UPDATE command, 34

V

value-based filtering, 115–116
valuesets
  definition, 157–158
  limiting directly, 161
  loading from an external source, 266–267
  many-to-many relationships, healthcare example, 162–163
  multidimensional, storing information in, 161–162
  one-dimensional, storing a series of filtering results, 160
  status and, 159, 161
  variables and, similarities, 157–158, 162
variables
  creating, 54
  data type, show, 111
  defining, 110–111
  definition, 109
  dimensionality, 109, 110, 111, 112
  dynamically assigning with formula, ampersand substitution, 130
  fact tables vs., 213–214
  filtering, value-based, 115–116
  getting information about, 111–112
  local vs. global, 241, 243–244
  storing data
    number of cells created, 113, 122
    order, 113–115
    performance considerations, 114–115, 117–118
    requirement, show total in bytes, 112
    sparsity, 122–124
  valuesets and, similarities, 157–158, 162
Venn diagram, LIMIT ADD, 140
visibility of data in the GUI, 228

W

Wikipedia, BI definition, 14
writing programs supporting BI applications, reasons for, 241–242
www.AnalyticalAlchemy.com, copyright page
www.learn-oracle-olap.com, 6
www.olapreport.com, 12
www.oracle.com/technology/software/index.html, 21

X

XML, saving metadata information to an XML file (AWXML), 272

About the Author

John Paredes is president of OLAP World, Inc. He has developed analytical applications for a diverse range of client corporations over a 15 year time frame and is also a trainer and developer of instructional materials for Oracle OLAP. He is an experienced speaker on the use of multidimensional analytical models, data mining, and expert systems. John Paredes holds a BSEE in electrical engineering from Rice University and an M.Phil. degree in statistics from Yale University.

He is available to do in-person trainings, or with his associates, assist you with your Oracle OLAP, OBIEE, or Hyperion Planning projects. Your comments, feedback, and suggestions on the book are most welcome. Please visit www.AnalyticalAlchemy.com for contact information.